APPROACHING THE SUNNAH: COMPREHENSION AND CONTROVERSY

APPROACHING THE SUNNAH:
Comprehension and Controversy

•

YUSUF AL-QARADAWI

Translated by Jamil Qureshi

THE INTERNATIONAL INSTITUTE OF ISLAMIC THOUGHT
LONDON • WASHINGTON

THE INTERNATIONAL INSTITUTE OF ISLAMIC THOUGHT
P.O. BOX 669, HERNDON, VA 20172, USA

LONDON OFFICE
P.O. BOX 126, RICHMOND, SURREY TW9 2UD, UK

ISBN 1–56564–418–2 PB
ISBN 1–56564–419–0 HB

Cover Design by Saddiq Ali
Printed in the United Kingdom by
Cromwell Press Limited, UK

Foreword

The International Institute of Islamic Thought (IIIT) has great pleasure in presenting this scholarly work on the Sunnah, originally published in Arabic in 1990 under the title *Kayfa Nataʿamal maʿa al-Sunnah.* The author, Yūsuf al-Qaraḍāwī, a graduate of al-Azhar University, is an internationally renowned scholar and specialist in the field.

In this work he brings his extensive scholarship and experience as a teacher to elucidation of the Sunnah, emphasizing its harmonious, integrative nature, its balance and moderation. His argument is subtle and challenging, applying traditional knowledge of the Shariʿah to issues faced by Muslims in the present day. He discusses the controversies around various interpretations of hadiths, exposing the confused, often misinformed, reasoning that underlies the (unfortunately widespread) misunderstanding of them. He examines the problem of weak hadiths, clarifying their relationship to legal injunctions, and their relevance and authority for moral instruction. He argues for ease in applying the Sunnah to our daily lives; for, as he points out, the Sunnah is a vehicle for the mercy of the Qur'an, meant to offer hope, not hardship. Muslims must, he argues, recover from their neglect and backwardness in understanding the Sunnah; strive to become proficient and discriminating in their knowledge of it, and apply it with the proper wisdom, decorum, sincerity and moderation.

The IIIT, established in 1981, has served as a major center to facilitate serious scholarly efforts based on Islamic vision, values and principles. Its programs of research, seminars and conferences over the last twenty-five years have resulted in the publication of more than 300 titles in English, Arabic, and other languages.

Our thanks to Jamil Qureshi for his commitment to producing a close, careful translation, and for his co-operation with the team at the IIIT's London Office. Our thanks to all those involved, directly or indirectly, in the preparation and production of this book, including Shiraz Khan and Maryam Mahmood. May God reward them all, as well as the author, for their efforts.

April 2006

Anas S. Al-Shaikh-Ali,
Academic Advisor,
IIIT London Office, UK

CONTENTS

Translator's Note

ACKNOWLEDGEMENT

This translation would not have been undertaken, still less could it have been completed, without the supervision of Mohammad Akram Nadwi, currently research fellow at the Oxford Centre for Islamic Studies. I am glad to express my appreciation and gratitude for his encouragement, and his help in rescuing me from many errors. Any errors, shortcomings that remain are my fault, not his.

TRANSLATION OF QUOTED MATERIAL

Shaykh al-Qaraḍāwī's book is, necessarily, filled with cited hadiths, and extensive quotations of related discussion among the scholarly experts of past and present. In almost all cases, these quotations are presented as authoritative, intended to inform contemporary application of the Sunnah. Accuracy in presenting this material was more important than readability. Verbatim translation, fettered to the Arabic words, word order and structures, resulted in English that was quite often unintelligible. Accordingly, for the quoted material, I traded a verbatim rendering for an intelligible one. This means: where necessary, pronouns have been replaced with the nouns they stand for; connectors serving as punctuation have been replaced with punctuation; connectors with a logical function have been rendered according to meaning (as I understood it) in the context, so the same connector may be differently translated in different passages; verbs have been put into the tenses/moods that made most sense for the context; cascades of dependent clauses in some texts have been divided up, where this was feasible, into smaller sentence units.

With so much compromise for intelligibility, what remains of 'accuracy'? What remains will be evident in the use of square brackets to mark instances where the original sentence has been divided, or a pronoun paraphrased, etc. It should be possible to sense the form and structure of the original, and so quickly locate any errors in the translator's reading. For texts with great moral authority, this matters – and it matters most to Muslims.

This way of presenting Arabic in English is well established, indeed it is now accepted convention for parallel text publications intended for readers expected to refer also to the original. Although the analogy is imperfect, this style of translation may be compared to transliteration: with effort and practice it is possible, even without the Arabic to hand, to sense the original. For readers unfamiliar with this style, a good rule to follow is: *simply read through the square brackets without thinking of them as parentheses.* (By contrast, words or sentences in round brackets are parentheses in the original and should be read as such.)

As for the main text: this has been rendered, with due deference, into intelligible English, but without marking up departures from the original. Author's notes and bibliographical information are presented as found in the original. A few notes, which had to be added in order to explain a point that would not be obvious to an English readership, are clearly marked '—Trans.'

TWO DIFFICULT TERMS: 'LAW', 'ACTION'

Shaykh Qaraḍāwī's discussion contains many terms of the science, which has its particular idiom. Arabic words are used sparingly in this translation, glossed at first occurrence in the usual way, and nuances should be comprehensible in context. However, there are two usages (related to each other) which need a note: 'Law' and 'action'.

'Law' (with initial capital) and its derivatives translate 'Shariʿah' and its derivatives. 'Shariʿah', though widely known, is widely misunderstood to mean 'the law in traditional Muslim societies'. But Shariʿah does not mean 'law' only in the sense of what the state enforces to regulate the actions of people under its jurisdiction. It means 'way' or *the* Way, and is nearly synonymous with *dīn*, or religion. It includes social norms as well as (actionable) legal rules, the two together forming the ethos which, in an Islamic society, is supposed to identify and bind Muslims, individually and collectively. The English word 'law' and its derivatives do not convey this radical association of norms and laws, except negatively in the word 'outlaw', and in the weak meanings of 'lawful' or 'unlawful'. The use of 'Law' (with initial capital) seemed a reasonable compromise, given that 'Way' does not have the derivatives needed for this text.

The reader will regularly encounter phrases like 'this is acted upon' or 'hadiths related to actions'. The meaning here is more than 'actionable' matters in the narrow sense of what can be appealed to the courts or other legal process. In some instances, that is indeed the meaning. More often, however, the meaning of 'it is acted upon' is that the text in question commands or commends behavior that should be normal practice (*sunnah*). This may relate to personal manners (e.g. speech or dress), to worship (e.g. in the obligatory rites or in supererogatory acts such as supplications), to norms of public behavior (e.g. whether or how to disagree or express censure), as well as to transactions in which the law is relevant (e.g. contracts). Shaykh Qaraḍāwī distinguishes between hadiths that are adduced in the derivation of Law, and those referred to for moral instruction. Of the former, the question hardly arises, assuming that the hadiths are authenticated and their meaning unequivocal, that they are 'acted upon' in the appropriate situation. But of the latter, the question does arise: sometimes it is a historical issue (is there a majority or consensus view?), sometimes a textual issue (preference among competing texts; distinguishing universal intent behind particular wording), sometimes a philosophical one (how far can the action be practiced as a norm?)

Jamil Qureshi

Oxford. September, 2005

Author's Preface to the Second Edition

Praise and thanks are due to God: it is by His favor that righteous deeds are accomplished, by His grace that all good and blessing reach us, and it is by His enabling that any objectives are realized. God's blessing, prayer and peace be upon him – who is God's mercy to all creatures and their solace, His ever-continuing favor to the believers, and His profound argument against all humankind – our master, leader and model, our beloved and teacher, Muhammad, and upon his family and Companions, and whoever travels upon his path, being rightly guided by his Sunnah, toward the Day of Judgment.

The Sunnah is the second or 'unrecited revelation', the Prophet's exposition of the Qur'an. It is, for Muslims, the second source of Legal judgments and ethical directives. It is therefore a duty for Muslims to hold to the Sunnah with full understanding, conviction and firm adherence, in what they do and how they behave, as also in how they invite to and teach the religion. This is especially so in light of the fact that the regard of the Muslims for their Prophet's Sunnah has deteriorated through ages of backwardness, just as their regard for the Qur'an of their Lord has also deteriorated.

It is incumbent upon the scholars of the Muslims – and their preachers and thinkers, and those concerned about the renewal of the religion and the reform of the Community, the enlightenment of their minds, the awakening of their hearts, the stirring of their powers – that they stand by their obligations in this field.

This book (I wrote it originally at the request of the International Institute of Islamic Thought) is by way of my contribution to this field. Over the eleven years since, a dozen or more impressions of it have appeared in Egypt and in Beirut. I thought I should look into it after this period with a view to revision, improvement and completion – hardly an easy matter for me owing to the limitation of my time by other pressing cares and commitments. Fortunately for this book, however, I was able to work on it uninterruptedly, to add to it whole sections, and otherwise complete the text and the notes, rectifying and revising, until the book grew by nearly a third of its original size. This is by the grace of God, Exalted is He, and by His enabling. I hope that my brothers in religion who have translated this book into other languages will rely on this edition to revise the earlier translations and complete them so that they do not diverge from the Arabic original of this edition.

I praise and thank God, Exalted is He, that He has enabled me to serve the Sunnah through a number of books, among them: "The Sunnah, the Source of Knowledge (*maʿrifah*) and Civilization"; "Introduction to the Study of the Sunnah"; "The Messenger and Knowledge (*ʿilm*)"; "Selection from the *Targhīb wa-tarhīb* of al-Mundhirī"; "The Highest Authority in Islam according to Qur'an and Sunnah" … and through other books indirectly related to the Sunnah, for example: "The Shariʿah of Islam is Right for Every Time and Place"; "Introduction to Study of the Islamic Shariʿah"; the first part of "Fiqh Made Easy for the Modern Muslim" …

It was a comfort to me that Dār al-Shurūq took on the publication of this expanded and revised edition. I appeal to God, Exalted is He, to bring good by it to its writer, to its readers and to its publishers, and to whoever has a part in diffusing the good in it. God is surely All-Hearing and Responsive.

And, first and last, all praise and thanks are owed to God.

Yusuf al-Qaradawi

Cairo. Jumada I, 1421AH/August, 2000CE

From the Qur'an:

> God has certainly bestowed grace upon the believers in that He has sent to them a Messenger from among themselves – who recites to them His revelations, and thereby prospers and purifies them, and who teaches them the Book and the Wisdom – though, before that, they used to be in manifest error.

(*Āl ʿImrān*, 3: 164)

> O believers: obey God and obey the Messenger, and those among you who are in authority. Then if you are in dispute over something, refer it to God and His Messenger, if you are indeed believers in God and the Last Day.

(*al-Nisā'*, 4: 59)

> And whatever the Messenger gives to you, take hold of it; and whatever he forbids to you, abstain [therefrom]. And fear God.

(*al-Ḥashr*, 59: 7)

From the sayings of God's Messenger,
ṣalla Allāhu ʿalayhi wa sallam

"All of my Community will enter Paradise except one who 'refuses'." [People] said: "Who is that who 'refuses', O Messenger of God?" He said: "Whoever obeys me enters Paradise. And the one who disobeys me – then he [is the one who] has refused [Paradise]."
(al-Bukhārī reported it from Abū Hurayrah)

"I have left two things among you. You shall not go astray following them: the Book of God and my Sunnah."
(al-Ḥākim reported it from Abū Hurayrah)

"I have left to you the shining path; [the path being so clear] its night is like its day. You must follow my Sunnah and the Sunnah of the righteous, rightly-guided successors following me: [hook yourselves into it firmly] *."
(Aḥmad ibn Ḥanbal, and the authors of the different *Sunan*, reported it from al-ʿIrbāḍ)

* Literally: "bite into it with your incisors".

CHAPTER ONE

The Status of the Sunnah in Islam

I

GENERAL CHARACTERISTICS OF THE SUNNAH

The Qur'an is the supreme sign and the greatest miracle of Muhammad (ṢAAS),[1] the preserved everlasting Book, into which falsehood cannot enter from any direction. Its permanency from first to last makes it the primary fixed source validating all the sources of Islam and its further secondary proofs – one never argues from the latter to validate it. The Sunnah of the Prophet comes as a source following along with the Qur'an and making it clear, as God said, addressing His Messenger: "We have sent down to you the Remembrance so that you make clear to humankind what has been sent down for them" (*al-Naḥl*, 16: 44). Through the Prophet's sayings, his actions and his acceptance (*taqrīr*),[2] the Sunnah functions as the practical exegesis of the Qur'an, the application in reality, as well as the ideal, of Islam. In sum, the Sunnah is the Qur'an interpreted and Islam embodied. ʿĀ'ishah (RAA),[3] through her understanding and insight, and her living in the household of God's Messenger, was aware of this, and gave expression to it in a brilliant turn of phrase. When asked about his character, she said: "His character was the Qur'an!"[4]

Whoever desires to know the practical way of Islam, in its particulars and its pillars, should therefore know it as elaborated and embodied in the Prophet's Sunnah. The term *sunnah* means 'way' or 'method' or 'pattern'. It represents the Wisdom of the Prophet, in explaining the Qur'an, in commenting on the truths of

Islam, and in his teaching of the Community.[5] God revealed to His Messenger "the Book and the Wisdom", both; and He made conveying that Wisdom one of his most important duties in the formative life of the Community.

A COMPREHENSIVE PATTERN

God said: "And we sent down to you the Book as a clarification of everything" (*al-Naḥl*, 16: 89). Accordingly, the Sunnah is a pattern distinguished by its comprehensiveness and completeness in relation to the whole of human life in all its dimensions, 'length', 'breadth' and 'depth'. We mean by 'length' the temporal or vertical dimension, from birth to death, indeed from the embryonic stage to what comes after death. By 'breadth' we mean the horizontal dimension, which comprehends all spheres of life. The Prophet's guidance proceeds with all of them: in the home, in the market-place, in the mosque, on the road, at work; in relations with God, with oneself, with family, with Muslims, non-Muslims, and human-kind generally, with animate creatures and inanimate things. We mean by 'depth' the deeper dimensions of human life, but this covers body as well as mind and spirit, the outward as well as the inward, and it embraces speech and action as well as intention.

Unfortunately, some Muslims hardly know anything of the Sunnah except keeping the beard long and the robe short, and using the *siwāk* from the *arāk* tree to clean the teeth. They forget the comprehensiveness of the Prophetic pattern, in which every-one, however different their conditions or circumstances, can find scope for something to serve as their model.

A BALANCED METHOD

The Sunnah is distinguished also by balance – between spirit and body, mind and heart, this world and the hereafter, the ideal and the actual, theory and practice, the unseen and the visible, freedom and responsibility, individualism and collectivism, conformity and inventiveness... So it has to be and is a moderate pattern for a moderate society, with neither overdoing in it nor doing too little. God commanded: "That you do not exceed the measure, but establish the measure with equity, and do not fall short of the balance" (*al-Raḥmān*, 55: 8–9).

When the Prophet caught sight of any among his Companions inclining towards either extreme, he turned them back firmly to moderation, and cautioned them against the consequences of excess or insufficiency. He disapproved the three men who questioned his worship as if they disdained it and their appetite for acts of devotion was not satisfied. One of them resolved that he would fast for life and not break his fast; another that he would stand in vigil for the night and not rest; the third that he would keep apart from women and not marry. When their saying so was reported to him, he said: "Be aware! I am more fearful of God than you, more God-aware than you, yet I fast and I break fast, I stand in vigil and I rest, and I marry women. Then whoever prefers [something else] above my *sunnah* is not one of mine."[6] On seeing the excess of ʿAbd Allāh ibn ʿAmr in fasting, keeping vigil and recitation of the Qur'an, he returned him to moderation, saying: "Indeed, your body owns a right over you (that is, of relaxation), your eyes own a right over you (that is, of sleep), your family own a right over you (that is, of everyday pleasures and sociability), and your visitor owns a right over you (that is, of hospitality and companionship)."[7] In other words: give to every owner of a right his right.

The Prophet himself set the highest standard of balance and moderation throughout his life – as demonstrated by his Sunnah and the history of his life – with his Lord, with his self, with his family, with his Companions, and with people as a whole. Most often what he prayed for was in the Qur'anic invocation: "Our Lord, grant us good in this world and good in the hereafter, and save us from the punishment of the Fire" (*al-Baqarah*, 2: 201). Among his prayers was: "O God, set right my religion, which is the protection of my affair; set right for me my world, wherein is my life and livelihood; and set right for me my hereafter, to which is my return; and make my life prosper for me by every good; and make my death a rest from every evil."[8]

AN INTEGRATIVE WAY

The Sunnah of the Prophet is a harmonizing or *integrative* way. It integrates within itself faith with intellection, or revelation with reason, so that from both of them there flows "light upon light" (*al-Nūr*, 24: 35). It combines also legislation and moral instruction. The Sunnah is involved in the forming, foundation and direction of instruction. In legislation, it is involved in defence, the application of force, discipline and punishment. Moral instruction is of little avail without the support of legislation; and legislation is of little avail without moral guidance. The Prophet was responsible for both together.

The Sunnah integrates within itself might and right, the authority of the state with the Qur'an, the call to religion. For indeed God restrains by that authority what he does not restrain by the Qur'an. If good conscience of the right does not prevent some people from wrongdoing, then might can prevent them, and whoever rebels against this call, the state can discipline. For every situation there is a limit of tolerance beyond which it is not permitted that it be overrun by the false. The Messenger held together the call to religion and the power of state: he it was who led the people in the prayer, and on the battlefield; who judged between them in disputes, and led them in administration in peace and in war. He was not as the Israelites were at certain stages in their progress – a prophet guiding them and leading in the call to religion, with a king administering and leading in their affairs of state – as the Qur'an has narrated to us that their prophet said to the Israelites: "God has raised for you Saul as king" (*al-Baqarah*, 2: 247).

Nor has there come about the Prophet in the Islamic tradition, what has come about the Messiah, regarding the partitioning of life (and responsibilities) between God and Caesar, so that the religion is for God, and for Caesar political power. Rather, God informed him so that he said: "My prayer, my sacrifice, my living and my dying are for God, the Lord of the worlds. He has no partner (or peer). By that am I commanded, and I am the first of those who surrender (to God)" (*al-Anʿām*, 6: 163–64).

Thus the Community was administered and its life guided in its entirety by the Book and the Balance. Whoever rebelled against either was disciplined, as God said, by "iron" of "mighty strength": "We sent our Messengers with the clear signs and sent down with them the Book and the Balance so that people should establish just measure, and We sent down iron in which are mighty strength and benefits for people" (*al-Ḥadīd*, 57: 25). Ibn Taymiyyah said: "People must have a book to guide, and iron to support. 'And God suffices as Guide and Helper' (*al-Furqān*, 25: 31)."

The leadership and the people are also brought together. The leader is not as an angelic being circling in the sky, but a human being dwelling on earth. Nor is it desirable for the leader to live in a hermitage secluded from the people. Rather, it is incumbent upon him to be with and among them, sharing in their sorrows and joys, their crises and troubles. That is indeed how the Prophet was. In times of scarcity he was the first to go hungry and the last to satisfy his appetite; in battle he was at the front of the ranks; in the prayer he was the people's leader; and in manners their model. When a stranger came, he could not distinguish the Messenger among the people and so he asked: "Which of you is Muhammad?" When the people were constructing the mosque and hauling stones, he hauled with them, sharing with them his toil in the building, so that some of them said:

> If we sit while the Prophet labors, it will be reprehensible on our part.

In the shade of this pattern the believers are united in order to make their society what it seeks to be, to make it the ideal, so that they may proclaim their message to the world. This important task is demanded of them collectively, with solidarity and mutual agreement, each in his place, and each according to his capacity: the learned one gives freely of his knowledge, the rich one of his wealth, the one who has celebrity of his celebrity, and each from whatever he has of power or ability gives freely according to his means: and God does not burden a soul except with what He has given it. The responsibility of the weaker ones among the people is honored, drawing the stronger among them to help the others, and together they are a help against whoever is other than them. So they are friends of one another, as God said: "And the believing men and the believing women are friends of one another, they enjoin the right and forbid the wrong, and they establish the prayer and pay the alms-tax (zakah), and they obey God and His Messenger. On those God will have mercy" (*al-Tawbah*, 9: 71).

A REALISTIC METHOD

The Sunnah is also a realistic method. It does not regard people as if they were winged angels, but as human beings who eat food and live in the markets, who have their dispositions and passions, their necessities and their needs – just as they also have elevated spiritual aspirations and are elevated by them to the host of heaven. They were created from clay and molded mud, but also there is in them a breath from the spirit of God. Little wonder then that a human being ascends and descends, that he makes progress and he stumbles, that he is guided and goes astray, that he stands firm and he deviates, that he disobeys God and he repents.

One of the Companions supposed that he had become a hypocrite because his state when at home was at variance with his state when in the presence of the Messenger. He rushed out till he reached God's Messenger and said: "Ḥanẓalah has become a hypocrite." He explained to the Messenger this 'hypocrisy' in that, when he was with him, his heart was softened, and his eyes moistened with tears, and he remembered his Lord, and the hereafter was present to him as if he saw it with his eyes. Then, when he returned to his house, he joked with his children, and played with his wife, and he would forget the state that he was in before. Then the Messenger said: "O Ḥanẓalah! If you were able to endure in the state you are in [when] with me, angels would be shaking hands with you on the roads. But, O Ḥanẓalah, there is a time [for this] and a time [for that]."[9]

It is a familiar fact that the human being is lucid and clear, then dozes and nods off. There is no harm in that if his time and life are apportioned between what is good for himself and the right of his Lord, or between this world and the hereafter, as is said in the proverbial saying: 'An hour for your heart, and an hour for your Lord.'

In recognition of that, the Sunnah makes allowance for human weakness. It widens the circle of the permitted and narrows that of the forbidden, as in the hadith: "What God has made lawful in His Book, that is lawful; and what He has forbidden, that is forbidden; and what He is silent about, that is exempt [from ruling]. So accept from God His latitude. For surely God never is forgetful of any thing." Then he recited: "And your Lord is never forgetful" (*Maryam*, 19: 64).[10] In further recognition of human weakness, the Sunnah makes permissible, according to circumstances, the necessities among those things normally restricted. It even makes permissible according to necessity certain of those things normally forbidden: for example, the Messenger permitted to two of his Companions the wearing of silk in light of their complaining of a skin ailment.

The Sunnah makes allowance for the reality of the human being and it relents for him when he lapses into disobedience. It does not close the door in the face of repentance. Rather, it opens it wide before him so that he can knock on that door, repentant and remorseful before his Lord. As in the hadith: "God spreads out His hands through the night so that He may accept repentance for the offences of the day; and He spreads out His hands through the day so that He may accept repentance for the offences of the night – until the sun rises in the west."[11] And in another: "By Him Who holds my soul in His hand, if you do not sin and seek forgiveness, He will remove you, and bring [instead] a people who do sin and seek His forgiveness, and He will forgive them."[12]

The Sunnah makes allowance for the different conditions of human beings, and the differences between them, whether innate or acquired. In consideration of such differences the Messenger would answer a single question from a number of persons with multiple answers – so he did not apply to an old man a ruling on the matter (*muʿāmilah*) appropriate to a youth; or to someone in conditions of necessity a ruling appropriate to one in abundance and enjoying freedom of action. Similarly, he considered the customs of peoples and their diversity: so he let the Abyssinians play with their spears in his mosque on the day of ʿId; and he let ʿA'ishah watch them from behind his shoulder. In the same way he urged the girls to come and play with her, as a concession to her being young. So too he made lawful entertainments at weddings, and at celebrations for the return of someone long absent, and other such occasions, as a concession to the need of human beings for amusement and recreation.[13]

The realities engaged by the Sunnah are too many for examples to encompass them. But all of them inform us of the realism of this divine Prophetic pattern.

A WAY MADE EASY

Another of the special, distinguishing qualities of the way of the Sunnah is its facility, its convenience and tolerance. Among the virtues of this Messenger mentioned in the earlier scriptures, in the Torah and the Gospel, are that he "will enjoin on them that which is right and forbid them that which is wrong; he will make lawful for them the good things and make prohibited for them the foul things; and he will release them from their burdens and from the fetters that were upon them" (*al-Aʿrāf*, 7: 157). So nothing exists in the Sunnah of this Prophet that hinders the people in their religious life (*dīn*), or oppresses them in their worldly life (*dunyā*). Rather, he says about himself: "Indeed I am a mercy proffered [to you]",[14] interpreting the verse: "And We have not sent you except as a mercy to the worlds" (*al-Anbiyā'*, 21: 107). He said: "Assuredly God did not commission me for affliction, nor for bringing affliction to others; on the contrary, He commissioned me as an educator and as a means of ease for others."[15]

He dispatched Abū Mūsā and Muᶜādh to the Yemen with a succinct, comprehensive instruction: "Urge ease, and do not urge hardship; offer good hope [lit. glad tidings], and do not provoke aversion; listen to one another, and do not provoke differences."[16] By way of teaching his Community, he said: "Urge ease, and do not urge hardship; offer good hope, and do not provoke aversion."[17] To his Companions, after they became agitated with a Bedouin who had urinated in the mosque, he said: "You are commissioned as people who make things easy, not as those who make things hard."[18] And about his Messengership, he said: "Assuredly I have been commissioned [to impart] a tolerant true-religion."[19] He said: "O people! [what is incumbent] upon you is actions that you can bear. For surely God does not tire [cease to persevere] until you tire [cease to persevere]."[20]

The Prophet made things easy in light of the pattern of the Qur'an, which proclaims that God desires ease for His slaves, not hardship, and that He did not lay upon them, in their religious duties, any distress. Thus, He said in the conclusion of the verse of purification: "God does not desire to lay upon you any distress" (*al-Mā'idah*, 5: 6); and after the verses on the forbidden degrees in marriage: "God desires to make (the observance of His decrees) light for you, for man was created weak" (*al-Nisā'*, 4: 28).

So the Prophet warned against pedantry and excess in the religion. It is why he did not prescribe celibacy and seclusion from the world or prohibit the good things of life. Rather, he called for the enjoyment of life with balance. He said: "God is beautiful and He loves beauty."[21] "God loves to see traces of His favors on His servant."[22] He prescribed concessions and making duties lighter in the rites of purification, prayer, fasting and pilgrimage. So he prescribed *tayammum* in place of *wuḍū'*; he prescribed the shortening and the combining of prayers; and the prayer sitting or lying down or by gesture, depending on the ailment and the person's capacity; and he prescribed breaking the fast in Ramadan for the invalid and the traveler, for the pregnant woman and the wet-nurse. He said in the case of the man who saw people shading him and spraying him with water while traveling: "There is no virtue in fasting while traveling,"[23] that is, while traveling in the kind of journey that is strenuous and exhausting.

He permitted the combining of the *ẓuhr* and *ʿaṣr* and the *maghrib* and *ʿishā'* prayers while in Madinah and without their being constraining circumstances such as traveling or rain. When Ibn ʿAbbās, the narrator of the hadith, was asked: "What did he intend by that?" He said: "He intended to not distress his Community."[24] In other words, he purposed to lift the distress from his Community. He said: "God loves that you act according to His indulgence, just as He hates that you act in disobedience to Him."[25] And: "God loves that you act according to His indulgence, just as He loves that you [act according to] His decrees."[26]

Once, some of his Companions complained to him that ʿAmr ibn al-ʿĀṣ had fallen into *janābah* (the state of major ritual impurity) and then prayed with them after doing *tayammum* but not taking a bath. When he asked ʿAmr about that he said that the night had been severely cold, adding: "And I had in mind God's saying, Exalted is He: 'And do not kill yourselves – surely God is ever-merciful to you' (*al-Nisā'*, 4: 29)." On hearing this, God's Messenger smiled – an indication of his acceptance of ʿAmr's action.

In another incident: a man suffered wounds, then he fell into *janābah*. Some people ruled for him that he be given a bath in spite of his wounds; his condition was aggravated as a result, and he died. When the Prophet was informed, he said: "They killed him! May God kill them! Why do they not ask when they do not know? For the only cure for witlessness is asking a question."[27]

II

THE MUSLIMS' DUTY TO THE SUNNAH

The Sunnah of the Prophet is, as we said, the detailed pattern for the life of the individual Muslim and of the Muslim society, and represents the Qur'an interpreted, and Islam embodied in life. Among the Muslims' duties is that they should know this detailed Prophetic pattern, with its distinguishing features, namely its comprehensiveness and completeness, its balance, its realism, and its facility. They should know what is clearly displayed therein of the virtues of deep-rooted piety, noble humanity, and authentic morals. And they should take him as the good example to follow in the entirety of their lives:

> Assuredly there is in the Messenger a good example for one who anticipates with hope God and the Last Day and remembers God much. (*al-Aḥzāb*, 33: 21)

> And whatever the Messenger gives to you, take hold of it, and whatever he forbids you from, reject it. (*al-Ḥashr*, 59: 7)

> Say: If indeed you love God then follow me. God will love you and forgive you your sins. (*Āl-ʿImrān*, 3: 31)

This makes it incumbent on Muslims to learn how to become proficient in insight into this Sunnah, how to apply it, with understanding and proper decorum, as the best generations of this Community applied it, who studied in the school of Muhammad, the Companions and their Successors, with sincerity. They excelled in learning, thereafter they put into action what they learned, and they excelled in action, thereafter they taught the leaders of Islam, and they excelled in teaching.

The foremost crisis facing the Muslims in this time is the crisis in thought. In my opinion it takes precedence over the crisis in conscience. It is always the thought that sets bounds to perception and sketches out the way. Then comes movement, after that, reconciling perception with what the thought sketched out. What most clearly represents that crisis in thought is the crisis in insight into the Sunnah and in application of it. This is especially the case among some movements in the Islamic re-awakening. The more discerning are looking to those movements and hanging their hopes upon them, and the heads of the Community the world over are turned toward them in expectation. Often, those movements present issues from the direction of their wrong understanding of the Sunnah. Their view of it is a deficient view. It all but limits the Sunnah to outward shows and formalisms, without penetrating to the understanding of the wisdom of the Prophetic pattern, whose special qualities we recounted earlier.

WARNING AGAINST THREE EVILS

It is narrated from the Messenger that he indicated that knowledge of Prophethood and the legacy of the Message would be targeted by extremists, and by falsifiers and by the ignorant. This has come in what Ibn Jarīr narrated, also Tammām in his *Fawā'id*, and Ibn ʿAdī, and others, from the Prophet. He said: "From every generation its just and upright [ones] will carry this knowledge, expelling from it the distortion of the extremists, the deviation of the falsifiers, and the interpretation of the ignorant."[28] Those are indeed three destructive sledgehammers, each a danger to the Prophet's legacy.

a) The distortion of the extremists

Distortion originates in extremism and obduracy, in shunning the moderation which distinguishes this religion, the tolerance which is an attribute of this righteous community, and the facility which characterizes the obligations in the Law. It is extremism that, before us, destroyed the People of the Book, some of whom went to excess in matters of creed, or of worship, or of conduct. They expelled from the religion its facility, prescribed what God never urged, and prohibited what God made lawful, thus burdening people with obligations and covenants that God never made incumbent on them. The Qur'an recorded that against them when it said: "Say: 'O People of the Book, do not go to extremes in your religion without right; and do not follow the caprices of a nation that certainly went astray before and caused many to stray, and strayed from the level path'" (*al-Mā'idah*, 5: 77).

Ibn ʿAbbās narrated from the Prophet: "Beware yourselves against extremism in the religion, for certainly those before you were destroyed by extremism in religion."[29] Ibn Masʿūd narrated from him that he said, and said three times: "The obdurate were destroyed."[30]

What is noteworthy here is that the hadith deems extremism to be distorting the religion. That is because it turns it away from its characteristic temperament of ease, facility and moderation to another temperament, burdening the people to excess and bringing hardship upon them.

b) The deviations of falsifiers

The deviations are those to which the falsifiers resorted in order to bring into the Prophetic pattern what is not of it, and to attach to it certain novelties and innovations which its temperament does not accept, its creed and its Law strongly reject, and its roots and branches shy away from. Now the falsifiers proved incapable of adding anything to the Qur'an, since it has been memorized by the hearts, inscribed in the written copies, and recited by the tongues, of the believers. So they reckoned their route to deviations in the Sunnah would be smooth, that it would be possible for them to say 'the Messenger of God said' without any evidence.

But the critical scholars of the Community and guardians of the Sunnah lay in wait for them at every lookout, and shut up against them every loophole leading to deviations. They did not accept a hadith without a *sanad* (chain of narrators, pl. *isnād*), and without scrutinizing its narrators one by one until his person and character were known from birth to death. They would find out about his teachers, associates and students. They would evaluate his trustworthiness and fear of God (*taqwā*), his exactitude in preserving what he heard, his consonance with trusted well-known reports, and the quality of his solitary reports on unfamiliar matters.

For this reason the scholars said: "The *isnād* is part of the religion." For, without an *isnād*, whoever wished might say whatever he wished! They likened seeking knowledge without seeking its *isnād* to 'looking for firewood in the dark'. So they did not accept any hadith except that whose *sanad* was thoroughly connected from its beginning to its end, reliably so, and from fair-minded narrators with exactitude in preserving what came to them, with no gaps evident or hidden, and with the requirement of its being safe from all irregularity or defect or objectionable content.

This exactitude in the quest for the *isnād*, with its criteria and its qualifications, is among the special qualities of the Community of the Muslims. They were far ahead of contemporary civilization in that it was they who established the foundations of the methodology of scientific history.

However, what is regrettable is that the Community circulated false hadiths without source and *isnād*. It is regrettable also that the knowledgeable scholars were adjudged to have been fabricating or falsifying them. Moreover, this became common currency among the general public. For example, the hadiths such as those about women, like: "the burial alive of daughters is among the honorable actions"; and "consult with [women], then oppose them"; and "do not allocate upper-story rooms for [women] and do not teach them writing", etc. Certain of these hadiths even violated the creed of *tawḥīd*. For example: "If one of you has believed firmly in a stone, it will surely benefit him." And some are false superstitions, for example that the rose is created from the perspiration of the Prophet.

This situation prompted a number of the scholars of the Community to compile books of fabricated hadiths so as to warn against them, and especially since the books of moral guidance, softening of the hearts, *taṣawwuf* (Sufism), and others, are filled with them – even some books of hadith themselves. Among those scholars were: al-Ṣaghānī, Ibn Jawzī, al-Suyūṭī, al-Qārī, Ibn ʿArāq, al-Shawkānī, and al-Laknawī, and al-Albānī in our time. So it is an obligation to make use of their books.

c) Interpretation of the ignorant

Wrong interpretation is that by which the reality of Islam is deformed, in which words are twisted from their proper contexts, and by which the main elements of Islam are diminished so that what issues from its fundamentals and directives is pushed out.

Just as the people of falsehood deviated so as to bring into Islam what is no part of it, these did so by deforming its priorities, putting back that whose right is to come forward, and bringing forward that whose right is to be put back.

Wrong interpretation and rotten understanding are a preoccupation of those who are ignorant of this religion, who never imbibed its spirit, and never pierced with insight to its realities. They do not have anything firmly-rooted in knowledge, nor impartiality towards the truth. They do not refrain from deviation and perversion in understanding. They refrain from the Qur'anic verses with explicit injunctions, the *muḥkamāt*, and run after the *mutashābihāt*, the allegorical or figurative verses. They do so for the sake of dissension, of interpreting those verses in accordance with the caprice that leads astray from the path of God.

That is indeed the interpretation 'of the ignorant' – though they put on the garments of learned scholars, or present themselves with the titles of wise philosophers. It is obligatory to be alert to it, and warn against it, and to put in place the discipline necessary for protection from falling into it. The majority of the doomed sects and factions, split off from the Community, from its creed and its Law, and the groups deviated from the level way, were doomed by such error in interpretation.

At this point it is worthwhile to turn to Ibn al-Qayyim's enlightened discourse on the need for quality of insight about the Messenger of God. He mentioned this in the book *al-Rūḥ*. We cite from it what he said:

> It is necessary that one understand from the Messenger his intent without exaggeration and without abridgement, for his speech does not carry that which it cannot sustain, nor falls short of his intent or his purpose in giving guidance or explanation. Neglect of that and abandonment of it has assuredly achieved straying in error from the right direction, which is not known except by God. Rather, wrong understanding about God and His Messenger is the root of every heretical innovation and error growing up within Islam. Indeed, it is the root of every failure in the roots and branches [of the religion], especially if conjoined with wrong purpose. Wrong understanding was in

> certain matters abetted by the leaders despite their good purpose, and because of their evil purpose by those who follow [the leaders]. O the tribulation [that has visited] the religion and its people! And God is appealed to for help! The Qadaris, the Murji'is, the Khārijis, the Muʿtazilis, the Jaḥmis, and the Rāfiḍis, and all the rest of the factions of the heretics, appeared [and] caused discord only because of wrong understanding about God and His Messenger. [This situation persisted] until the religion became, in the hands of most of the people, that to which these misunderstandings led. But that [religion], as the Companions understood it, and those who followed them, from God and His Messenger, was then forsaken and those people did not turn to it nor pay attention to it [... ...] so far so that if you peruse the writing [of these people] from its beginning to its end, you do not find that its author has, in [even] a single place, understood from God and His Messenger his intent as it should be [understood]. And this only he knows who has known what [opinion] is held by the people, and laid it out beside what has come from the Messenger. As for one who has reversed the matter – thus, laid out what has come from the Messenger beside what he has believed with conviction and come to profess, and blindly followed therein the conjecture of whoever is more attractive to him – then it is not gaining a thing to speak with him. So reject him and what he has chosen for himself, and assign to him what he has assigned to himself. And give thanks to Him who has kept you untainted by this.

Bad interpretation of the texts – whether a text of the Qur'an or of the Sunnah – is a long-standing evil. Muslims have suffered from it, as the communities before them suffered. It steered them into deviation from the religion of God, distortion of His radiant words, and the derailment of the purposes He intended thereby, namely to lead humankind out of darkness into light.

The Muslims suffered from the interpretations of the differing sects, each of whom strove by tricks to direct the text so as to fit their sectarian doctrine, without concern for critical principles and the decisive basic rules of Law or language or reasoning. Among them were some who went beyond all bounds. For example, the Bāṭinis, who displaced words from their meanings, and walked off with them on a road undisciplined by reason or tradition.

Hence the differing interpretations of the rationalist schools of philosophers and theologians, and most particularly the Muᶜtazilis. Hence too, among the jurists, those who forced the interpretation of the texts – notably the texts of the Sunnah – in support of their schools' doctrines, which they captured with guile. They adopted their schools' doctrines as sources and the texts as their branches. This was a dangerous invention. For it is obligatory that schools or doctrines refer back for authority and direction to the texts, not the other way around. The basic principle is that the non-infallible is referred back for authority and direction to the infallible: "And if you have a dispute on a thing refer it to God and His Messenger if you are believers in God and the Last Day" (*al-Nisā'*, 4: 59).

Interpretation is surely indispensable, but it has its place, its conditions, and its discipline. We have set this out in detail elsewhere.[31]

The cause of some of the bad interpretation was ignorance or absent-mindedness or the pursuit of conjecture – in other words, indolence of mind or deficiency in knowledge. Then there is another kind of bad interpretation whose cause is the pursuit of caprice. An example of that is what Aḥmad ibn Ḥanbal narrated: that a hadith of ᶜAmmār ibn Yāsir was mentioned to Muᶜāwiyah – "The group in rebellion will kill you". Then he said to ᶜAmr ibn al-ᶜĀṣ: "Only the one who brought him killed him" meaning ᶜAlī. This is an interpretation to be rejected from every aspect. Otherwise, we must say that the Messenger was himself the slayer of whoever was martyred with him in his expeditions, such as his uncle Ḥamzah and Muṣᶜab ibn ᶜUmayr and others.[32] This interpretation is without doubt one whose motive is caprice.

The interpretations of the religious and theological sects are diverse. Their motive was only to support the school doctrine, even if by means of affectation and arbitrariness. In our time we have found the people inconsistent in embracing the authentic hadiths, even the verses of the noble Qur'an – so they may interpret them with meanings that are strange for them. This they do for the caprice in their souls. And caprice makes blind and deaf:

"And who is further astray than one who follows his caprice without the guidance from God?" (*al-Qaṣaṣ*, 28: 50).

III

PRINCIPLES FOR THE APPLICATION OF THE SUNNAH

It is necessary for one who applies the Sunnah of the Prophet to expel from it the deviations of the falsifiers, the distortions of the extremists, and the interpretations of the ignorant, and adhere to the few matters regarded as the fundamental principles in this field.

1: VERIFYING THE FIRMNESS OF THE SUNNAH

The first such principle is that one verify the proof of the *sunnah* and its soundness according to the comparison, scientific method and painstaking detail, which the learned scholars applied to such proofs. This includes both *sanad* and *matn* (the academic apparatus and the text proper of the hadith), and equally whether it be the Sunnah of speech or deed or acceptance. The diligent researcher must have recourse to the people of renown and experience in this field of work. They were the assayers of the hadith, who exhausted their lives in study of it and teaching of it, in distinguishing the sound from the unsound, the accepted from the rejected. "And none can inform you like [One] Aware" (*al-Fāṭir*, 35: 14).

The scholars established for the hadith a science well-founded in its roots and well-ordered in its branches. It is the science of the principles of hadith (*uṣūl al-ḥadīth*), or the idiom and terminology of hadith (*muṣṭalaḥ al-ḥadīth*). It holds for the hadith the place that *uṣūl al-fiqh* holds for fiqh. In point of fact it is an assemblage of disciplines. Ibn al-Ṣalāḥ expanded it to 65 'kinds'. After him others added to that, until al-Suyūṭī (in *Tadrīb al-Rawī ʿalā Taqrīb al-Nawawī*) numbered as many as 93 'kinds'.

It is well-known that some questions in this science of *uṣūl al-ḥadīth* are agreed upon and on others there is difference of opinion.

The obligation on the learned is to be reserved on the disputed matters, and give preference therein according to the balance of evidence. Here, I report giving more weight to the approach of the forerunners among the scholars of the Community in the most resplendent of its epochs, over the approach of the later scholars. I do so because the former were more strict and bold in rejecting weakness in the hadiths, and more often firmly established than the latter.

They discussed a number of issues in the science. Among them are the following:

Ziyādat al-thiqah fī al-ḥadīth: additions in the hadith by a reliable narrator. Up to what point should one accept the additional material reported from such a narrator?

Taqwiyyatu al-ḥadīth bi-taʿaddudi al-turuqi al-ḍaʿīfah: strengthening a hadith by the addition of weak routes of transmission. Which hadith is strengthened by such addition? Which category of the weak may one use for such addition?

Ḥadīth mawqūf: where the chain of narration goes back to a Companion and stops there, not going higher to the Prophet himself. Then, the question of its being understood as *marfūʿ* (as if from the Prophet himself) when its subject-matter has to do with that in which there is no room for opinion (*ra'y*).[33] But some of the scholars permitted latitude in that, in hadiths in which it is possible that there is room for opinion.[34]

Maḍmūn: study of the topic of the hadith, or (in the terminology) its *matn* or content. Some of what the forerunners accepted in accordance with the characteristics of their epoch is not reckoned acceptable today in accordance with the development of knowledge in our epoch.

2: PROFICIENCY IN UNDERSTANDING THE SUNNAH

The second principle is that one be proficient in understanding the Prophetic text. Understanding it means understanding in harmony with the meanings indicated by the language; in the light of the path (the general intent) of the hadith, the particular circumstance and aim of it; in the shade of the Qur'anic and Prophetic texts in turn; and in the framework of the general principles and the totality of the purposes of Islam. All that, together with the necessity of distinguishing what has come by way of the preaching of the Message, and what has not come in that way – according to the distinction of the learned doctor of Islam from India Aḥmad ibn ʿAbd al-Raḥīm, known by the name Shāh Walī Allāh al-Dahlawī (d. 1176 AH). That distinction can be put in a different way (according to the expression of our teacher Maḥmūd Shaltūt, former Shaykh al-Azhar): what was part of the legislative Sunnah and what was not legislative; then, within the legislative Sunnah, what has attributes of general and permanent import, and what has attributes of particular and time-bound import. Confusion of the two kinds is among the worst defects (*al-āfāt*) in understanding the Sunnah.

Such defects did not come about as a result of the Sunnah not being firmly established – it was already firmly established and authenticated – but as a result of errors in understanding. Such error is an ancient disease – it touched the Sunnah just as it touched the Qur'an. It is what prompted the truth-seekers among our scholars to warn against error in understanding from God and from His Messenger.

3: THE TEXT BEING SAFE FROM CONTRADICTION BY WHAT IS STRONGER

The third principle is that one assure oneself of the safety of the text from contradiction by what is stronger than it. 'What is stronger than it' may be a text from the Qur'an, or other hadiths, more abundant in number of sources, or more sound in proof of their authenticity, or more consonant with original principles (*uṣūl*), or more fitted to the purpose of the Legislative measures. Or it may be the general purposes of the Law, which have acquired definitiveness because they are not derived from one or two texts, but from an assemblage of them, giving the advantage – through conjoining some with others, together with the authenticity of their proofs – of certainty and definitiveness.

This is connected to an important legal issue in both *uṣūl al-fiqh* and *uṣūl al-ḥadīth*, that is, *al-taʿāruḍ wa al-tarjīḥ* (contradiction and preference on balance of evidence). The texts in outward form sometimes contradict each other but in their reality are not contradictory. It is incumbent on the jurist or scholar to remove the apparent contradiction, wherever possible, by reconciling the texts or, failing that, by judging on the balance of evidence. Al-Suyūṭī stated in *Tadrīb al-Rāwī* that judgments on the balance of evidence are of more than one hundred kinds.

THE SOURCE OF BOTH LEGISLATION AND GUIDANCE

The Sunnah is the second source of Islam for its Legislation and its guidance. Jurists refer to it to discover the Legal injunctions. In the same way preachers and educators do so, to draw from it inspiring meanings, worthy instructions and profound wisdom, and ways to persuade people to the good and dissuade them from the evil.

So that the Sunnah can carry out this important duty, one must give greater weight to its being proven to be from the Prophet. This is expressed in the idiom of the science of hadith as the hadith's being attested as *ṣaḥīḥ* (authentic, sound) or *ḥasan* (good). The *ṣaḥīḥ* is equivalent to the rank of 'excellent' or 'very good' (as such terms are understood for university degrees); the *ḥasan* to the rank of 'good' or 'acceptable'. Beyond that, the higher level of the *ḥasan* is considered as being close to the *ṣaḥīḥ*; in the same way its lower level is considered close to the *ḍaʿīf* (weak).

A *ṣaḥīḥ* hadith is one narrated by a narrator well-known for probity and for the completeness of his preserving from another narrator, from the beginning of the *sanad* to its end, when it connects to God's Messenger, without gap or rupture. Also, a *ṣaḥīḥ* hadith is safe from irregularities and defects.

Thus, one does not accept a hadith narrated by a narrator of unknown origin or whose circumstances are unknown, or whose probity, or the completeness of whose preserving, are doubted. Or if there is a gap or rupture in any link of his chain of narrators. Or if the hadith reported from him is irregular (*shādhdh*) in that it contradicts a reliable narration from someone more trustworthy than himself. Or if there is in the hadith some hint of defect or something else objectionable in its *sanad* or its *matn* (the text being reported).

Let no one suppose about this knowledge, or about the people who conveyed it, that the Community's scholars used to accept anything from whoever might bring it to them, that one would come to them and say 'from So-and-So from So-and-So from God's Messenger', and they would answer: 'You have spoken the truth!' Rather, about everyone who came to them with a hadith, they were sure to ask a number of questions: Which circle of scholars and students is he from? Who are his teachers? Who are his fellow-students, who accompanied him in the study of the science? What are his character and his conduct in the view of his teachers, his companions and his pupils? Do people attest to his uprightness and his fear of God (*taqwā*)? To his thoroughness in preserving? Did he continue so throughout his life or did he change in the last years of his life? Who among his pupils studied under him in his old age, and who studied under him before he changed? And so on.

The learned scholars of the Community are in agreement that hadiths adduced in Legal injunctions affecting actions, which is a pillar of the science of fiqh and a foundation of the lawful and the unlawful, must be *ṣaḥīḥ* or *ḥasan*. However, they disagree in respect of the hadiths that are related to the merits of actions, invocations, what softens the hearts, *targhīb* (inspiring longing for God) or *tarhīb* (inspiring fear of God), and the like, which do not enter unequivocally under the heading of Legislation.

Among the learned scholars of the early generations (*salaf*) there were some who were relaxed about the reports of this class of hadiths, and did not see harm in publicizing them. But this being relaxed is not absolute, as some have supposed. Rather, it has its grounds and its conditions. However, many abused this relaxation of standards (for hadiths not connected with actions stipulated by the Law), and thereby veered people off the level path, and polluted the wellspring of pure Islam.

The books of preaching and what softens the hearts, and the books of Sufism, abound in this kind of hadiths. However, we are of the opinion that most of them are not satisfied with weak or flimsy hadiths. Rather, these books follow sayings that have no source or *sanad*, some of them even contradict and belie God's Messenger. Hadith scholars warned against such hadiths, and composed books clearly setting out their spuriousness. They were unanimous on the prohibition of narrating such weak or false reports, except in order to expose their falsehood and nullity. As a result of their work, there was no circulation of them among the mass of people.

The same kind of flimsy and rejected sayings are found in many books of *tafsīr*, to the extent that they habitually presented the notorious fabricated saying on the merits of certain Qur'anic *surah*s. They did so even though senior hadith experts (*ḥuffāẓ*) had exposed its defect and explained its invalidity, leaving no further excuse for anyone to report it or blacken the pages of his book with it. Yet the likes of al-Zamakhsharī, al-Thaʿālibī, al-Bayḍāwī, Ismāʿīl Ḥaqqī, and others persisted in presenting the false hadith.

A DEFENCE OF FABRICATED HADITHS REFUTED

More common than such presentation of the false hadith is to find a Qur'an commentator – for example the author of *Rūḥ al-Bayān* – willing to justify quoting the hadith and to defend it. This author, at the end of the commentary on *Sūrat al-Tawbah*, with an enviable daring, goes so far as to say:

> Know that, about the hadiths that the author of *al-Kashshāf* cited at the end of this surah (and al-Qāḍī al-Bayḍāwī and al-Mawla Abū al-Saʿūd followed him [in doing so], may God have mercy on them, the cream of Qur'anic commentators), the learned scholars often [had] discussion [and differences], with some [of the scholars] affirming [those hadiths], others rejecting them on the basis of their being fabricated, like Imam al-Ṣaghānī and others. [… …]

What is apparent to this poor slave of God, may God be indulgent with what is decreed for him, is that those hadiths are bound to be either sound and strong, or enfeebled and weak, or falsified and fabricated.

If they are sound and strong, then no discussion on them [is proper or necessary]. But if their *isnād*s are weak, then the hadith scholars have agreed that action is permitted on the weak hadith for *targhīb* and *tarhīb*, as in al-Nawawī's *al-Adhkār* and ʿAlī ibn Burhān al-Dīn al-Ḥalabī's *Insān al-ʿUyūn* and Ibn Fakhr al-Dīn al-Rūmī's *al-Asrār al-Muḥammadiyyah*, and other [works].

If they are fabricated: then it has been mentioned by al-Ḥākim and others that a man from among the ascetics took it on himself to compose hadiths on the virtue of the Qur'an and its surahs, and then it was said to him: "Why do you do this?" He said: "I saw people renouncing the Qur'an, and I longed to inspire them to it." Then it was said to him that the Prophet said: "One who has with premeditation forged a lie against me, let him provide for his seat in the Fire." Then he said: "I did not lie *against* him; rather, I lied *for* him."

He meant: that lying *against* him leads to the destruction of the foundations of Islam and undermines the Law and the injunctions, and is not like the other – lying *for* him. [That, the lying for him,] is for encouragement to following his Law and following in his tracks in his path. Shaykh ʿIzz al-Dīn ibn ʿAbd al-Salām said: "Speaking is a means to [attain] objectives. Then every praiseworthy objective may arrive at its objective by means of either of the two, [speaking] truth and [speaking] falsehood. Now [speaking] falsehood is prohibited. Then, if arriving at [the objective] is possible by [speaking] falsehood and not [possible] by [speaking] the truth, then telling a lie in that [instance] is permitted (*mubāḥ*) provided the attaining of that objective is permitted, and it is obligatory (*wājib*) provided the objective is obligatory. So this regulates it [i.e. this is the ruling principle in such situations]."[35]

Here we cannot help but express our consternation by saying *lā ḥawla walā quwwata illa bi Allah* and *innā li Allah wa innā ilayhi rājiʿūn*: 'There is no might or power except with God' and 'To God we belong and to Him we are returning'.

One marvels at the sin of pride that publishes the like of this discourse from a man self-enrolled among commentators on the

Book of God. Some people have described him as *faqīh* (a jurist, one who understands the Law of Islam) and *uṣūlī* (an expert in the *uṣūl* or principles of fiqh)! But what understanding (*fiqh*) does this man have who is ignorant of what are, according to the exacting scholars, the primary things? This shaykh (he has a Sufi leaning) does not know that God perfected the religion for us, and thereby completed the blessing upon us. So we do not recognize any need for someone to complete it for us by manufacturing hadiths of his own, still less that he presume to correct God, or to strengthen his Messenger. In effect he says to the Prophet: 'I lie for you so as to make up for you the shortcomings of your religion, and I fill up any gaps in it with the hadiths I contrive.'

As for the statement of Ibn ᶜAbd al-Salām: it is being taken quite out of context. Among what it permits are certain sorts of speaking – such as deception in war, and making peace between two parties, and giving help to an innocent fleeing a tyrant, and other situations like that mentioned appropriately in the context.

In any case, the statement of Ibn ᶜAbd al-Salām itself rebuts the claim of this claimant. For Ibn ᶜAbd al-Salām has stated that for every praiseworthy objective that may be arrived at by both telling the truth and telling lies, telling lies is prohibited. So here, in the context of this discussion, he would say: if all of the desired, preferred objectives which the fabricated hadiths persuade to, and all of the repudiated objectives which they dissuade from, are without doubt capable of attainment by means of hadiths that are *ṣaḥīḥ* and *ḥasan,* then falsehood is therefore prohibited, indeed it is one of the greatest of the great sins.

REJECTION OF THE *ṢAḤĪḤ* IS EQUAL TO ACCEPTANCE OF THE FABRICATED

Just as accepting invalid and fabricated hadiths and attributing them to God's Messenger is an offence, an absurdity and danger, so too, equal to it in nullity, is rejecting the *ṣaḥīḥ* and established hadiths – out of caprice or pride or presuming to know better than God and His Messenger. Doing so entails an evil conjecture about the Community, its scholars, and the leaders of its best generations and noblest summits. In time past, the mass of people tended to accept weak and fabricated hadiths. As for the general public in this time: they tend to reject the authenticated hadiths – with no knowledge, no guidance, and no enlightened book. We do not mean by 'general public' the illiterate and those like them – for those are not the ones thrusting themselves into what they are not good at. We mean by 'general public' only the self-exalted and deluded ones – who 'never leave a house by the door' (that is, who love indirection and complication), who never strengthen knowledge by referring to its sources, who know the outer husk of knowledge, grabbing it by snatches from secondary references, or from orientalists and missionaries and their like. The important thing here is that rejection of a *ṣaḥīḥ* hadith is, in the religion, like the acceptance of a rejected hadith: they are on a par.

Acceptance of falsified hadiths enters into the religion what is not of it; rejection of authenticated hadiths drives out of the religion what is of it. Without doubt, both are reproached and censured alike – acceptance of the false and rejection of the true.

THE DOUBTS OF THE OLD ENEMIES OF THE SUNNAH

Since ancient times heretics and innovators have raised doubts and allegations in refutation of the Sunnah. The learned scholars and truth-seekers turned upon them to ruin and frustrate them. One such scholar was al-Shāṭibī:

Imam al-Shāṭibī said:

> Within the insurgency of heretical innovators [certain] factions have at times justified rejection of hadiths with [the argument] that they avail themselves of conjecture, and conjecture is censured in the Qur'an – as in His saying, Exalted is He: "They follow but a conjecture and what their selves fancy" (*al-Najm*, 53: 23); and He said: "They follow only conjecture and conjecture does not avail a thing against the truth" (53: 28); and what has come with that meaning [in other verses]. [They exaggerate in this line of argument] to the point that they make

permitted what God has made forbidden by the tongue of His Prophet, though it is not made forbidden in the Qur'an textually. They surely purposed thereby to affirm themselves in, from what was appealing to them, some notions of their own minds.

The conjecture meant in the verse, as also in the hadith, is other than what they have alleged. We have found that it has three means [ways in which it is used and can be looked at]:

Firstly. Conjecture about the *uṣūl* [root principles or fundamentals] of the religion. According to the scholars it is of no use because of the likely possibility of [the truth's] being opposed to [what] the one conjecturing has conjectured. [A conjecture is by definition either true or false; the mere possibility of its being false makes it useless for establishing the fundamentals of the Law]. Conjecture in respect of the *furūᶜ* [the branches or derived matters in the Law] is different. For, according to specialists in the Law, it is acted upon because of the evidence that demonstrates it. So conjecture is censured except for what is connected to the *furūᶜ*, and this is correct – the learned scholars have mentioned it in this context [i.e. they have allowed a conditional role for conjecture in connection with the details of the Law, not its fundamentals].

Secondly. Conjecture prefers, out of two contradictory [possibilities], one over the other, with no demonstration for the [one] preferred. [There is] no doubt that it is censured because it is an arbitrary judgment. For that reason, "conjecture" is followed in the verse by "the self's fancy" in His saying: "They follow but a conjecture and what their selves fancy." So they incline to a matter on bare prejudice and fancy. A conjecture whose steps are demonstrated is different. Then it is not censured in the generality [of cases] because it moves out of [bare] following fancy. For that [reason], it is affirmed and acted upon, according to its requirement, whenever it is fitting to be acted upon, for example as in the *furūᶜ*.

Thirdly. Conjecture is of two varieties: [1] conjecture dependent upon definitive principle. These are the conjectures [that are] acted upon in the Law wherever they occur, since [such conjecture] is dependent upon a well-known principle, and it is of a species whose kind is well-known. And [2] conjecture not dependent upon a definitive [principle]; rather, it is based on something other than principle, and it is censured – as has been set out [above]. If [it is] dependent on a[nother] conjecture like itself, and if that conjecture is based also on a

> definitive [principle], then as before. [On the other hand, if it is based] upon something other [than definitive principle], then it is censured.
>
> So, by the implication of all [the foregoing]: for a solitary report with an authenticated *sanad* – which must be dependent upon a principle definitive in the Law – acceptance of it is obligatory, and so we accept it absolutely. In the same way, as the conjectures of the unbelievers are without basis on anything, then one must reject them, and their meriting being considered is non-existent. (This last response is borrowed from an original whose full exposition is in *Kitāb al-Muwāfaqāt*, and to God belongs the praise.)
>
> Some of those who have strayed surely go too far in rejection of the hadiths. They rejected the opinion of [one who] relied upon what is in [the hadiths] to the extent of unjustly attacking [his] opinion as [being] opposed to reason, and accounted the one who said [it] as insane.
>
> Abū Bakr ibn al-ᶜArabī has narrated about some whom he met in the East who are deniers of the *ru'yah* [the believers' seeing of God in the Garden]: that it was said to [a denier of the *ru'yah*]: "Is unbelief attributed to one who affirms the [possibility of] *ru'yah* of the Creator, or not?" Then [this denier] said: "No! For he has said what is unacceptable to reason, and whoever has said what is unacceptable to reason has not unbelieved." Ibn al-ᶜArabī said: "Then this is our status according to them [i.e. they think us mad]!" So let the fortunate reflect on what the pursuit of fancy leads to. May God protect us from that by His favor.[36]

Ibn Qutaybah has mentioned in his book *Ta'wīl Mukhtalif al-Ḥadīth* many of the specious doubts, severally and individually, which the enemies of the Sunnah stirred up. He invalidated them, specious doubt by specious doubt, nor did he take leave of them until he transformed their fire to ashes.

THE DOUBTS OF NEW ENEMIES OF THE SUNNAH

In our times new enemies of the Sunnah have arisen. Some are from outside our lands, like the missionaries and the orientalists. Others are from within our lands, from among those tutored by missionaries and orientalists, or influenced by them, directly or indirectly. These people have made use of the weaponry of older adversaries of the Sunnah and joined to it new weaponry inspired by the culture of the present. They called on these and those with their 'cavalry' and their 'infantry' against the Sunnah and its books, its narrators and its methods. They have been helped in that by places and institutions with power and shrewd policies. However, God has sent for the Sunnah, from among great contemporary scholars, those who, with overwhelming truths and telling arguments on their side, have made a stand against the doubts of the skeptics, and their vanities and frauds. "So the truth was brought to pass and what they were doing made obsolete, and there they were vanquished and overturned [to become] the ridiculed" (*al-Aʿrāf*, 7: 118–19).[37]

BEING CONTENT WITH THE GUIDANCE OF THE QUR'AN

Among the doubts of the enemies of the Sunnah, which they repeat continually, is their claim that the Qur'an suffices without the Sunnah – in consideration of the fact that there is detailed exposition in it of everything, as God said: "We revealed to you the Book as a clarification of everything and as a guidance and as a mercy and good tidings for those who have surrendered" (*al-Naḥl*, 16: 89). And He said: "Assuredly in their story there is a lesson for people of understanding. It is not a made-up story; rather, it is a confirmation of that which is before you and a detailed exposition of everything, and a guidance and a mercy for a people who believe" (*Yūsuf*, 12: 111). They make the same claim also because (they say) God vouchsafed the preservation for us of the Qur'an, but not that of the Sunnah.

The answer to that claim is that the Sunnah is without a doubt the clarification of the Qur'an. It is that which details what is summary in the Qur'an, particularizes what is general in it, and qualifies what is absolute in it. If the Sunnah were not there, we would not know the details of the rites (prayer, fasting, alms-tax, pilgrimage) and other necessary and essential duties. For this reason, God said: "And We are revealing to you the Remembrance so that you make clear to the people what We have revealed to them, and perhaps they may reflect" (*al-Naḥl*, 16: 44). Moreover, it is the Qur'an itself that has enjoined on us obedience to the Messenger, just as it has enjoined on us obedience to God: "Say: 'Obey God and obey the Messenger'" (*al-Nūr*, 24: 54); "O believers: Obey God and obey the Messenger, and the people of authority among you; and if you have a dispute on any matter, refer it to God and the Messenger" (*al-Nisā'*, 4: 59). The scholars were unanimous on the point that referring to God means referring to His Book, and referring to the Messenger means referring to his Sunnah. God said: "Let those be warned who deviate from his [the Messenger's] commands lest a trial afflict them or a painful punishment afflict them" (*al-Nūr*, 24: 63).

As for the claim that God has preserved only the Qur'an – namely, that He guarantees its preservation, and does not guarantee the preservation of the Sunnah. This has already been explained by al-Shāṭibī in *al-Muwāfaqāt*: that the preservation of the Qur'an vouchsafes that of the Sunnah because the latter is the exposition of the former. For the preservation of what is clarified necessarily entails the preservation of what is clarifying it.

REJECTION OF HADITHS BECAUSE OF MISCOMPREHENSION

What I wish to draw attention to here is rejection of the Sunnah and *ṣaḥīḥ* hadiths as a result of miscomprehension arising in the mind of one not specialized and not well-grounded in this science. That has confirmed for us that the need of the approaching time is investigation and closely-detailed study of how the Sunnah should be understood, with intelligent recourse to its sources and its authorities. It is what we will be calling attention to in subsequent pages.

Rejection of the ṣaḥīḥ on account of poor understanding

Among the harms to which the Sunnah is exposed is that some rash individual reads a hadith, presumes for it a meaning of his own and interprets it accordingly. That meaning being unacceptable to him, he then rushes to reject the hadith, along with the discarded meaning. But if he had been fair, looked attentively and investigated, he would know that the meaning of the hadith is not as he understood it. He would know that he had prescribed for it, as suited his own judgment and taste, a meaning which neither Qur'an nor Sunnah present, which the language of the Arabs does not compel, and which no esteemed learned scholar from before him advocated.

The hadith of ʿĀ'ishah: "He would command me to put on izār, then would be intimate with me, while I was having my monthly period"

An example is the hadith, narrated by al-Bukhārī and others, from ʿĀ'ishah, that she said: "God's Messenger would command me, while I was having my monthly period, to put on the *izār* (lower garment), then he would be intimate with me."

Someone writing in the Kuwaiti journal *al-ʿArabī* nearly a third of a century ago rejected this hadith. He based his argument on the claim that it was at variance with the Qur'anic verse: "They ask you about menstruation. Say: it is a hurt; so keep apart from the women in menstruation, and do not go near them until they are cleansed (of it)" (*al-Baqarah*, 2: 222). The writer said the Qur'an commands the keeping apart from women in a state of menstruation, whereas the hadith says that the Messenger was intimate with his wife above the *izār.*

We have already rebutted this argument in detail elsewhere.[38] The gist is that there is no contradiction between the hadith and the Qur'an, as the writer had understood there to be. Rather, the hadith provides commentary on the Qur'an; it clarifies the meaning of the *iʿtizāl* (the keeping apart) that is commanded. The intent is not complete avoidance (*ijtināb*) of women – as the Jews do, who will not spend the night with the wife when she is in this state. The purpose in respect of the *iʿtizāl* that is commanded is that one forsakes the bodily intimacy of sexual intercourse. As for mutual pleasure in what is other than that – it is not part of that which is prohibited.[39]

Hadith: "O God, have me live as a miskīn ..."

Another example is the hadith that Ibn Mājah reported from Abū Saʿīd al-Khudrī and al-Ṭabarānī from ʿUbādah ibn Ṣāmit: "O God, have me live *miskīnan* (as a poor person) and have me die *miskīnan* and gather me [hereafter] in the company of the *miskīn*."[40] Someone read this hadith and he understood *al-maskanah* (poverty) to mean want of material wealth, with consequent neediness before other human beings. Now, this understanding of the meaning repudiates the supplication of the Prophet against the affliction of poverty,[41] and his asking from God, virtue and prosperity,[42] and his saying to Saʿd: "Indeed, God loves the slave [who is] prosperous, God-fearing and not ostentatious,"[43] and his saying to ʿAmr ibn al-ʿĀṣ: "Excellent indeed is the righteous wealth of a righteous man!"[44]

Because of the apparent contradiction, this person rejected the hadith mentioned. But the reality is that *al-maskanah* here does not mean 'poverty' in that sense. How could it mean that when he supplicated God against it, and associated it with unbelief – "O God, I seek refuge with You from unbelief and poverty"?[45] And his Lord entrusted him with prosperity: "And He found you destitute and enriched you" (*al-Ḍuḥā*, 93: 8). What is meant by *al-maskanah* is as Ibn al-Athīr said: "He meant by it lowliness and humility before God, and lest one should become one of the oppressors and the arrogant."

That is how the Prophet lived – far from the life of the arrogant ones, whether in look or form: he dressed as the slaves and the poor dressed; and he ate what they ate; and when a stranger came he (the stranger) did not distinguish him from his Companions for he was with them as one of them; and at home he mended his shoe with his own hand; and he patched his cloak; and he milked his sheep; and he turned a millstone to grind grains alongside the woman neighbor and the slave.

When a man entered to him and, being in awe of him, was trembling, he said: "Be at ease, for I am not a king. Rather, I am the son of a woman of the Quraysh who used to eat dried meat in Makkah."

The hadith on the renewal of the religion every century

Another example is the hadith, which Abū Dā'ūd and al-Ḥākim reported, and more than one scholar authenticated, from Abū Hurayrah from the Prophet: "God will send to this Community at the head of every century one who will renew for it its religion."[46] Someone read this and understood renewal (*tajdīd*) as meaning that the renewer develops the religion and alters it so as to adapt it to the age. He argued: 'But the religion is not subject to renewal, it is firmly established and does not change. It is not the duty of the religion to adapt to progress; rather, it is the duty of progress to adapt to the religion.'

Now, if 'renewal' meant that, in every age, we bring out (so to speak) a 'new edition' of the religion, its principles and teachings, going along with the needs of the people and in convoy with developments – and this overturns the truths of the religion – then a hadith that urges this should indeed be discarded. The person would be right if the intent of *al-tajdīd* had been what he interpreted it to be. But it is not.

The renewing meant – as I have explained elsewhere[47] – is of the understanding of the religion, and of faith and action. For the renewal of a thing is that by which an effort is made to return it to what it was like on the day of its origination, and then it emerges so as to seem new despite its antiquity. This is achieved by the strengthening of what has weakened, and the repairing of what has deteriorated over time, and the patching of what has frayed, so that it reverts closer to its original form. So the meaning of renewal is not the alteration of its ancient nature, or the replacement of it by another thing, novel and newly created. For that has nothing to do with renewal.

Let us take an example from among tangible things. If we intended renewal of an ancient historical structure, that would mean: letting its substance, its character and functions, and everything that survives of its distinguishing features, remain; repairing everything that decay has done to it; improving its entrances, facilitating the approaches to it; improving the specification of it; etc. It is nothing to do with renewal that we should demolish it, and erect a prestigious building in the latest style in its place.

It is the same with the religion: its renewal does not mean the issuing of a 'new edition' of it. Rather, it means the reversion of it to where it was in the epoch of the Messenger and his Companions, and of those who followed them with sincerity. It means: the revival of ijtihad in it, and recourse to its original wellsprings, liberation from inflexibility and imitativeness (*taqlīd)*, and examination of the legacy with a critical eye so as to benefit from its positive qualities and guard against any points of deficiency in it. Close to this renewal of thinking is another renewal, and that is the renewal of faith in the religion, devotion to its precious values and its principles, and renewing the invitation to it in harmony with the circumstances and necessities of the age – as has come in the hadith: "The faith wears out inside you, as the robe becomes worn out [outside you] – so beg God that He renew the faith in your hearts."[48]

"Islam is founded on five [foundations]"

Among the strangest instances in our time of the rejection of *ṣaḥīḥ* hadith, on account of incompetent understanding, is that some people have rejected the most famous hadith – one that Muslims young and old have memorized, the generality and the elite – and it is the hadith of Ibn ʿUmar and others: "Islam is founded upon five [foundations]: testifying that there is no god except God and that Muhammad is the Messenger of God; and the establishing of the prayer; and the paying of zakah; and fasting Ramadan; and pilgrimage to the House for whoever is able to [make] a way thereto."

The pretext for this bold foolhardiness in rejecting the hadith is that the hadith does not mention jihad, despite its great importance in Islam. And that is the basis for rejecting it!

This view is ignorant of the obvious fact that jihad is obligatory on some, not on others; that it is not an individual duty except in special circumstances for most particular considerations. That is very different from the five foundations, which are imposed on the generality of all people.

If the reasoning of the one who rejects the hadith were correct, it would entail rejecting the verses of the Qur'an which describe the good qualities of the believers: the God-fearing, the bondsmen of the Merciful, the virtuous and upright, the good-doers, those who possess spiritual intellect; and other qualities, which God has extolled in His Book, and promised for them most abundant recompense, but among those good qualities He does not mention jihad.

Read on that: the qualities of the God-fearing, in the first verses of *al-Baqarah*, 2: 2–5, of the people of virtue and veracity in the verse "it is not virtue ..." (2: 177); the qualities of the believers at the beginning of *al-Anfāl*, 8: 2–4; the qualities of those who possess spiritual intellect in *al-Raʿd*, 13: 20–22; the qualities of the believers and the inheritors of *Firdaws* (Paradise) at the beginning of *al-Mu'minūn*, 23: 1–10; the qualities of the bondsmen of the Merciful at the end of *al-Furqān*, 25: 63–77; the qualities of the God-fearing and the good-doers in *al-Dhāriyāt*, 51: 15–23; the qualities of the most-honored in the Gardens of God in *al-Maʿārij*, 70: 22–35. In all of these occurrences and others in the Book of God, jihad is not mentioned. Then will that enormous ignorance which rejects the hadith also expel these verses from the Book of God?

Shaykh al-Islam Ibn Taymiyyah has gone to some length in explaining the confinement of Islam to the five foundations mentioned, and why other fundamental obligations are not mentioned, such as jihad, or the virtue of looking after one's parents, the bond of near kinship, and matters similar to that. He said:

> In what was asked about is that: if there is, among the outward actions that God made obligatory on him, more than these five, then why did he say: Islam is these five? Some people have answered that these [five] are the more visible and the more powerful symbols of Islam, and by the slave's accom-

plishing of them his *islām* is completed; and by his leaving them is indicated the dissolution of the bond of his being bound [in Islam].

The more precise explanation is: that the Prophet mentioned the religion that renders up the slave to his Lord absolutely, namely the right of God, upon individuals, of exclusive worship. So He made it a duty for each one who was capable of it that he worship God by it, dedicating the religion purely to Him; and this [religion] – it is [made up of] the five. [As to] what is similar to that [in being obligatory], then it is what is obligatory according to occasions and exigencies, and so the duties thereof [being connected to occasions and exigencies] do not extend universally to all people.

Rather: [these other obligations comprise] either [1] the collective obligations – such as jihad, and commanding the good and forbidding the evil, and what [necessarily] follows [from] that by way of authority, and governance and the issuing of Legal dicta, and [scholarly or philosophical] inquiry, and transmission of hadith, and other [such duties] –

Or [2, those obligations which are] obligatory by occasion of the right of individual persons. By [that right] is specified the one on whom it is obligatory to fulfil it [i.e. the right of one individual specifies another individual for whom that right becomes a duty], and it is voided by annulment, and when the matter is achieved, or by acquittal – whether by his releasing or by the accomplishment of the matter.

Then the rights of the slaves [of God] – for example: settlement of debts; and restitution of the usurped [thing], and of loans, and of deposits for safe-keeping; and just restitution of wrongs respecting blood relations and properties and lands – indeed these are rights of individual persons, and when they release from them, [these rights] are voided, being binding on one person, not on another, in one circumstance, not in another. They are not incumbent upon every competent slave as is unmixed worship of God. That is why the Muslims share in them with the Jews and the Christians. The five [however, are obligations of a kind quite] different, for indeed these are among the distinguishing [things] of the Muslims [i.e. unique and restricted to the Muslims].

In the same way, what is obligatory respecting the bonds of close kinship, and the rights of wives and children and neighbors and [business] partners and the poor; and what is obligatory respecting the rendering of testimony, and the

> issuing of Legal dicta, and the giving judgment, and governance, and commanding the good and forbidding the evil, and jihad: all of that is obligatory by the contingent occasions, and upon some and not others. [This kind of obligation exists] in order to attract benefits or repel harms; if [the aims are] achieved without action by a person, [then] they are not obligatory. For that which is shared between people, then it is obligatory collectively; and what is particular then it is obligatory upon [a particular individual] Zayd, not upon [another individual] ᶜAmr. The people do not share in obligations [laid] upon each competent individual to discharge in person, except for the five. For indeed the wife of Zayd and his near kin are not the wife of ᶜAmr and his near kin, so it is not obligatory upon this one the like of [what is] obligatory upon this other. Different is fasting Ramadan; and pilgrimage to the House; and the five services of prayer; and the zakah. Indeed the zakah, though it is a right on property, yet it is due to God, and the eight categories [of recipients] are its [only lawful] heads of expenditure. This is why intention is obligatory therein, and [why] it is not permissible that another person do it [i.e. discharge the duty of zakah] without one's permission, and why it is not demanded from the unbelievers.[49]

On reckless haste in rejecting the ṣaḥīḥ and its being dubious to do so

In our view, haste in rejection of any hadith, though it is *ṣaḥīḥ* and affirmed, makes its having been understood doubtful. Those deep-rooted in knowledge do not venture recklessness in rejecting *ṣaḥīḥ* hadiths. Rather, they approve the opinion held by the early generations of the Community (*salaf*). For when it is established that they accepted a hadith, and no esteemed leader censured it, then necessarily they did not recognize any criticism of it on grounds of irregularity nor any cause of objection to it.

A fair-minded scholar must let the hadith stand, and study the intelligible meaning or the appropriate interpretation of it. This is the point of division in this field between the Muᶜtazilis (rationalists) and Ahl al-Sunnah (the Sunnis, those who followed the Sunnah). The former were prompt to dismiss every difficulty of hadith that resisted what they had accepted as principles of knowledge and religion. But Ahl al-Sunnah applied their minds to interpretation of the difficult hadith, and to bringing together what, outwardly, was at variance, and reconciling what was contradictory.

For that purpose Abū Muhammad Ibn Qutaybah (d. 267 AH) composed his well-known book *Ta'wīl Mukhtalaf al-Ḥadīth*, refuting the stormy assaults stirred up by the Muᶜtazilis around some hadiths, which they reproached for being contradictory to the Qur'an or to reason, or false in light of sense-perception, or for being opposed to other hadiths. After Ibn Qutaybah, the Ḥanafī hadith scholar Abū Jaᶜfar al-Ṭaḥāwī (d. 321) composed his book *Mushkil al-Āthār* in four bound volumes,[50] endeavoring to locate the points of difficulty in these hadiths, interpreting them and making them acceptable, and distinguishing them as conformable to reason.

Once the evidence of a hadith's being from the Prophet has been affirmed, a far-reaching, thorough examination into how it may be understood is obligatory; and there must be every caution against dismissing it merely to please far-fetched arguments, which may themselves have a mistake hidden in them.

The stance of ᶜĀ'ishah on certain hadiths

The clearest example of that is some of what has come from ᶜĀ'ishah. She censured some hadiths on the basis of her conjecture that they were opposed to the Qur'an, or to the established principles of Islam, or for other reasons. At times, it is the case that she censured hadiths narrated by the Companions, even though there is no doubting their veracity or their exactitude in preserving, and despite the hadiths' general import being sound. Take for example the hadith of the cat, and what has come about the punishment for tormenting it until it died. Aḥmad ibn Ḥanbal narrated it from ᶜAlqamah, he said:

> We were with ᶜĀ'ishah. Then Abū Hurayrah entered, so she said: "Are you the one who narrated the hadith – that a woman tormented a cat, confining her and then not feeding her, not giving her water – ?" Then he said: "I heard it from him" meaning the Prophet. Then she said: "Do you know

> what the woman was? At the time she did [that] she was an unbeliever. Indeed the believer is more noble with God, the All-Powerful and Sublime, than that He would punish him for a cat! So when you narrate a hadith from the Messenger of God, then watch how you are doing so!"[51]

ʿĀ'ishah censured Abū Hurayrah for his reporting of this hadith with his fashioning of it, and she reckoned that he did not preserve its wording as he heard it from the Prophet. Her argument is that she judged it too much that a believing human being be punished because of a cat; that a believer is nobler with God than that He would enter him into the Fire because of a dumb animal! May God forgive ʿĀ'ishah, for she was forgetful of a thing here in this matter that is the most important of the most important things. It is this: what demonstrates against the woman is the deed – namely that the cat was imprisoned until it died starving. It is proof plain of the hardness of heart of that woman and her cruelty to God's weak creatures, and that the rays of compassion did not reach into her bosom. None enters the Garden except the compassionate, and God does not show mercy except to those who show mercy. If she had shown mercy to one that is on the earth, then the One Who is in the heavens would have shown mercy to her.

This hadith and others of the same import should be counted in the sphere of humane values with pride in Islam, which respects every living creature, for Islam establishes a reward for human kindness to every group of creatures with a moist liver. What completes this meaning is what has come in another hadith, which al-Bukhārī also reported: that a man gave water to a dog, God acknowledged it from him and forgave him; and that a prostitute gave water to a dog, and God forgave her.

On top of that is the fact that Abū Hurayrah is not alone in the reporting of this hadith, so that it might be supposed he did not retain its words correctly – how could that be, when he is without exception the strongest in memory of the Companions? Furthermore, Aḥmad ibn Ḥanbal, al-Bukhārī and Muslim have reported from Ibn ʿUmar that he said: "A woman is punished for a cat. She confined her so that she died starving. Then she entered the Fire on account of [the cat]. God said: You did not feed her, and did not give her water, when you had tied her up. Nor did you let her go forth that she might eat of the vermin of the earth."[52] Also, Aḥmad has narrated from Jābir that he said: "A woman tormented a cat and tied him up until he died, and she did not let him go forth so he might eat of the vermin of the earth."[53]

So Abū Hurayrah is not alone in the reporting of this hadith. But even if he had been alone it would not have impaired at all the quality or meaning of his report.

CHAPTER TWO

The Sunnah as a Source for Jurisprudence and Preaching

I

IN JURISPRUDENCE AND LEGISLATION

The Sunnah is, after the Qur'an, the second source for jurisprudence and legislation. There is apposite and wide-ranging discussion of the fact in all the books on the principles of jurisprudence of all the schools. Al-Awzāʿī (d. 157 AH) said: "The Book is more in need of the Sunnah than the Sunnah is of the Book."[1] He said so because the Sunnah clarifies the Qur'an by detailing what is summary in it, qualifying what is absolute in it, and particularizing what is general in it. Some people even went so far as to say: "The Sunnah is decisive over the Book."[2] However, Aḥmad ibn Ḥanbal disapproved this turn of phrase: "I should not dare to say that. Rather, I say: 'The Sunnah is the exposition of the Book'."[3] That expression of the relation between the Book and the Sunnah reflects well Ibn Ḥanbal's understanding and piety together. It is the balanced position. For in one sense the Sunnah is making clearer what is there in the Book; but then, even on matters not directly in the Qur'an, the Sunnah remains so consistently within its orbit, that its teaching still serves as an exposition of the Qur'an.

Certainly there is no dispute about the Sunnah's being a source of legislation in the rites of worship and general affairs for the individual, the family, the society, and for the state and political relations. Al-Shawkānī said: "The conclusion is that the need for the Sunnah is established, and its independence [as a source] for the legislation of the injunctions is a religious necessity. No one disagrees on that except one who has no share in the religion of Islam."[4]

The books of Islamic jurisprudence – of whatever school – are overflowing with proofs from the Sunnah of speech, practice, and acceptance. There was no difference on this point between those known in the history of fiqh as the school of *ahl al-ḥadīth* ('the people of hadith') and those known as the school of *ahl al-ra'y* ('the people of opinion'). The fundamental principle was accepted by both, any differences arising only in the detail and the practical application, a consequence of the differences between them on the criteria for acceptance of hadiths and for acting in accordance with them.

The books of the Ḥanafī school (which exemplifies the school of *ra'y*) abound in hadiths which their learned doctors use as proofs. A typical book is *al-Ikhtiyār Sharḥ al-Mukhtār* by Ibn Mawdūd al-Ḥanafī al-Mawṣilī (d. 683 AH). It was prescribed, in schools linked with al-Azhar, for our secondary studies (I mean for the Ḥanafī students). Another is *al-Hadīd* by al-Marghīnānī, prescribed for Ḥanafī students at the Shariʿah faculty of al-Azhar, and the commentary on it, *Fatḥ al-Qadīr*, by the established Ḥanafī scholar Kamāl al-Dīn ibn al-Humām. A careful study of the hadiths in such books provides ample assurance that *ahl al-ra'y* looked to the Sunnah for corroboration, just as did *ahl al-āthār* ('the people of the traditions').

Yet, some people in our time have said that Abū Ḥanīfah affirmed the authenticity of only seventeen hadiths. This opinion makes no sense to anyone who knows the temperament of the schools of knowledge of that age, and the nature and formation of the scholars in them. Abū Ḥanīfah came out of the Kufan school of knowledge, which had combined jurisprudence and hadith since its foundation by the noble Companion ʿAbd Allāh ibn Masʿūd. The school grew in knowledge and blessing with the advent of the caliph, ʿAlī ibn Abī Ṭālib. It was he who said: "May God have mercy on Ibn Umm ʿAbd (meaning Ibn Masʿūd) for he has certainly filled this township with knowledge."

It is particularly strange that those who hold that opinion about Abū Ḥanīfah attribute it to the learned Ibn Khaldūn. This is due to a tendency (with which many test our forbearance) to extract certain phrases without attending to, or being informed about, the whole of the relevant passage, or even the immediate context. If we refer to Ibn Khaldūn we find that opinion expressed in the passive voice (a common device to distance the opinion being reported and to imply its weakness); he does not offer (or adopt) it as his own opinion; moreover, he says after it what rejects it. The passage in question is in the section *ʿulūm al-ḥadīth* ('the sciences of hadith') in his *Muqaddimah*:

> Know also that the leading *mujtahid*s differed in how much and how little of this material [i.e. hadiths, they accepted and transmitted]. Now about Abū Ḥanīfah, it is said that he transmitted the narration of seventeen hadiths or thereabout (up to fifty); and Mālik – may God have mercy on him – pronounced as authentic according to himself only what is in his book (*al-Muwaṭṭā*), and the utmost number of them is 300 hadiths or thereabout. Whereas Aḥmad ibn Ḥanbal – God have mercy on him – [accepted] in his *Musnad* 30,000 hadiths. And each of them exercised his judgment on whatever was conveyed to him.
>
> Yet some raging zealots say: Among them, one [meaning Abū Ḥanīfah] had little in hadith material and for this [reason] was less in narration [of it]. But there is no way for this view in regard to the great imams, because the Law is derived only from the Book and the Sunnah, and whoever had little in the goods of hadith was bound to seek and narrate it, and be assiduous and strenuous therein, so that he could derive the religion from the authentic sources, and receive the injunctions from the one who had them [as passed to him from one] who [in turn] conveyed them from God. And among [the great imams], whoever was less in narrating [hadith] was so only on account of the taunts that were opposing him in [narrating], and the defects which impeded its route – especially when criticism [challenging and questioning sources] was a priority [at that time] for many. Then personal judgment led him to rejection of the acceptance [of a hadith] because of an opposi-

> tion of that sort to it, among the hadiths and the routes of their transmitting authorities. There was a great deal of that [at that time]. Thus his narrating was [so] little for reason of the weakness of the routes [of transmission]. This notwithstanding, the people of the Ḥijāz narrated much more of hadith than the people of Iraq, because Madinah had been the focus of the Hijrah and the refuge of the Companions. Those of them who relocated to Iraq were often preoccupied in jihad. Imam Abū Ḥanīfah was only so little in narrating [hadith] because he was severe in the criteria for narrating and for [assessing] the firmness [of hadiths], and he would pronounce the hadith weak if settled reasoning opposed it, and so he considered it difficult. He reduced on account of that his narrating [of hadith], and so reduced [the number of] his hadith. It is not that he abandoned narrating the hadith as a deliberate policy – for he was far removed from that. That he was among the great *mujtahid*s in the science of hadith is demonstrated by their approbation of his school and by the dependence on him and on his judgments in respect of rejection or acceptance [of hadiths]. As for others among the hadith specialists (*muḥaddithīn*) – and they were the majority – they relaxed the criteria [for accepting hadith] and increased the number of their hadith, and all [did so] on the basis of their personal judgment. And indeed his colleagues [his students and fellow-scholars among the scholars of Iraq] after him relaxed the criteria [for accepting hadith] and increased the amount of their narrating. Al-Ṭaḥawī [for example] narrated and [did so] in great volume, and wrote his *Musnad.* He is one of lofty rank, except that he does not match the two *Ṣaḥīḥ*s, for the reason that the criteria that were settled upon by al-Bukhārī and Muslim in their two books have been widely accepted among the Community just as they [the hadith specialists] have said, whereas the criteria of al-Ṭaḥawī have not been agreed upon, such as narrating from one of hidden condition, and other than that.[5]

That is what the learned Ibn Khaldūn really said about Abū Ḥanīfah and his school. It is the discourse of a knowledgeable historian, well-informed and fair-minded.

ALL JURISTS REFER TO THE SUNNAH

We can state with complete assurance that all the jurists of the Muslims – from different schools, from diverse cities, whose doctrine survives or has been cut off, is followed or is not followed – have been in agreement on acceptance of the Sunnah and the appeal to it in making rulings. On this point (as noted above), those affiliated to the school of *ra'y* and those affiliated to the school of *ḥadīth* were the same. The following reports from al-Bayhaqī illustrate this unanimity:

> From ʿUthmān ibn ʿUmar, that he said:
> A man came to Mālik and asked him about a matter. Then [Mālik] said to him: "God's Messenger said so-and-so." Then the man said: "Is that your opinion?" Then Mālik said: "Let them beware who oppose his [the Messenger's] command lest a trial afflict them or a grievous punishment" (*al-Nūr*, 24: 63).
>
> From Ibn Wahb, that he said:
> Mālik said: "There never used to be among those giving fatwas to the people that one said to [the people], 'Why did I say that?' The people were satisfied with the narration and pleased with it."[6]
>
> From Yaḥyā ibn Ḍurays, that he said:
> I was a witness [when] a man came to Sufyān, and said: "What do you have against Abū Ḥanīfah?" He said: "What is [supposed to be wrong] with him? I have heard him say: 'I take from the Book of God, and if I do not find [what I am seeking], then from the Sunnah of God's Messenger; then if I do not find [what I am seeking] in the Book of God or the Sunnah of His Messenger, I take from the sayings of his Companions. I take from the saying of whomever I like, and I leave the saying of whomever I like. But I do not depart from their saying to the saying of other than them. Then as for when the matter reaches to Ibrāhīm or al-Shaʿbī and Ibn Sīrīn and al-Ḥasan and ʿAṭā', and Ibn al-Musayyab' – and he enumerated the men – 'people do ijtihad, and I do ijtihad as they do.' "
>
> From al-Rabīʿ that he said:
> One day al-Shāfiʿī narrated a hadith and a man said to him: "Do you accept this, O Abū ʿAbd Allāh?" Then [al-Shāfiʿī] said: "When I report from God's Messenger a *ṣaḥīḥ* hadith and

> I do not accept it, then I attest to you that my mind has definitely gone!"
>
> From al-Rabīᶜ that he said:
>
> If you find in my book an opposition to the Sunnah of God's Messenger then maintain a view according to the Sunnah and leave what I say.[7]

THE NECESSITY OF LINKING HADITH AND FIQH

Since the Sunnah is a fundamental source of fiqh, it is one of the duties of jurists to go deeply into the science of hadith. In the same way it is a duty of hadith specialists to master the science of fiqh. There have been gaps of knowledge between these two that should be closed up: this is something I called for long years ago.

The best practitioners of fiqh do not master the arts of hadith or go deeply into the knowledge of its disciplines. In particular, they do not go into the disciplines of *jarḥ* and *taᶜdīl* (critical scrutiny of narrators leading to rejection or acceptance), and so fail to appreciate the consequence of narrators being classed as reliable or weak. Accordingly, certain hadiths, which are not considered established according to the leading figures in the assaying of hadith, are common currency with them. Moreover, they settle such hadiths in their books, adducing them in what they decide of injunctions in the Legal categories of the permissible and the forbidden, the obligatory and the commended. At times they even argue from hadiths without benefit of any reserve or discipline from what has been said about them in the books – hadiths whose sources and *sanad* is not known. Among the hadith specialists a saying has long circulated: "This is from the hadiths of the jurists" – by which they mean it does not have a well-known source.

On the other side, the best practitioners of hadith are not good in the knowledge of fiqh or its principles. They have no aptitude for discovering its rules and deriving its precious treasures and subtleties. They are not thoroughly familiar with its leading figures, the multiplicity of their schools and their objectives, or the diversity of their personal judgments.

Both sides, the specialists in fiqh and those in hadith, are in pressing need of the knowledge of the other so as to complement what each has. The jurist must know hadith, since the bulk of the judgments of fiqh are established according to the Sunnah. The *muḥaddith* must know fiqh so as to understand what he is conveying, to not be a mere conveyor (*nāqul*), and to avoid understanding in an improper way what he is conveying.

Islamic scholars of the early period took note of this need. They censured whoever disregarded it, to the extent that some of the most learned of them, for example Sufyān ibn ʿUyaynah, are reported to have said: "If this matter were in our hands, we would beat with a palm-rod (*jarīd*) every *muḥaddith* who did not busy himself with fiqh, and every *faqīh* (jurist) who did not busy himself with hadith."

It is strange that there are many weak hadiths in the books of fiqh. Now many accept the use of a weak hadith to teach the merits of certain deeds (*faḍā'il*), or to inspire longing for God (*targhīb*) and dread of Him (*tarhīb*). But there is general agreement that a weak hadith cannot be used to derive injunctions. Nevertheless, in the books of fiqh, one finds hadiths that are weak, extremely weak, and fabricated, and some with no source at all. That prompted those great hadith specialists who did busy themselves with fiqh to write books of source-critique (*takhrīj al-ḥadīth*) on the hadiths that the jurists adduced in their books. These hadiths were cited *muʿallaq* (hanging, unsupported), that is, without any *sanad*s. Al-Jawzī wrote such a source-critique in his book *al-Taḥqīq fī Takhrīj al-Taʿālīq*, which, after him, Ibn ʿAbd al-Hādī refined in his *Tanqīḥ al-Taḥqīq*.

Several *ḥuffāẓ* compiled books of source-critique of the hadiths used in admired and famous fiqh writings. An example is *Naṣb al-Rāyah li-Aḥādīth al-Hidāyah* by al-Ḥāfiẓ Jamāl al-Dīn al-Zaylaʿī (d. 762 AH). It has been printed many times in four volumes. Al-Ḥāfiẓ Ibn Ḥajar abridged it in his book *al-Dirāyah fī Takhrīj Aḥādīth al-Hidāyah*, adding to it some informative and instructive notes. It is published in a single volume. The *Hidāyah* is one of the principal textbooks in Ḥanafī fiqh. Another example is Ibn Ḥajar's source-critique of the hadiths in *Fatḥ al-ʿAzīz fī Sharḥ al-Wajīz*. *Sharḥ al-Wajīz* is the great commentary by al-Rāfiʿī on al-Ghazālī's *al-Wajīz*. A group of scholars, including Ibn Ḥajar in his famous book *Talkhīs al-Ḥabīr*, have exposed its sources. Al-Rāfiʿī's commentary is among the principal textbooks of Shāfiʿī fiqh.

To be sure, some jurists relied upon hadiths that only those after them established as weak – so they are to be excused for relying on them. But for those to whom their weakness had been disclosed, there is no excuse for their repeated recourse to them. It is right to abandon a ruling based upon hadiths established as weak, when there is not, for that ruling, another proof (*dalīl*) from the texts of the Law or its general principles or its objectives as a whole. Why it is right to do so can be easily seen from the works of source-critique on books of fiqh of high repute in the still-followed schools. For example: *Naṣb al-Rāyah li-Aḥādīth al-Hidāyah* by al-Zaylaʿī; *Talkhīs al-Ḥabīr fī Takhrīj Aḥādīth Sharḥ al-Rāfiʿ al-Kabīr* by Ibn Ḥajar; *Irwā al-Ghalīl fī Takhrīj Aḥādīth Manār al-Sabīl* by al-Albānī (*Manār al-Sabīl* being among the texts of Ḥanbalī fiqh); and *al-Hidāyah fī Takhrīj Aḥādīth al-Bidāyah* by Aḥmad ibn Ṣiddīq al-Ghamarī (*al-Bidāyah* refers to Ibn Rushd's *Bidāyat al-Mujtahid*).

I myself have noted, while researching the fiqh of zakah, a number of hadiths that scholars of fiqh of still-followed schools rely on, and which have been challenged by the leading scholars of hadith. For example:

> There is no *ṣadaqah* on vegetables.
>
> *ʿUshr* and *kharāj* do not combine.
>
> There is no duty [right] on wealth besides zakah.

The last hadith is well-known among the jurists. Some of their great ones cite it, for example al-Māwardī in *al-Aḥkām al-Sulṭāniyyah*; al-Shīrāzī in *al-Muhadhdhab*; and Ibn Qudāmah in *al-Mughnī*. Al-Nawawī (in *al-Majmūʿa*) said about it: "It is a very weak hadith; it is not known." Before him, al-Bayhaqī said, in *al-Sunan*: "Our colleagues narrate it in commentaries, but I do not remember any *isnād* in it." The original form of the hadith, according to al-Tirmidhī and Ibn Mājah and al-Ṭabarī in his *Tafsīr*, is: "There is a duty (right) on wealth besides zakah." Subsequently, a familiar sort of copyist's error occurred in a particular transcription of Ibn Mājah, and the word 'is not' (*laysa*) got interpolated at the beginning of the hadith. The error circulated and persisted. Abū Zarʿah ibn al-Ḥāfiẓ Zayn al-Dīn al-ʿIrāqī pointed out the error in *Ṭarḥ al-Tashrīb fī Sharḥ al-Taqrīb* (vol. 4, p. 18). Aḥmad Shākir explained it in his source-critique of al-Ṭabarī's *Tafsīr* (report no. 2527), and he furnished against it some proofs that settle the mind and heart.

In many books of fiqh and its divisions (*abwāb*) there are hadiths of this category, that is, those whose *sanad* was unknown to the *ḥuffāẓ*. In *Naṣb al-Rāyah*, al-Zaylaʿī marked such hadiths as *gharīb* ('unknown'). It is a term peculiar to him, indicating that he did not find a *sanad* for the hadith. To indicate the same thing, Ibn Ḥajar in *Dirāyah* used the expression "I did not find it" or "I did not think it *marfūʿ*" or words close to that. There are many such hadiths in some divisions of fiqh, indeed so many that it draws attention.

While studying hadiths on the subject of ritual slaughter, I found in *al-Dirāyah* more than twenty hadiths, some of them *ṣaḥīḥ* and some weak; and about some, Ibn Ḥajar has said he "did not know it" or "did not find it". Some examples:

> The hadith:
> Adopt in relations with them (the Magians) the same way (*sunnah*) as with the People of the Book except marrying their women and eating [of the meat from animals] that they have slaughtered.
> (Ibn Ḥajar said: "I did not find it in these words." He means: with the addition of the words "marrying their women", etc.)
>
> The hadith:
> The Muslim slaughters in the name of God [whether] he has invoked or has not invoked [God's name].
> (Ibn Ḥajar said: "I did not find it in these words.")
>
> The hadith of Ibn Masʿūd:
> Strip the *tasmiyah* [of everything else, i.e. say only the *tasmiyah*].
> (Ibn Ḥajar said: "I did not find it in these words.")

> The hadith:
> The immolation [i.e. the incision] should be [at the point] that is between the top of the chest and the bottom of the chin.
> (Ibn Ḥajar said: "I did not find it.")
>
> The hadith:
> Cut the veins with what you wish.
> (Ibn Ḥajar said: "I did not find it.")
>
> The hadith:
> That the Prophet prohibited you to dislodge the phlegm of the goat when you slaughter. (The author said: "That is, [when] you reach the phlegm with the knife.")
> (Ibn Ḥajar said: "I did not find it.)
>
> The hadith:
> That he prohibited ʿĀ'ishah from [eating] lizard when she asked about eating it.
> (Ibn Ḥajar said: "I did not find it.")
>
> The hadith:
> That he forbade the sale of crayfish.
> (Ibn Ḥajar said: "I did not find it.")

And so on – there are other hadiths like that.[8]

Such laxity in adducing weak hadiths is not confined to books of *ahl al-ra'y* as they are called. Rather, one finds generally among the books of the surviving schools of Law, weak hadiths and even those with no source. But, to be sure, the ascription of laxity varies from school to school.

In *Talkhīs al-Ḥabīr*, Ibn Ḥajar has traced the hadiths in the commentary by al-Rāfiʿī on al-Ghazālī's *al-Wajīz* (both of whom were leading Shāfiʿīs). He pronounces as weak many of the hadiths on which the argument in the book rests. Now Ibn Ḥajar was himself a Shafiʿi – but the truth has more right to be followed than one's school. Similarly, al-Ḥāfiẓ Abū Bakr Aḥmad ibn al-Ḥusayn al-Bayhaqī (d. 457 AH) sent to Abū Muhammad ʿAbd Allāh ibn Yūsuf al-Juwaynī (d. 438 AH; the father of Imam al-Ḥaramayn) a courteous critique of some of the erroneous hadith conjectures that had befallen him in his book *al-Muḥīṭ.* The very first hadith in the book, on the prohibition of bathing with water exposed to sunlight, is an example: it is a hadith not authenticated as *ṣaḥīḥ*.

It is a tribute to the fair-mindedness of al-Bayhaqī that he criticized also hadith specialists among his Shafiʿī colleagues. He criticized their laxity in abandoning the distinction between reports on which it is correct to base argumentation, and reports on which it is not correct to do so. He criticized them also for narrating from weak and unknown narrators, and for other failings presented in his treatise, *al-Rasīnah al-Rakīnah*.[9]

Most strange indeed is that even books on the subject of the principles of jurisprudence (*uṣūl al-fiqh*) are not lacking in hadiths that are fragile and fabricated and without source. An example is the hadith: "My Companions are like the stars: whichever of them you are led by, he will guide you." This is very weak. Indeed, Shaykh al-Albānī has judged it to have been fabricated. Another is: "Whatever is seen by Muslims as good, it is good in the sight of God." This is in fact from the discourse of Ibn Masʿūd, not a *marfūʿ* hadith (so it should not be attributed to the Prophet). Yet another is: "My Community's differences are a mercy."[10] And there are several others, familiar from the books of *uṣūl al-fiqh* well-known to students.

THE DUTY OF SCHOLARLY REVISION OF THE LEGACY OF FIQH

It is a duty of the learned community in our time, the *ʿulamā'*, to go back over the fiqh inheritance – in the light of knowledge of the hadith combined with fiqh and its principles, with penetrating and perceptive reasoning – and look into the injunctions based on weak hadiths. For it is a point of agreement that a weak hadith cannot support an injunction, that one cannot build upon it the obligations of the lawful and the unlawful. Through this effort, those injunctions (relating to Legal dicta and to collective duties) that have no authoritative basis other than weak hadiths will be uncovered. Some examples follow:

Bloodwit for non-Muslims

Take for example, in the criminal code, how one determines the Legal bloodwit for the *dhimmī*s. The majority of jurists hold that the bloodwit for the *dhimmī*s of the People of the Book – more precisely, from those of them under Islamic jurisdiction (*dār al-Islām*, as the jurists put it) – is one half the bloodwit for Muslims.[11] Their proof for that is some hadiths that appear in the *Musnad* and the *Sunan*. Of them, there is not one in both *Ṣaḥīḥ*s or in either of them (that is, in one but not the other). Rather, they are hadiths that some scholars accepted but others rejected. For example, the hadith of ʿAmr ibn Shuʿayb from his father from his grandfather that the Prophet said: "The bloodmoney for the unbeliever is half the bloodwit for the Muslim." Aḥmad ibn Ḥanbal reported this, as did al-Nasāʾī and al-Tirmidhī. Again Aḥmad and al-Nasāʾī, and also Ibn Mājah, have reported a variant: "He judged that the blood-money of the People of the Two Books (and they are the Jews and the Christians) is half the bloodmoney of the Muslims." (The meaning of the two terms used, 'bloodmoney' and 'bloodwit', is the same.)

Other scholars held that the bloodwit for a Jew or Christian is a third of the bloodwit for a Muslim. Their doing so demonstrates that, in their view, the hadith just cited was not established.

By contrast, al-Thawrī, al-Zuhrī, Zayd ibn ʿAlī, and Abū Ḥanīfah and his influential followers, held that the bloodwit of the *dhimmī* is equal to that of the Muslim. They adduced hadiths and reports (*āthār*) that the Prophet made the bloodwit of the person under covenant of protection by the Muslims the bloodwit of the Muslim, and that he paid out the bloodwit of a Muslim as the bloodwit due for a *dhimmī*. But then, those scholars who disagreed with this pronounced these hadiths weak.

The reality is that the hadiths of neither of the two opposing viewpoints attain the rank of *ṣaḥīḥ*, and none of them can sustain a ruling. Therefore, recourse is obligatory to the general texts of the Law and its objectives as a whole. Now, if we refer to the Qur'an, we find for accidental killing it is the same – whether it be a Muslim or one of the peoples between whom and the Muslims there is a compact. The obligation in both cases is "bloodwit surrendered to his people and the emancipation of a believing captive (slave)" (*al-Nisā'*, 4: 92), and it does not differentiate between Muslim and non-Muslim. This is consonant with the Law's restraining bloodshed among both Muslims and non-Muslims, and with equal treatment of people in line with the noble sentiments of humanity, especially among the people of the land, the land of Islam, co-nationals under a single political authority. It is the doctrine according to which Islamic governments ruled for long centuries, throughout the periods of the ʿAbbāsid and ʿUthmānī caliphates. However, the great powers of the present want to exploit the legal status of non-Muslim minorities, alleging that they are oppressed, and that equal treatment for them does not exist in the criminal code in Islamic jurisprudence.

Bloodwit for the woman

In the case of bloodwit for a woman, the majority of the greatest jurists hold that it is half that for a man. They rest their case on hadiths mentioned from Muʿādh *marfūʿan* (reporting from the Prophet) that he said: "The bloodwit for a woman is half the bloodwit for a man." Al-Bayhaqī said of its chain of authorities: "An *isnad* like its *isnad* is not [accepted as] established." He reported from ʿAlī, that he said: "The bloodwit for a woman is [calculated] as one half the bloodwit for a man." This is a narration of Ibrāhīm al-Nakhaʿī from ʿAlī. It is also narrated by Ibn Abī Shuʿayb, who narrated it through Shaʿbī from Ibrāhīm. It is in every case *mawqūf* (stopped at a Companion), and in Law there is no compelling proof in the non-*marfūʿ* (that is, in what is not from the Prophet himself). There is not in the details of the penalty for a woman and the penalty for a man – that is, for injuries and the like – a single hadith established or demonstrated as being *ṣaḥīḥ*.

As for the minority, they rest their case on an appeal to ijmaʿ or consensus. Now ijmaʿ is a proof in which there is no doubt. But in this instance ijmaʿ is not established. For people have narrated that on this subject there is a different opinion from two of the scholars of the *salaf* (the early generations of Muslims). The two are al-Āṣim and Ibn al-ʿAlbah: according to them, the bloodwit for a woman is the same as the bloodwit for a man.[12]

Explanation of the attitudes of Islam

Just as a *ṣaḥīḥ* hadith is sought to explain the injunctions in the rites of worship and in everyday affairs and in the lawful and the unlawful, it is sought to explain the attitude of Islam in decisions relating to ideas, education, good manners, and other matters. If, for example, we wish to explain the attitude of Islam on 'the life of the world' – in respect of renunciation of it or absorption in its good things – then weak hadiths do not suffice. Among similar examples are the attitude of Islam to reliance on God, as against making use of (the so-called 'natural' or 'secondary') causes; to preventive medicine or therapeutic medicine; to the conservation of animals and plants; to instances of material or intellectual progress; to supernatural phenomena and miracles.

For these cases and their like, it does not suffice to adduce hadiths that are subject to disagreement. Rather, recourse must be to hadiths that are strengthened and authenticated in their proofs, clear and unambiguous in what they demonstrate. Also, one should not be satisfied with a single relevant hadith. Rather, the principle is that there should be many hadiths contributing their light to the picture, and illuminating the attitude of Islam on this or that matter – except, of course, when there is a Qur'anic verse, and then it will be the source and reference point.

II

IN PREACHING AND GUIDANCE

The Sunnah of the Prophet is, after the Qur'an, the inexhaustible resource and treasury on which religious teachers, preachers and guides can draw for their lessons and sermons. For, as the Sunnah is the agreed-upon source for the legislation of the injunctions, and for the fiqh of the rites of worship and of everyday affairs, so too it is the agreed-upon source for the purification of the soul. That is why all those engaged in the education of the spirit, including the great men of *taṣawwuf* of the early period who were respected among the Community, are unanimous on binding the traveler on the road to God to the Sunnah, in his thought and worship, and in his relations with God, with himself, and with people. Imam al-Junayd, may God have mercy on him, said: "All roads are closed off except [the roads taken by those] who follow the tracks of God's Messenger." And: "One who does not memorize the Qur'an and write down the hadith should not be followed in this business [Sufism], because this our knowledge is bound to the Book and the Sunnah." Abū Ḥafṣ, one of the leaders of those who followed a Sufi way, said: "One who did not give weight in his actions and his states to the Book and the Sunnah, who did not rebuke his desires, he was not counted in the register of men." Abū Sulaymān al-Dārānī said: "It may be that an anecdote from the anecdotes of the people may enter my heart for a few days: but I do not accept [anything] of it except according to the two just witnesses: the Book and the Sunnah." Aḥmad ibn Abī al-Ḥawārī said: "Whoever does his deed without following the Sunnah, his deed has wasted."

So the educators and the preachers are needy of the Sunnah, as are the students and practitioners of fiqh. In the Sunnah they find illuminating guidance, cogent argument, and eloquent wisdom; epitomes and maxims, affecting admonitions, salient similitudes, and instructive stories; diverse kinds of command and prohibition, and promise and threat to inspire longing for God and dread of Him, to soften stiffened hearts, give life to exhausted resolve, and awaken forgetful minds. Running within the framework of the Qur'an, the Sunnah addresses the whole being, mind, heart and conscience, striving for the formation of the perfected Muslim personality – a mind that is alert, a heart that is pure, a resolve that is strong, and a body that is fit.

Foremost of what those relying on this material should do is to take it from the source of it, from the books of the Sunnah. First of all, the two *Ṣaḥīḥ*s: the *Ṣaḥīḥ* of al-Bukhārī and the *Ṣaḥīḥ* of Muslim, both of which the Community has met with acceptance. Neither has been criticized except for a few hadiths mostly on matters of form and fine technical detail. After these two, selection from the other books of the Sunnah: the four *Sunan* (of Abū Dā'ūd, al-Tirmidhī, al-Nasā'ī and Ibn Mājah), the *Muwaṭṭā* of Mālik, the *Musnad* of Aḥmad ibn Ḥanbal, the *Sunan* of al-Dārimī, the *Ṣaḥīḥ* of Ibn Khuzaymah, the *Ṣaḥīḥ* of Ibn Ḥibbān, the *Mustadrak* of al-Ḥākim, the two *Musnad*s of Abū Yaʿlā and al-Bazzār, the *Maʿajim* of al-Ṭabarānī, and *Shuʿab al-Īmān* of al-Bayhaqī. Then there are other works, whose hadiths the hadith experts have confirmed as *ṣaḥīḥ* or *ḥasan*. Every preacher is under obligation not to rely on hadiths that are feeble or rejected or classed as fabricated. It is a matter of severe regret that such hadiths appear time and again as the common merchandise of preachers of sermons and religious counselors.

By the grace of God, a number of the basic texts have already been published in print editions. Thanks to the labors of the servant of the Sunnah, Muhammad Fu'ād ʿAbd al-Bāqī, may God have mercy on him, *Muwaṭṭā Mālik*, *Ṣaḥīḥ Muslim* and *Sunan Ibn Mājah*, have been edited and published, with the hadiths numbered and indexed. Also edited and published are *Sunan Abī Da'ūd* and *Sunan al-Tirmidhī*, again with the hadiths numbered and indexed, by ʿIzzat ʿUbayd al-Daʿʿās. ʿAbd al-Fattāḥ Abū Ghuddah, may God have mercy on him, has edited al-Nasā'ī's book, and numbered its hadiths in accordance with *al-Muʿjam al-Mufuhris li al-Alfāẓ al-Ḥadīth*.

An even more important task is source-critique and exposition of the rank of the hadiths, distinguishing the *ṣaḥīḥ* from the faulty. The following critical works, by the hadith-scholar Shaykh Nāṣir al-Dīn al-Albānī, have appeared: *Ṣaḥīḥ Ibn Mājah*, *Ṣaḥīḥ al-Tirmidhī*, and *Ṣaḥīḥ al-Nasā'ī*. His *Ṣaḥīḥ Abī Da'ūd* has all but come out. So too, all but completed, are parts of *Ṣahih Ibn Ḥibbān*, edited with source-critique by Shuʿayb al-Arna'ūṭ. Before that, Muhammad

Muṣṭafā al-Aʿẓamī edited what was found of *Ṣaḥīḥ Ibn Khuzaymah*, and published it together with source-critique by al-Albānī.

Before that, there had appeared fifteen volumes of the *Musnad Aḥmad*, edited with source-critique by Aḥmad Muhammad Shākir, about one-third of the whole. Shaykh Aḥmad ʿAbd al-Raḥmān had earlier arranged the *Musnad* by topic, written a commentary on it, and published it in 23 volumes. He called it *al-Fatḥ al-Rabbānī*, and its commentary *Bulūgh al-Amānī*. Shaykh Shākir made an effort to bring out some of the *tafsīr* of Ibn Kathīr, selected, corrected and source-critiqued. He called it *ʿUmdat al-Tafsīr*, he published five parts of it but was unable to complete it. He, and his most learned brother, Maḥmūd Muhammad Shākir, brought out rather more than ten parts of *Tafsīr Imam al-Ṭabarī* (d. 310 AH), with editing and source-critique of the hadiths and reports (*āthār*) it contains. After the older brother Shaykh Aḥmad died, Professor Maḥmūd brought out, after him, another two parts. Then this great scholarly work came to a halt.

Al-Muṣannaf by ʿAbd al-Razzāq al-Sanʿā'nī (d. 211 AH) has appeared in eleven parts, edited by the Indian hadith-scholar, Shaykh Ḥabīb al-Raḥmān al-Aʿẓamī; so too *Muṣannaf Ibn Abī Shaybah* (d. 225 AH) from al-Dār al-Salafiyyah in India, edited by Shaykh Mukhtār al-Nadwī.

Some of the important secondary collections have also come out. *Mishkāt al-Maṣābiḥ* by Shaykh al-Khaṭīb al-Tabrīzī (d. 732 AH) has been edited by al-Albānī with an abridged source-critique. Al-Albānī has distinguished the *ṣaḥīḥ* from the *daʿīf* in al-Suyūṭī's *Ṣaḥīḥ al-Jāmiʿ al-Ṣaghīr* and its *Supplement*, and published them in two separate volumes. *Jāmiʿ al-Uṣūl* of Ibn al-Athīr (d. 606 AH) has been edited and brought out by ʿAbd al-Qādir al-Arnā'ūṭ.

Majmaʿ al-Zawā'id of Nūr al-Dīn al-Haythamī (d. 807 AH) came out earlier, but it was not edited. Its distinction is that it judges between *ṣaḥīḥ* and *ḍaʿīf* hadiths, and brings together material from outside the Six Books of hadith: *Musnad Aḥmad*, and *Musnad al-Bazzār*, and *Musnad Abū Yaʿlā*, and the three *Maʿājim al-Ṭabarānī*. I wish that this useful book had been edited, although I am apprehensive of present-day editors of our useful books: they edit the book with additions to its bulk of commentary, of which there is little need, and which they repeat in every book, the consequent lengthening of the work providing scope to get money from its poor readers!

Among the important books which are repeatedly printed – but not edited, nor their sources checked – are: *Mustadrak al-Ḥākim* (d. 405 AH) and the abridgement of it by al-Dhahabī (d. 748 AH). Among examples of the important ones that are edited and source-critiqued, are: *Zād al-Maᶜād* by Ibn al-Qayyim (d. 751 AH), edited by Shuᶜayb al-Arnā'ūṭ, published in five volumes by al-Risālah, with a sixth for the index; and *Riyāḍ al-Ṣāliḥīn* by al-Nawawī (d. 676 AH). It is a book blessed and splendid in usefulness. Shuᶜayb al-Arnā'ūṭ and al-Albānī edited it and checked all its sources.

More important still is the source-critique of the book *al-Iḥsān fī Taqrīb Ṣaḥīḥ Ibn Ḥibbān*, edited by Shaykh Shuᶜayb al-Arnā'ūṭ in sixteen volumes, with a two volume index. Al-Risālah published it.

Greater than that is the concordance of similar hadiths in *Musnad Imam Aḥmad*, published in more than forty volumes, edited by Shaykh Shuᶜayb and five of his distinguished learned colleagues. It is on the point of completion, and al-Risālah are publishing it with the support of the Kingdom of Saudi Arabia.

Here one has a duty to refer to old source-critiques and benefit from them. For example: the critique by Zayn al-Dīn al-ᶜIrāqī (d. 807 AH) of the hadiths in *al-Iḥyā'* of al-Ghazālī (d. 505 AH), who called it *al-Mughnī ᶜan Ḥaml al-Asfār fī Takhrīj mā fī al-Iḥyā' min al-Akhbār*. It was printed with marginal notes to the *Iḥyā'*; it is necessary for the reader of *al-Iḥyā'* to refer to it. One knows the rank of the hadiths that were adduced by al-Ghazālī, and how many extremely weak hadiths there are in it, others with no source for them, and others pronounced fabricated! Another example is the source-critique by Ibn Ḥajar al-ᶜAsqalānī of the hadiths in the *tafsīr*, *al-Kashshāf*. It is useful from the viewpoint of the many hadiths that the Qur'anic commentators adduce, and which were subsequently copied by other commentators.

Among the important and famous books for preaching and admonishment is the book *al-Targhīb wa al-Tarhīb* of al-Mundhirī (d. 606 AH) – may God have mercy on him. The defect of the book is that there are many weak hadiths in it, and some of them extremely weak. It may be that it even descends to the level of the fabricated – to the extent that this is the opinion of al-Mundhirī himself. But many givers of admonishments and sermons have not read al-Mundhirī's Preface so that they would know his technique and terminology. This is what drove me back to serve this book by making critical selections from it (*muntaqā*). The selection includes the *ṣaḥīḥ* and the *ḥasan* in it, with notes on what is obscure in it, and explanations of its purposes, and answers to the questions it asks itself. In short, it erases doubts and corrects misunderstandings. Its title is *al-Muntaqā min al-Targhīb wa al-Tarhīb.*

As for the commentaries on the well-known books: the greatest of them is *Fatḥ al-Bārī fī Sharḥ al-Bukhārī* by Ibn Ḥajar. This is the book about which (with a pun on the well-known hadith) al-Shawkānī said: "*la hjirah baᶜd al-fatḥ*" ('No emigration after the Conquest'). There are available other commentaries on al-Bukhārī earlier than it, contemporary with it, and later than it. One should make use of them all. Examples are: al-Kirmānī (d. 675 AH), al-ᶜAynī (d. 855 AH), and al-Qasṭalānī (d. 923 AH).

Among commentaries on Muslim are the *Sharḥ* of al-Nawawī, and those of al-ᶜIyāḍ, and al-Abbī and al-Sanūsī. A recent commentary by an Indian scholar, Mawlānā Shabbīr Aḥmad al-ᶜUthmānī, is called *Fatḥ al-Mulhim bi-Sharḥ Ṣaḥīḥ Muslim.* He had issued four parts but not completed it. Our friend Shaykh Muhammad Taqī al-ᶜUthmānī, undertook its completion. He attached to his commentary some knowledge of the time and solutions for its difficulties, which makes the commentary unique in its divisions (*fī bābi-hī*). He has brought out six volumes.

Of commentaries on the *Muwaṭṭā*, we would mention *al-Muntaqā* the commentary of Abū Walīd al-Bājī (d. 474 AH), and the commentary of al-Suyūṭī, *Tanwīr al-Ḥawālik.*

Among the greatest of the commentaries on Abū Dā'ūd is *Maᶜālim al-Sunan* by al-Khattābī (d. 388 AH). The commentary of Ibn al-Qayyim is entitled *Tahdhīb Sunan Abī Da'ūd.* Among the hadith commentaries of the scholars of India are: *ᶜAwn al-Maᶜbūd* by al-Diyānwī, and *Badhl al-Majhūd fī Ḥalli Abī Da'ūd* of al-Sahāranpurī (d. 1346 AH), with the commentary of Shaykh al-Ḥadīth al-Kāndhlawī, and a Foreword by Sayyid Abū Ḥasan al-Nadwī. The *Manhal al-ᶜAdhb al-Mawrūd* of Shaykh Maḥmūd Khaṭṭāb al-Subkī (founder of al-Jāmiᶜah al-Sharīᶜah) is a copious, full commentary. He issued ten parts of it, but did not complete it, may God have mercy on him.

Among the greatest of the commentaries on al-Tirmidhī, and old, is *ᶜĀriḍat al-Ahwidhī* of Imam Abū Bakr ibn al-ᶜArabī (d. 543 AH). Of new commentaries: *Tuḥfat al-Ahwidhī* by al-Mubārakpurī, the well-known Indian hadith scholar.

Al-Nasā'ī has not been commented on, as Abū Da'ūd and al-Tirmidhī have. However, there are the marginal notes of al-Suyūṭī, and another set of marginal notes by al-Sindī (d. 1139 AH). Both of them have been printed with the text of al-Nasā'ī. (When I visited India about twenty years ago, an Indian scholar there was busy in the preparation of a commentary on al-Nasā'ī. I do not know whether he finished it.)

Of the commentaries on *Mishkāt al-Maṣābiḥ*, the best known is the commentary of ᶜAlī al-Qārī (d. 1014 AH), entitled *Mirqāt al-Mafātīḥ.* It is printed in five parts. There is a new, complete commentary, entitled *Mirᶜāt al-Mafātiḥ*, by ᶜUbayd Allāh al-Mubārakpurī, one of the scholars of India. (The work is distributed by al-Jamiᶜah al-Salafiyyah in the city of Benares in India, nine volumes as I remember.)

Among the respected commentaries useful for the preacher is that of ᶜAbd al-Ra'ūf al-Manā'wī on al-Suyūṭī's *al-Jāmiᶜ al-Ṣaghīr.* It is the one published under the title *Fayḍ al-Qadīr fī Sharḥ al-Jāmiᶜ al-Ṣaghīr* in six volumes. It is a useful book but needs some editing.

On *Riyāḍ al-Ṣāliḥīn* the well-known commentary is *Dalīl al-Fāliḥīn* by Ibn ᶜAllān (d. 1054 AH), printed in eight parts. There is a new commentary by Ṣubḥī al-Ṣāliḥ (may God have mercy on him) called *Manhal al-Wāridīn*. Another by Muṣṭafā al-Khann and his colleagues is called *Nuzhat al-Muttaqīn*.

For al-Nawawī's book *al-Adhkār*, there is a commentary by Ibn ᶜAllān, namely *al-Futuḥāt al-Rabbāniyyah*, printed in seven parts. For his small and famous work, *al-Arbaᶜīn al-Nawawiyyah*, there are very many commentaries. However, the most esteemed of them, and the most popular and beneficial, is the commentary of Ibn Rajab al-Ḥanbalī (d. 790 AH): *Jāmiᶜ al-ᶜUlūm wa al-Ḥukm*. The forty hadiths having been completed became fifty, and Muhammad al-Aḥmadī Abū al-Nūr began an edition of them.[13] Shaykh Shuᶜayb al-Arnā'ūṭ edited and source-critiqued the hadiths in *al-Arbaᶜīn al-Nawawiyyah*, and attached marginal notes. Mu'assasat al-Risālah in Beirut published it in two volumes.

Among the most useful books in this context, one that comments on what is behind the hadiths – their secrets, and the religious and social wisdom in them – is the book *Ḥujjat Allāh al-Bālighah* by al-Dahlawī (d. 1176 AH).

A perceptive preacher will know which books and chapters from the sources of the hadiths he is more in need of than others. No doubt the books and chapters on faith and *tawḥīd*, on the rites of worship, and knowledge, and good manners, and renunciation (*zuhd*), and the softening of the hearts, and the remembrance and invocation of God, and the Qur'an, and virtue, and the rite of prayer, and the states of the hereafter, the Garden and the Fire, and the life-story and the battles of the Prophet, and the exemplary stories and history, and the like – all these captivate the attention of the preacher, most often with hadiths that relate to the injunctions directly. If the preacher is adept and has extensive knowledge, he will make use of all the divisions of the hadiths, even those on the injunctions.

PREPARATION BEFORE PRESENTING A HADITH AS EVIDENCE

The important thing for a preacher is that he seek out the import of the hadith he is presenting as evidence – find out its meaning, its value, its stance. Indeed, the obligation is on all knowledgeable persons to rely on authenticated sources, and to rid themselves of hadiths that are feeble or rejected or fabricated, and those with no source. It is with just such hadiths that many of the books in Muslim religious education are stuffed to overflowing, then mixed with others that are *ṣaḥīḥ* and *ḥasan*, without distinguishing between the kinds, the accepted and the rejected. Some are deceived by a hadith's being widely known. It circulates in books or on tongues, and people reckon this is sufficient for its being established, and license for its further passing around and acceptance. But it is well known to serious scholars that a hadith that has circulated widely on the tongues, even in the books of the learned, and been copied by some from others, may nevertheless be extremely weak, lacking a source altogether, even fabricated.

This is what prompted a number of hadith scholars to write accounts of the hadiths made famous on the tongues. Examples are: *al-Tadkhirah bi al-Aḥādīth al-Mushtahirah* by al-Zarkashī (d. 794 AH); *Tamyīz al-Ṭayyib min al-Khabīth fī mā Yaduru ʿalā Alsinat al-Nās min al-Ḥadīth* by Ibn Dībaʿ; *al-La'ālī' al-Manthūrah fī al-Aḥādīth al-Mashūrah* by Ibn Ḥajar (d. 852 AH); *al-Durar al-Muntashirah fī al-Aḥādīth al-Mushtahirah* by al-Suyūṭī (d. 911 AH); and *al-Maqāṣid al-Ḥasanah fī mā Ishtahra min al-Ḥadīth ʿalā al-Alsinah* by al-Sakhawī (d. 902 AH), which was abridged by al-Zurqānī (d. 1122 AH). Al-ʿAjlūnī (d. 1162 AH) collected these books in *Kashf al-Khafā' wa-Muzīl al-Albās ʿAmma Ishtahra min al-Ḥadīth ʿalā Alsinati al-Nās*. Also important in this field are the books, by Ibn al-Jawzī, al-Suyūṭī, al-Qārī, al-Shawkānī, Ibn ʿIrāq, al-Albānī, and others, that address fabricated hadiths.

In books of *taṣawwuf*, admonishment, and softening of the hearts, the authors cite many in this category of hadith (weak, flimsy, fabricated). So too in books of *tafsīr*, and especially in what concerns the merits of the surahs, stories about the prophets and the righteous, and the occasions of Revelation, we find the same category of hadiths being used. Very few of them have been authenticated as *ṣaḥīḥ*.

In a recent conference one of the attending scholars presented the story of Thaʿlabah ibn Ḥāṭib, which the Qur'an commentators mention as the occasion for the revelation of the verse: "And among them those who pledged to God: if He grants us from His bounty then we shall spend in charity and most certainly be among the righteous. Yet when He gave them of His bounty, they were niggardly with it, and turned away, and they were contradicted. So He made their outcome hypocrisy in their hearts until the day when they shall meet Him, because they broke with God what they had pledged to Him, and because they were liars" (*al-Tawbah*, 9: 75–77). But the *isnād* for the story – as Ibn Ḥajar has said in his source-critique of *al-Kashshāf* – is extremely weak.[14]

THE DEFECTS OF MANY ADMONISHERS

A failing common to admonishers and preachers of sermons in the mosques in most Islamic lands is that they are "gathering firewood in the dark". They mumble from the hadiths what moves people, while there is not among those hadiths one with a source that has been confirmed as *ṣaḥīḥ* or *ḥasan*. I have not witnessed a Friday sermon or a lesson of admonishment but, almost always, I have heard a bundle of weak, or severely weak, hadiths, and at times even fabricated ones. In one country, I attended a sermon that I think was on the occasion of celebrating the life of the Prophet, and so its theme was his personality, the purity of his life, the charm of his attitudes, and the greatness of his character. It is a subject-matter richly endowed, overflowing with established truths from the Qur'an, and the authentically reported Sunnah. But the preacher remembered barely two or three of the hadiths established as *ṣaḥīḥ* or *ḥasan*. Instead, he emptied from his store a big number of hadiths that are feeble, rejected or fabricated, or whose source is not known. The scholars have said about such material:

"It has no nose-ring or bridle [meaning it has no control, restraint or discipline]." Here are some examples of that:

> The first [entity] that God created is the light of the Prophet.
>
> God brought his parents to life, and they accepted Islam at his hands.
>
> Whoever is called by the name 'Muhammad', intercession for him is obligatory.
>
> (Various sayings reporting supernatural phenomena in relation to his birth, etc.)

Among the strange things that I heard about the excellence of the Community of the Prophet is the hadith: "The scholars of my Community are like the prophets of the Israelites." The preacher argued for the correctness of this hadith by telling a story. The gist of it is: that Abū Ḥamīd al-Ghazālī met the prophet Moses in a dream or in the spirit world. Moses (whom God addressed directly) said to him: "What is your name?" He said: "Muhammad ibn Muhammad ibn Muhammad al-Ghazālī al-Ṭūsī…etc." He said: "I asked you for your name, and I did not ask you for your genealogy." He said: "And you, when God asked you about what is in your right hand, you did not say to Him 'My staff' and go quiet. Rather, you said: 'It is my staff. I lean on it, and I beat down with it leaves for my sheep, and I have other uses in it'." The preacher commented: "So al-Ghazālī disputed with Moses, upon him be peace." That is how this man established the truth of the false hadith ("The scholars of my Community are like the prophets of the Israelites")! And that is how merchandise unworthy to be brought to market – made up of strange material from stories and dreams and Israelite traditions – is spread and circulates, in the absence of the good merchandise, namely hadiths established as *ṣaḥīḥ* and *ḥasan*. Then, as the economists say, bad currency drives out the good!

The failing is a familiar one. It touches even some scholars who are people of knowledge and worthy of trust, and most strict in the narration of hadith, but who, nevertheless, when they write on topics related to admonishment, are lax to the extreme of laxity.

We have seen the like of that in the books on admonishment of Abū Faraj ibn al-Jawzī (d. 597 AH), for example *Dhamm al-Hawā*; whereas the same al-Jawzī is strict in *al-Mawduʿāt* and *al-ʿIlal al-Mutanāhiyah fī al-Ḥadīth al-Wāhiyah* and the like. Another example is al-Naqqād Shams al-Dīn al-Dhahabī (d. 738 AH), who was lax very often in *al-Kabā'ir* because this book has the character of admonishment. Similarly, al-Ḥāfiẓ al-Mundhirī in his comprehensive book *al-Targhīb wa al-Tarhīb*. He cites in it a great number of feeble, rejected hadiths, even fabricated ones. He had no need of them. In his Preface, he informs readers about the matter through the pointers and terminological classifications he mentions there. So he discharged his responsibility in that way, God have mercy on him. However, his readers are not mindful of that, especially in our age. That is what drove me to prepare *al-Muntaqā* – a two-part selection from al-Mundhirī's book, with source-critique of the *ṣaḥīḥ* and *ḥasan* hadiths in it.[15]

THE FATWA OF IBN ḤAJAR AL-HAYTHAMĪ

Ibn Ḥajar al-Haythamī, the well-known Shāfiʿī jurisprudent, surely did an excellent thing when he straightforwardly asked the rulers of his time to forbid from preaching every preacher who did not make clear the sources of the hadiths he cites, and who mixed up true and authenticated reports with invalid and false ones.

A questioner came to Ibn Ḥajar al-Haythamī about a preacher who climbs the pulpit every Friday and recites many hadiths, and does not clarify their sources or their narrators (the questioner mentioned a particular hadith by way of example), and asked: "So what is obligatory [to be done] about him?" And his answer in his words:

> What he has cited of hadiths in his sermon without clarifying their narrators, or who said them, is permissible on condition that he is [himself] one of the people of knowledge in hadith, or he is quoting from a book written by one like that [knowledgeable in hadith]. But as for relying on the narration of hadiths on [the basis of] the mere seeing of them in a book whose author is not of the people of hadith, or in sermons

> whose author is not like that [a hadith scholar] – then it is not lawful. Whoever does that is to be rebuked for it with a severe rebuke. And this is the condition of many sermon-givers. For indeed they, from a mere seeing of a sermon with hadiths in it, memorize [those hadiths] and preach with them [in their own sermons], without their knowing whether those hadiths are properly sourced or not. So it is a duty on the governors of all lands that they restrain their sermon-givers from that. And it is a duty of the governors of the land of this sermon-giver to forbid him from that if he commits it to excess.
>
> It is [incumbent] upon this sermon-giver that he make clear his *sanad* in his narrations. Now if his *sanad* is correct, then [there is] no objection against him. Otherwise it is permissible for the person in authority that he remove from him the entitlement to give sermons, holding him back from being so bold as to hold this handsome status without right.[16]

If only this were put into effect on the sermon-givers of our time! Then surely many of them – for their ignorance of the hadith, and their confusion of the accepted and the rejected hadiths – would be removed.

III

NARRATING WEAK HADITHS IN *TARGHĪB* AND *TARHĪB*

I am of the view that the cause of the wide circulation, among so many of those who give sermons, reminders and admonishments, of feeble, rejected and even fabricated hadiths, is adherence to the opinion of the majority of scholars, which permits the narration of such hadiths. They permit weak hadiths related to the virtues of deeds, softening of the hearts, renunciation, and *targhīb* and *tarhīb*, and stories tending to that, so long as these hadiths have nothing in them connected to the commands of the Law, to any of the five kinds of injunctions, namely the permitted, the forbidden, the reprehensible, the obligatory, the commendable. In the Preface to *al-Targhīb wa al-Tarhīb* al-Mundhirī wrote: "The scholars accept relaxation of the categories of hadith in respect of *targhīb* and *tarhīb*

– to the extent that many of them cite the fabricated [one] and do not make clear its condition!"

That is near to what al-Ḥākim says in his *Mustadrak* at the beginning of *Kitāb al-Duʿā'* (the book of supplication): "And I, by the will of God, shall set flowing the reports which the two Shaykhs [al-Bukhāri and Muslim] are silent about in the Book of Supplications – following the doctrine of Abū Saʿīd ʿAbd al-Raḥmān ibn Mahdī on their acceptance." Then he lays out his *sanad* to Abū Saʿīd ʿAbd al-Raḥmān and quotes his opinion:

> If we relate from the Prophet on the lawful and the unlawful and the injunctions, we are strict about the *isnād*s and we criticize the [narrators]. And if we narrate on the virtues of deeds, and the reward and the punishment [hereafter], and the commended [acts] and the supplications, then we make easy the *isnād*s.[17]

Al-Khaṭīb narrates in *al-Kifāyah*, with his *sanad* from Aḥmad ibn Ḥanbal, the same opinion in nearly identical words,[18] then says: "The hadiths on the softening of hearts tolerate one's relaxing [the conditions] for them up to the point [in the hadith where] there comes in it anything of an injunction." Similarly, Abū Zakariyyā al-ʿAnbārī says: "[If] the report when it came did not make the permitted forbidden and the forbidden permitted, and did not make an injunction obligatory, and if it was on *targhīb* and *tarhīb*, or the intensification or relaxing [of elements or forms of worship], [then] it is obligatory to close one's eyes to it [in forbearance], and to make the narration of it easy."[19]

But how far should this closing of the eyes, and making easy of the *isnād*s, go?

Some people understand from this that one should accept a hadith on *targhīb* and *tarhīb* without condition – even if its narrator is alone in narrating it, or one atrocious in his errors, or who has a lot of rejected reports credited to him, or who has been accused of being a liar. Some of the ignorant ones of the Sufis even permitted the narration of fabricated hadiths – hadiths concocted and manufactured – provided only that they inspired to the good and frightened away from the evil. Some of them (as we noted earlier) went so far as to excuse themselves with that motive, for contriving hadiths on the merits of particular surahs of the Qur'an or of particular good deeds. When people cited the well known hadith reported *mutawātir* – "One who lies against me with premeditation, he has provided his place in the Fire" – they said with all impudence: "We never lie *against* him, but we only lie *for* him." That is an excuse more ugly than sin: it implies a judgment that his religion is deficient and they are completing it for him. But God said: "This day I have completed for you your religion" (*al-Mā'idah*, 5: 3).

Therefore, the scholars dedicated to establishing the truth made the purpose, and the limits, of relaxing the conditions for *isnād*s very clear. We cite here brief examples of the reflections of some of those scholars:

> Ibn Rajab al-Ḥanbalī said (commenting in his *Sharḥ ʿIlal al-Tirmidhī* on al-Tirmidhī's saying that he did not adduce in an argument hadiths narrated from someone accused of dishonesty, or known for forgetfulness, or for many errors in his reports):
> As for what al-Tirmidhī has mentioned … his point is that he does not adduce [such hadiths] in the Legal injunctions and matters of practice. But if narrators had narrated some of those [hadiths] on the softening of the hearts and *targhīb* and *tarhīb*, then many of the imams permitted the narration of [such hadiths] from weak [narrators]; among [those imams were] Ibn Mahdī and Ibn Ḥanbal.
>
> Rawwād ibn al-Jarrāḥ said:
> I heard Sufyān al-Thawrī, he said: "Do not take this knowledge in the lawful and the unlawful except from the heads, the ones most famous for their knowledge, those who know the addition and subtraction [the adjustments needed to understand the quality of a report]; and there is no objection in what is other than that [i.e. the lawful and the unlawful] to taking from respected elders [men known for their piety but not specialists in hadith]."
>
> Ibn Abī Ḥātim said:
> My father transmitted to us from ʿAbdah, he said: "It was said to Ibn al-Mubārak – when he had narrated a hadith from a

man – it was said: 'This man is weak!' Then [Ibn Mubārak] said: 'It is tolerated to narrate from [a weak narrator] this degree (*qadr*) or the like of these things.' [So] I said to ʿAbdah: 'Like which things might it be?' He said: 'On manners, on admonishments, on renunciation.' "

Ibn Maʿīn said about Mūsā ibn ʿUbaydah al-Rabdhī, a man known for his piety (not as a hadith scholar) and weakness in narration, that he wrote down from his hadiths those on the softening of hearts.

Ibn ʿUyaynah said:
Do not hear from Baqiyyah (meaning Baqiyyah ibn Walīd) what is in the Sunnah, but hear from him what is on the reward [hereafter] and other than it.

Aḥmad ibn Ḥanbal said about Ibn Isḥāq (Muhammad ibn Isḥāq, author of the famous *Sīrah*):
One writes down from him on the battles and things like them.

Ibn Mūsā said on Ziyād al-Bikā'ī:
No objection to him on the battles, but as for what is other than that: No.

Ibn Rajab said:
Indeed one only narrates on *tarhīb* and *targhīb* and renunciation and good manners the hadiths of those of the people who are forgetful [but] who are not suspected of lying. And as for the people who are suspect, one leaves their hadith. So said Ibn Abī Ḥātim and others.[20]

The sayings just quoted (and others like them) make it clear that not one of the imams of hadith accepts the narration of hadiths of *targhīb* and *tarhīb* from all and sundry indiscriminately, nor if their narrators were ignorant or accused of lying, nor if excessively prone to error in their reports. They only permitted the narration of some narrators, in whose capacity for memorization there was some pliancy or weakness, and though they were not (as Sufyān al-Thawrī put it) "among the famous heads of the knowledge", there was no doubt as to their trustworthiness and probity. There was doubt only about their capacity for memorization and their alertness and thoroughness.

For the acceptance of weak hadiths on the softening of hearts and *targhīb*, Ibn Ḥajar mentioned three conditions. Later, al-Suyūṭī copied them from him in *Tadrīb al-Rāwī*:

First: This condition is agreed upon. It is that the narrator or report may be weak but not extremely so. Thus, one who is alone in narrating is excluded, one who is from among the known liars, or from those accused of lying, and one who is preposterous in his error.

Second: that the hadith comes under a general principle (meaning, it conforms to and does not contradict the Law or the religion). Thus, that which has been innovated, for which there is no source at all, is excluded.

Third: that, in the course of acting upon such a hadith, it should not be believed to be established as from the Prophet. Thus, what the Prophet did not say will not be (incorrectly) attributed to him. As for any action taken in accordance with such a hadith, it is to be taken only as a precaution.

Al-Suyūṭī said: "The last two [conditions] are from Ibn ʿAbd al-Salām and from his student Ibn Daqīq al-ʿĪd. And the first: al-ʿAlāʾī reported the agreement about it."[21]

SOME IMPORTANT REALITIES

It is essential here that I alert readers to a number of realities of this subject, of which many people have a poor understanding. As a result, religious education has become confused for them, albeit some of them continue to serve as religious guides for large numbers of Muslims.

1: REJECTION OF WEAK HADITHS EVEN ON *TARGHĪB* AND *TARHĪB*

Among scholars, old and new, some do not accept hadiths other than the *ṣaḥīḥ* and the *ḥasan*, whatever their subject-matter. Ibn Rajab said in *Sharḥ al-ʿIlal*:

> It has appeared from what Muslim (d. 261 AH) has mentioned in his Preface [that] he judged [that] the hadiths of *targhīb* and

> *tarhīb* are not narrated except from one from whom the injunctions are [also] narrated.[22]
>
> In the Preface of his *Ṣaḥīḥ* he abhorred the narration of weak hadiths and rejected reports.[23]

Evidently, this was also the doctrine of Imam al-Bukhārī (d. 206 AH). It is the doctrine of the master of *jarḥ* and *taᶜdīl* (censure and approval of narrators), Yaḥyā ibn Maᶜīn (d. 233 AH). Among the later scholars who adhered to it were: Ibn Ḥazm (d. 456 AH) of the Ẓāhirī school, al-Qāḍī Ibn al-ᶜArabī (d. 543 AH) of the Mālikī school, and Abū Shāmah from the Shāfiᶜī school. Among contemporary scholars: Shaykh Aḥmad Muhammad Shākir and Shaykh Muhammad Naṣīr al-Dīn al-Albānī. Shaykh Shākir wrote about it in his book *al-Bāᶜth al-Ḥathīth*, in which he comments on Ibn Kathīr's *Ikhtiṣār ᶜUlūm al-Ḥadīth*. After stating what some people permitted in the narration of weak hadiths, and expounding its conditions (which we noted above), he says:

> What I [hold] is that the exposition of the weakness of a weak hadith is obligatory in all cases. Because leaving out the exposition puts the one approaching it in mind that it is a *ṣaḥīḥ* hadith – especially when the transmitter is one of the hadith scholars to whose opinion one refers in [such matters]. [I hold also that there should be] no difference between injunctions [on the one hand], and the merits of deeds and the like [on the other], as regards non-acceptance of a weak report. Rather, there is no argument from any [hadith] unless from what has been authenticated as from God's Messenger – from a *ṣaḥīḥ* or *ḥasan* hadith. As for what Aḥmad ibn Ḥanbal and Ibn Mahdī and al-Mubārak have said – "...If we narrate on the merits and the like we relax [the conditions of acceptability of reports]" – then they only meant by that (in what I consider on balance, and God knows better) the taking of hadiths that are *ḥasan*, which do not reach to the rank of *ṣaḥīḥ*. For, in point of fact, the terms *ṣaḥīḥ* and *ḥasan* were not in their epoch widely settled upon and evident. Rather, many of the early scholars did not rank the hadith except as *ṣaḥīḥ* or *ḍaᶜīf* and no more.[24]

Ibn Taymiyyah and Ibn al-Qayyim have a discourse of the same meaning. In it they interpret what is narrated from Aḥmad ibn Ḥanbal as meaning that he accepts a weak hadith in the sense of giving it priority over *ra'y* (personal opinion) and *qiyās* (analogical reasoning); moreover, that what he had in mind was the reports that (later) came to be classed as *ḥasan.* As is well known, it was al-Tirmidhī who popularized the distinction between *ṣaḥīḥ* and *ḥasan.*

As for Shaykh al-Albānī: he has given his authority to the same position in the prefaces to many of his books, in particular: *Ṣaḥīḥ al-Jāmiᶜ al-Ṣaghīr* and its *Supplement*, and *Ṣaḥīḥ al-Targhīb wa al-Tarhīb.*

2: NON-ADHERENCE TO THE CONDITIONS STIPULATED BY THE MAJORITY

The second reality is that, regrettably, the three conditions, stipulated by those who permitted the narration of weak hadiths on *targhīb* and *tarhīb*, softening of the hearts, and the like, have not been adhered to in a scholarly manner. Many of those who busy themselves with the hadiths in this field do not distinguish between the weak and the extremely weak. They do not scruple to ensure that the hadith conforms to Legal principle established from the Qur'an or the authenticated Sunnah. Rather, at times (as I said earlier) the infatuation with what there is in these reports of reminder and inspiration overwhelms them – even if a report is one rejected in the most severe degree of rejection, or if there loom about it signs of fabrication.

3: PROHIBITION OF NARRATING IN A STYLE OF CERTAINTY

The scholars have mentioned on this an important warning, namely not to say in a weak hadith 'God's Messenger said this and this' in the style of a positive, definitive statement. Ibn Ṣalāḥ said in category 22 of his *ᶜUlūm al-Ḥadīth*:

> If you intend the narration of the weak without *isnād*, then do not say in it 'God's Messenger said like this or like this' or what resembles that in words [expressive] of certainty. Rather, only say: 'It is narrated from God's Messenger this or this'; or 'it has reached us from him this or this'; or 'it has been mentioned from him' or 'has come from him'; or 'Some of them narrate'; or what resembles that [sort of phrasing].

> This manner is the rule for that whose being *ṣaḥīḥ* or *ḍaʿīf* you doubt. Indeed, only say 'God's Messenger said' in that whose being *ṣaḥīḥ* is clear to you in respect of its route [of transmission], which we clarified earlier. God knows better.[25]

What Ibn Ṣalāḥ said, al-Nawawī agreed with, as did Ibn Kathīr, and al-ʿIrāqī, and Ibn Ḥajar, and all the books on the technique and terminology of hadith. But the givers of reminders and sermons, and writers who narrate weak hadiths, do not give their hearts to this alarm. Instead, they start off their weak hadiths with the words 'God's Messenger said'.

4: THE SUFFICIENCY OF THE *ṢAḤĪḤ* AND THE *ḤASAN*

If, on a particular topic, we have to hand a single hadith or many from the category of *ṣaḥīḥ* or *ḥasan*, and the same from the category of the *ḍaʿīf*, then the more worthy course is to find the former sufficient. There is no call to load our memories with the *ḍaʿīf*. Indeed, doing so is at the expense of the *ṣaḥīḥ* and infringes one's duty to it. It has come from some of the Companions: "No effort do the people expend on innovation (*bidʿah*) but they lose the like of it from the Sunnah." And that is something that has actually happened: *bidʿah* is replacing *sunnah*, innovation taking the place of tradition. Al-Khaṭīb narrated in *al-Kifāyah* from Imam Ibn Mahdī that he said:

> One should not busy oneself in the writing down of the hadiths of the weak [narrators]. For indeed the least of what is in it – to the extent that he writes from the hadith of the people of weakness – is that the hadiths of [the people of] trustworthiness are missed by him.

If human capacity for memorization, reflection, comprehension and absorption, is limited – and there is no escaping that – then it is better to direct that capacity, and one's effort and time, to what has more right and priority. There is no disagreement that, of the two, the *ṣaḥīḥ* has precedence in this respect over the *ḍaʿīf*.

5: WARNING AGAINST UNBALANCING THE ORDER AMONG THE DEEDS

The hadiths on softening of the hearts, *targhīb* and *tarhīb*, may not have (in their texts) anything to do with an injunction that makes permissible or makes forbidden. Nevertheless, we find that they contain something else that has its own great importance and consequences. Our earlier imams did not attend to this – it is something that has emerged (over time) from 'the disordering of the relationships' among obligations and deeds, which the Law in its wisdom had settled. For every deed – commanded by the Law or forbidden by it – there is a weight or value specified, relatively to some other deed, in the view of the Law. We are not permitted to transgress a limit that the Law has stipulated as a limit – so that we shift a deed below or above the level prescribed for it, so as to make it more or less worthy, more or less important.

The most serious case is altering the weight of deeds: giving to some of the righteous deeds a value greater than their due, or more frequency than is proper to them, by inflating what is in them of reward, until it extinguishes what is more important and higher in rank in the view of the religion; conversely, giving undue weight to some of the proscribed acts, overstating what is in them of punishment, in such a way as damages one's perception of the importance of other proscribed acts. Such exaggerations in the promise of reward or the threat of punishment have resulted in distortion of the image of the religion in the view of the educated seekers of enlightenment. They relate what they hear or read of such exaggeration to the religion itself, whereas Islam is exempt from it.

Often what such exaggeration leads to (especially on the side of *tarhīb*) is psychological reversions and anxieties. They sow aversion and hatefulness between people, and frighten them from the religion, and distance them from its spaciousness. So we will find a father has complained of his twelve-year-old daughter waking up in the night alarmed and fearful, because she sees frightening dreams – the affect of having listened to a cassette of one admonisher about the punishments of the grave, a cassette in which there were many from this category of hadiths.

It is the Muslims' duty to maintain the deeds in their ordering in the Law – without falling into the web of exaggerations which drive us hard into either extreme of excess or neglect. As ʿAlī ibn Abī Ṭālib said: "Upon you [is obligatory] the middle way [of doing things]: which the one going too far (*al-ghālī*) returns to, and the one not going far enough (*al-tālī*) catches up with."

6: A WEAK HADITH CANNOT ITSELF ESTABLISH AN INJUNCTION

The scholars of the religion allowed the narration of a weak hadith only with conditions attached to doing so. According to the oldest of them: they were lenient in their scrutiny of the *isnād*s in the narration of a weak hadith, intending thereby only the urging of a righteous deed whose righteousness is already established by accepted Legal argument, or the restraining of an evil deed whose evil is already established by Legal argument. They did not intend to establish by the weak hadith the righteousness or evil of the deed. However, many of the general populace – indeed even some hadith scholars – did not differentiate between the permissibility of narrating a weak hadith (with the conditions attached) and the establishment of an action by it.

That is why we see, for example, people in most Muslim lands making much of the night of mid-Shaʿban. They make its night special by keeping vigil in it, and its day by fasting in it, on the basis of the hadith narrated from ʿAlī, *marfūʿan*: "When it is the night of mid-Shaʿban, then keep vigil during the night and keep fast during the day. For indeed God, Exalted and Blessed is He, comes down in it, at the setting of the sun, to the heaven of this world, and He says: 'There is not one who has sought forgiveness but that I forgive him [....].' " Ibn Mājah narrated it. Al-Mundhirī pointed to its being weak; al-Buṣīrī also affirmed its weakness in *Zawā'id Ibn Mājah.*[26]

Again, in most Muslim lands, we see people making much of the day of ʿĀshūra', sacrificing animals, considering it to be an ʿĪd or a day fixed for regular annual remembrance, and they give generously in it to kith and kin. They do all this relying on a weak hadith, nevertheless widely circulated among the common people: "Whoever is generous in giving to his kith and kin on the day of ʿĀshūra', God will be generous to him for the rest of his years." In the opinion of Ibn Taymiyyah and others, the hadith is fabricated. Al-Mundhirī said of it: "al-Bayhaqī and others narrated it by way of a group of the Companions." And al-Bayhaqī said: "Though [the] *isnād*s [of this hadith] are weak, when they are drawn together, some with others, they take strength. And God knows better." That is a statement that raises doubts. Ibn Jawzī and Ibn Taymiyyah and others were quite certain that the hadith is fabricated, but al-ʿIrāqī and others sought to defend it and establish it as *ḥasan li-ghayri-hi* (that is, not *ḥasan* in itself but by association with an *isnād* that supports it). Many later scholars found it difficult to judge a hadith as fabricated.

All of that, on balance of evidence, suggests to me, that this hadith is something that some ignorant one of the Sunnis invented to rebut the exaggerations of the Shiʿa. For them, the day of ʿĀshūra' is a day of sadness and mourning, so he turned it into a day for being bathed and brightly-dressed and giving gifts to children!

Many of the misunderstandings and widespread innovations among the Muslim masses can be traced back to such weak hadiths. These hadiths spread through generations of backwardness among them, influenced their minds and their hearts, and chased away the *ṣaḥīḥ*. Yet it is on the *ṣaḥīḥ* that Muslims are required – within the precincts of the Qur'an – to base their understanding and interrelationships. Al-Shāṭibī clarified that duty in his book, *al-Iʿtiṣām*.

Shaykh al-Islam Ibn Taymiyyah, may God have mercy on him, has a crystal-clear discourse on the intent of the scholars in saying that one may act according to a weak hadith on the merits of certain deeds (*faḍā'il*) or *targhīb* and *tarhīb*:

What the scholars are on [i.e. their considered opinion] is:

Acting in accordance with a weak hadith on the *faḍā'il* is not for the establishment of a recommended act by a hadith, which is not [itself] adduced as an argument. For the recommended act surely is a [category of] command in the Law and is not established except by Legal proof. One who reports from God that He loves some particular deed without Legal proof has surely prescribed as Law in the religion [something], for which he has no permission from God. It is just as if he established [actions in the category of] the obligatory or the forbidden. For this [reason] the scholars differed on the recommended [category], just as they differed on other matters. Indeed, [this] is a basic principle of the religion as defined in Law.

Their intention in that was only that the deed should be something of which it had already been established, by a text [of Qur'an or Sunnah] or by ijmaᶜ [consensus], that God loved it or that God abhorred it – [a deed of the former kind] such as reciting the Qur'an, and glorifying Him in His names, and making supplication, and giving in charity, and emancipating a slave, and treating people with kindness; and abhorred deeds such as lying or treachery, and similar to that... So when a hadith is narrated on the merit of some recommended deeds and the reward for them, and the abhorrence of some deeds and the punishment for them, and their reward and punishment and their kinds are established and decided, [and] if, in what is narrated, the hadith [is one that] we do not know to be fabricated, it is permissible to narrate it and act upon it. Meaning: that the soul may hope thereby for reward, or be fearful thereby of punishment. Just as a man knows that commerce brings profit, but [as a supplement to that knowledge] he is informed that it makes a great profit, then this if true benefits him, and if false it did not harm him.

An example of that: *targhīb* and *tarhīb* by [reliance on] the reports of the Israelites and [reports of] dream-visions, and the sayings of the *salaf* and of the scholars, and events associated with the scholars, and the like of that, does not permit the establishing of a Legal injunction – neither a recommended act nor anything else. However, that it be mentioned in *targhīb* and *tarhīb*, and the arousing of awe and fear is permissible [provided that] what is attractive or repulsive about it was [already] known by Legal argument. For indeed that is beneficial and not harmful. And it is the same whether in itself the matter is

> true or false. For what one knows to be false [and] fabricated, it is not permitted to give attention to it. For if [it is] a lie, then it is good for nothing; and if it is established that it is *ṣaḥīḥ*, then the injunctions are established by it. When both cases [it is true or it is false] apply, it is narrated on the possibility of its being true and the non-harmfulness of its being false. Aḥmad [ibn Ḥanbal] only said: "When there come [reports related to] *targhīb* and *tarhīb*, we relax [the normal standards] for the *isnād*s." His meaning: We only narrate of that [sort of reports] with the *isnād*s, and [we do so] even if they were not reported from trustworthy narrators [of the quality] that one would base [a Legal] argument on them. Similarly, the saying of the one who said: Act according to [those hadiths] in the merits of deeds, only doing according to what in them is of the deeds of righteousness, for example reciting the Qur'an and remembrance [of God], and avoiding what is abhorred in them of deeds of wickedness.
>
> But if the weak hadiths on the *faḍā'il* include [matters] determined and delimited [by the Law] – for example, [doing] the prayer at a specified time with a specified recitation or in a specified row – it is not permissible for you, because the recommendation of this specified quality was not established by Legal proof. [It is] different if what is narrated in it [is something like]: "Whoever has entered the market and said 'There is no god but God…', he will have such and such."[27] Now the remembrance of God in the market surely is [already known to be something] recommended, on account of what is therein of remembering God among the forgetful, as has come in the well-known hadith: "Remembering God among the forgetful is like a green tree among dry trees."[28]
>
> As for the measure of reward narrated in [a weak hadith]: its being established does not harm, nor does its not-being established.
>
> And the conclusion: that one narrates this category [of hadith] and one acts according to it in *targhīb* and *tarhīb*, but not in the recommended acts. Beyond that: conviction about the consequence of it – and [this] is the measures of reward and punishment [for it] – [that] is conditional upon Legal proof.[29]

Despite this clear exposition, we see many people establishing the bounds, and the terms and measures, of the lawful and unlawful, the recommended and the reprehensible, according to weak hadith.

7: TWO COMPLEMENTARY CONDITIONS FOR THE ACCEPTANCE OF WEAK HADITH

If we adopt the opinion of the majority on the permissibility of narrating weak hadith on *targhīb* and *tarhīb*, then it is proper, in my view, to polish the three conditions already mentioned with a further two, complementary conditions. (These are mentioned in my book *Thaqāfat al-Dāʿiyah*.) They are: (1) that the hadith should not contain exaggerations offensive to reason or Law or language; (2) that the hadith should not contradict a Legal proof stronger than itself.

What offends reason or the Law or the language. The leaders of hadith study have stipulated that a fabricated hadith is known by indications evident in the narrator or in what is narrated. Among the evident indications in what is narrated are: *a)* from the general evidence of fabrication, that the report is contrary to reason, hence its interpretation is not acceptable, and it is closely bound to what sense and perception reject. Or *b)*, that the report is contradictory to the definitive proofs of the Book or the Sunnah known as *mutawātir*, or to the definitive ijmaʿ (consensus), and there is no possibility of reconciling the contradiction between the two. Or *c)*, the report has to do with a large issue, about which there is a strong expectation of a group of people having been present to convey it, but it has been conveyed by only one person. Also among those evident indications, *d)*: the extremes of severe threat over a small matter, or of tremendous promise over a slight matter: this is common in the hadiths of story-tellers.

Even among hadith scholars, sadly, there are many who do not apply these basic criteria to what they narrate on *targhīb* and *tarhīb* and the like. Perhaps there was an excuse for them in the temperament of their age. As for modes of reasoning in our age, exaggerations are not acceptable, nor are they digested; and it is likely that the religion itself is blamed when such exaggerations are encountered in hadiths like these.

As to what offends the language: in this class are many of the hadiths that certain story-tellers narrate. For example: Darrāj Abū al-Samaḥ incorporated into Qur'anic commentary words whose meanings are patently clear in the language, but for which he narrated interpretations that are misleading in their strangeness and distance from the dictionary meanings. An example is the hadith from Abū Haytham from Abū Saᶜid, *marfūᶜan*: "*Wayl*: [its meaning is] a valley in hell – unbelievers fall in it for forty autumns, before its bottom is reached." Ibn Ḥanbal and al-Tirmidhī have narrated something similar except that they have the phrase: "seventy autumns". But *wayl* is a word meaning 'threat of destruction', well known before Islam and after it. Another example is what has come, according to al-Ṭabarānī and al-Bayhaqī, from Ibn Masᶜūd, from his commentary on *al-ghayy* in the verse: "Then has followed after them a generation who have ruined the rite of prayer and followed lusts: so they shall encounter error (*ghayy*)" (*Maryam*, 19: 59). Ibn Masᶜūd said: "A valley in hell"; and in a variant narration: "the fire in hell". But *ghayy* is a word well known, and it is the antonym of *rushd* (guidance), as in the verse: "The right way (*al-rushd*) has been clearly distinguished from the wrong way (*al-ghayy*)" (*al-Baqarah*, 2: 256). Similar to that is what al-Bayhaqī and others have reported from Anas ibn Mālik, on the verse "And We made between them a place of perdition (*mawbiq*)" (*al-Kahf*, 18: 52). Anas said, of the meaning of *mawbiq*: "A valley of pus and blood." Even stranger is what Ibn Abī Dunyā has narrated from Shafī ibn Mātiᶜ: that "there is in hell a valley called *athām*, containing snakes and scorpions [...]." He points to the verse: "And whoever does that will pay the penalty (*athām*)" (*al-Furqān*, 25: 68). But *athām* is only a word derivative from *ithm* (sin, offence).

It is regrettable indeed that al-Mundhirī, may God have mercy on him, should have cited all of these hadiths in his book *al-Targhīb wa al-Tarhīb*. No wonder that the sermon-makers hurried to them and made much of them. That is why we argued against them in our book *al-Muntaqā min al-Targhīb wa al-Tarhīb*.

It should not contradict a stronger Legal argument. An example of this is the weak hadiths that report about ʿAbd al-Raḥmān ibn ʿAwf that he entered Paradise on all fours on account of his wealth. It has been claimed that such hadiths conform to the general class of warning against the ordeal of property, and the arrogance of the wealthy. However, we must note that these weak hadiths are contradicted by *ṣaḥīḥ* hadiths that make ʿAbd al-Raḥmān ibn ʿAwf one of the ten who were promised Paradise, not to speak of widely attested events and well trusted reports, all of which establish that he was among the best of the Muslims, and the greatest in piety and God-fearing, of those who spent of their wealth freely in the way of God, and the model of the wealthy man properly grateful to God. For this reason God's Messenger exalted him and was pleased with him; and ʿUmar, appointed him as one of the six Companions of the Council and gave to his say, when the voices were equal, a weight and preference above that of others.

That is why al-Mundhirī rebutted these weak hadiths for their impropriety. He said:

> There has come [to us] something other than what is proper: from the hadith of a group of the Companions from the Prophet that ʿAbd al-Raḥmān ibn ʿAwf will enter Paradise on all fours for the great quantity of his wealth. The best of [those hadiths] is not safe from objection, and there never came from them anything by a single narrator of the rank of *ḥasan*. Most certainly his wealth was a quality that God's Messenger mentioned: "How excellent the righteous wealth of a righteous man!"[30] So how should his rank in the hereafter be diminished, or he be judged inadequate, but not others of the wealthy ones of this Community? And for sure this has not come about the person of any other than [ʿAbd al-Raḥmān ibn ʿAwf]. It is only correct [to affirm] the absolute precedence of the poor of this Community [over] their wealthy ones. And God knows better.[31]

Another example of this kind is the hadith '*al-gharānīq*'. To be sure, we have a hadith expert (*ḥāfiẓ*) of the stature of Ibn Ḥajar, author of the commentary on al-Bukhārī, saying of this hadith that, because it is narrated by a number of routes, it must have a source. But it is a hadith that clear reason refuses to accept, and authentic tradition rejects. Shaykh al-Albānī compiled about it the treatise *Naṣba al-Majānīq li-Nasf Qiṣṣat al-Gharānīq.* Also al-Shaykh Muhammad Ṣādiq ᶜArjūn, in his valuable book *Muḥammad Rasūl Allāh*, sets out in comprehensive detail the falsity of these stories, and describes them as a mere "stupid lie".

A WISE PREACHER DOES NOT TRANSMIT WHAT IS UNCLEAR TO PEOPLE

The inspired preacher should not transmit to the people everything that is known of the hadiths, even if they are *ṣaḥīḥ*. Jamāl al-Dīn al-Qāsimī said in his book *Qawāᶜid al-Taḥdīth*:

> Not every *ṣaḥīḥ* hadith is transmitted to the general public. The evidence for that is what the two Shaykhs [al-Bukhārī and Muslim] have narrated from Muᶜādh, that he said: "I was on a donkey [following] behind the Prophet, when he said: 'Muᶜādh! Do you know what is the right of God upon His slaves and what is the right of the slaves upon God?' I said: 'God and His Messenger know best.' He said: 'Indeed, the right of God upon his slaves is that they worship Him and do not associate with Him anything. And the right of the slaves upon God is that He shall not punish one who does not associate with Him anything.' I said: 'Messenger of God, shall I give the people this good news?' He said: 'No, do not give them the good news, lest they become listless!' "
>
> In a[nother] narration from both [al-Bukhārī and Muslim] from Anas that: "The Prophet said to Muᶜādh who was following directly behind him: 'There is not one who testifies that there is no god but God and that Muhammad is His Messenger, truthfully and from his heart, except that God prohibits him to the Fire.' He said: 'Messenger of God, shall I not inform the people of it so they will rejoice in the good news?' He said: 'Then they will become listless.' " Then Muᶜādh notified [someone] of it at his death, to avoid sinning [against the command to share knowledge and not hide it]. Al-Bukhārī reported [it] by way of a note [i.e. without an *isnād* attached] from ᶜAlī : "Convey to the people what they know [and so can

> understand]; do you want God and His Messenger to be denied?" There is a saying like it of Ibn Masᶜūd: "You have not transmitted a hadith to a people whose minds cannot attain it except that it is a trial for some of them." Muslim narrated it.
>
> Al-Ḥāfiẓ Ibn Ḥajar said: Of those who were averse to transmitting some hadith and not others: Aḥmad [ibn Ḥanbal was averse to doing so] in the hadiths whose outward meaning is rebelling against the ruler; and Mālik in the hadiths of the Attributes; and Abū Yūsuf in the strange [matters]; and before them Abū Hurayrah, [for example] in what is narrated from him on the two bags:[32] The point [that Abu Hurayrah was alluding to] is what happens during dissensions. Similar to it [is a report] from Ḥudhayfah. And from Ḥasan [al-Baṣrī]: that he disliked Anas conveying to al-Ḥajjāj the story of the ᶜUraniyyūn,[33] lest he should adopt it by his weak interpretation as an instrument [to justify] what he was intending in excess of shedding blood.
>
> The control[ling principle] of that is: that the outward [meaning] of a hadith may be strengthening heretical innovation, and its outward [meaning] is not the purpose in the original source; so what is wanted is keeping it back from one about whom one fears that he will seize upon its outward [meaning].

Thus the proscription (of conveying all hadiths to all and sundry) related to the public interest, and was not a prohibition in itself. Muᶜādh informed people as he did because of the generality of the command to convey knowledge about the religion.

Some of the scholars said that the proscription in his saying "Do not give them the good news" is particularized to some people, i.e. not universal. Al-Bukhārī adduced it in the argument that it was for the scholar to particularize the knowledge to some people and not others. The thing to be shunned is people not understanding what is conveyed to them. He adopted the position that hadiths like those of the all-permitting sorcerers (*al-baṭalah*[34] *al-mubāḥiyyah*)[35] provide a pretext for the abandonment of the religious obligations and the lifting of the injunctions, and that opens wide the way to ruin in this world on top of ruin in the next. For where are those who, when they are given the good news, increase greatly in worship? It was said to the Prophet "Why do you stand [in vigil] in the night when God has forgiven you?" Then he said: "Shall I not be a grateful slave?"'[36]

So I marvel at all the absurdities in the attitude of those preachers who do not cease to mention the hadith of the fly and dipping it in the food! Or the hadith that Moses slapped the angel of death! Or the hadith (in answer to one who asked, "Where is my father?"): "Indeed my father and your father are in the Fire." Or the hadiths in which the *salaf* and the *khalaf* (the early generations and the later) have differed about construing the Attributes of God as predicates (qualifying His essential being) or as actions (qualifying His acting in particular contingencies) – likely to be misconstrued anthropomorphically (in both cases, if carelessly expressed). Or the hadiths of the times of trouble which suppose in their outward meaning that the only or best course is giving up all hope of restoration of order, and the refraining from any action of resistance to the disorder. Or other hadiths whose meaning is too subtle for the majority of people.

There is no need for these hadiths. Injunctions are not arranged upon them. If the people live their long lives without hearing them, it does not diminish them in their religious life by a grain of mustard seed. If, for a particular reason, the preacher does have need of something from these hadiths then it is his duty to place them in the right framework, to elucidate them with some exposition, and to preface them and add commentary to them, so as to make their meaning clear and dispel from them any doubts and misgivings.

We have taken as an example of that a famous hadith that has often led the people to wrong understanding, and because of that understanding, they have arranged upon it commands of dangerous consequence. It is the hadith of Anas, as follows:

HADITH: THAT EVERY AGE IS WORSE THAN WHAT PRECEDED IT

Al-Bukhārī narrated it with his *sanad* to al-Zubayr ʿAdī. He said: "We came to Anas ibn Mālik and we expressed to him our misgivings about what we met from al-Ḥajjāj. Then he said: 'Be patient!

For indeed there will not come upon you a time except that what is after it is worse than it – until you meet your Lord. I heard it from your Prophet.' "

The importance of this hadith

Some people have taken this hadith to justify sitting back from taking action, from striving for reform, change and deliverance. They have urged that the hadith demonstrates that human affairs are in decline continually, in a permanent falling off, a successive decaying, from one level to another level lower than it; it is not carried from bad except to worse, nor from worse except to what is worse than that, until the Hour stands over the evil ones of the people and all people meet their Lord.

Others have held back from acceptance of this hadith. At times some of them have rushed to rebut it because, to their way of thinking, it was harmful or wrong for a number of reasons. First, it encouraged hopelessness and despondency. Second, it urged negativism in facing up to oppression from deviant rulers. Third, it opposed the idea of 'progress' upon which the whole of life and existence stands. Fourth, it moved away from the historical reality of the Muslims. And fifth, it opposed the hadiths that have come on the appearance of a *khalīfah* who will fill the earth with justice just as, now, it is filled with oppression and injustice (and he is the one known by the name *al-Mahdī*), and the hadiths on the coming down of the Messiah, ʿĪsā ibn Maryam, upon him be peace, and his establishing the political state of Islam, and the rule of its Law, and exalting its word throughout the earth.

The attitude of our scholars in older times to this hadith

It is our duty to say that the predecessors among our scholars held back from this hadith, regarding its 'generality' (*iṭlāq*) as dubious. By 'generality' they meant what is understood from the hadith, that *every* time is worse than the one before it, whereas some times have been less in evil than what preceded them, even if that happened only the once – in the time of ʿUmar ibn ʿAbd al-ʿAzīz. That was after, immediately after, the time of al-Ḥajjāj, about whom complaint was general. The good that there was in the time of ʿUmar ibn ʿAbd al-ʿAzīz has been made well-known. Even if what has been said about it – that in his time evil faded away – might indeed be going too far, it cannot be claimed by any means that his time was worse than what preceded it.

The scholars in earlier ages responded to these reservations as follows:

a) The interpretation of al-Ḥasan al-Baṣrī

Al-Ḥasan al-Basrī imputed to the hadith a meaning restricting it to the overwhelming majority of times, not all times. Asked about ʿUmar ibn ʿAbd al-ʿAzīz after al-Ḥajjāj, he said: "Some breathing space [i.e. a period of solace] was necessary for the people."

b) The interpretation of Ibn Masʿūd

There has come from Ibn Masʿūd: "There will not come upon you a time except that it will be worse than the one preceding it. Look now, I do not mean that one ruler is not better than another ruler and no year is better than another year, but your scholars and your jurists will go, then you will not find among [the people] a successor [to them], and there will come a people who give fatwas according to their personal opinion (*ra'y*)." And in a speech attributed to him: "Then they will defile Islam and wreck it". In *al-Fatḥ* Ibn Ḥajar weighed this argument in commenting on the meaning of good and bad in this context, and said: "He is the more appropriate to be followed."

But in fact he does not altogether uproot the difficulty. For, according to the texts, it is demonstrated that in the unseen future there will come times for Islam in which its banner will be raised, and its word exalted. Even if this happens only in the time of the Mahdī and the Messiah in the end days, still it suffices.

History records that there have come periods of stagnation and seizure in the world, succeeded by times of movement and renewal. It suffices to mention, for example, those scholars and reformers who appeared in the eighth century – after the fall of the caliphate in Baghdad. And the vicissitudes of the conditions in the seventh century, after which appeared, for example, Ibn Daqīq al-ʿĪd, and Shaykh al-Islam Ibn Taymiyyah and his pupil Ibn al-Qayyim, and the rest of his pupils in Syria; so too appeared al-Shāṭibī in al-Andalus; and Ibn Khaldūn in the Maghreb and Egypt, and others on whom Ibn Ḥajar wrote biographical notes in his book *al-Durar al-Kāminah fī Aʿyān al-Mi'at al-Thāminah.*

In the epochs that followed that, we find for example Ibn Ḥajar himself, and al-Suyūṭī in Egypt, and Ibn Wazīr in Yemen, and al-Dahlawī in India, and al-Shawkānī and al-Sanʿā'ī in Yemen; and Ibn ʿAbd al-Wahhāb in Najd; and other scholars of high rank in ijtihad, and leaders of the reformers. This is what prompted Ibn Ḥibbān to observe in his *Ṣaḥīḥ* that the hadith of Anas was not for the general public of his time, and he based his argument on the afore-mentioned hadith on the Mahdī, and how he will fill the earth with justice, after it has been filled with injustice.[37]

c) The interpretation that we favor on balance

On balance I favor the commentaries on this hadith that Ibn Ḥajar has given in *al-Fatḥ*:

> It is probable that the referent of the times mentioned is the time of the Companions, on the basis that it is they who were addressed by that [hadith]. Then as for those after them: they were not intended in the report mentioned. However, the Companion [i.e. Anas] understood [the words] in their generality, so for that [reason] he answered [in the way that he did] those who complained to him about al-Ḥajjāj. He commanded them to be patient, and they – or the greater part of them – were the *Tābiʿīn* [the Successors, the generation after the Companions].[38]

Ibn Ḥajar also brings to bear on this interpretation the discourse of Ibn Masʿūd, who was particularly of the time of the Companions and the Successors addressed in the hadith. (The assassination of ʿUthmān happened in that time, followed by the Dissensions.)

As for the particular claim that the hadith implies an appeal to silence before injustice, patience with abuse of power and tyranny, and contentment with wrongdoing and disorder, and that it supports negativism in the face of the arrogance of the tyrants in the earth – it is rebutted by a number of arguments:

First: that the speaker of "Be patient!" was Anas, so it is not a hadith *marfūʿ*. He inferred what he understood from the Prophet. And a Muslim is free to adopt or leave the discourse of every individual except the one who was free of sin.

Second: Anas indeed did not command people to be content before injustice and disorder, but only commanded them to be patient – and the difference between the two is great. Contentment before unbelief is itself unbelief, and before wrongdoing wrongdoing. As for patience, it is all but indispensable; one is patient with a thing that one is averse to, while endeavoring to change it.

Third: one who does not have the capacity for resistance to injustice and tyranny, has no way other than to seek refuge in patience and long suffering. At the same time he must strive to make preparations for appropriate action, for change, and to seize means and occasions, to take help from all who share his burden of concern. He must be ardent to exploit favorable opportunity, so that he may counter the power of the false with the power of the true, and the helpers of injustice with the helpers of justice. Certainly the Prophet was patient for thirteen years in Makkah against the idols and their worshippers. He used to pray in the Masjid al-Ḥarām, and circumambulate the Kaʿbah while there were three hundred and sixty idols in it. He circumambulated it with the delegation of his Companions in the seventh year of the Hijrah in the *ʿumrat al-qaḍā'*, and he saw the idols but did not touch them until the right time came on the day of the Great Conquest – the conquest of Makkah – and he destroyed them.

That is why our scholars have stipulated that if the elimination of a wrong leads on to a greater wrong, silence is obligatory upon one until the conditions change. Thus, it is not proper to understand the instruction to be patient as meaning an absolute surrender to injustice and arrogance. Rather: it means waiting and watching attentively until God gives his judgment, and He is the best of judges.

Fourth: patience does not forbid one from speaking the word of truth, and enjoining the right and forbidding the wrong before tyrants acting as gods. Yet there is no obligation to do so upon one who fears for himself or his family or those around him. It has come in a hadith: "The best jihad is a word of truth before an oppressive ruler."[39] And in another hadith: "The leader of the martyrs is Ḥamzah ibn ʿAbd al-Muṭṭalib, and a man who stands before an oppressive leader, then enjoins him [to do what is right] and forbids him [to do what is wrong] and kills him."[40]

CHAPTER THREE

Principles for Correct Understanding of the Sunnah

I

UNDERSTANDING IN THE LIGHT OF THE QUR'AN

To understand the Sunnah correctly, in a way that is secure from distortion, deviation and bad interpretation, we must understand it in the light of the Qur'an, in the framework of its divine instructions. Where the Sunnah gives us information, the Qur'an is decisive as to its truth; and where it commands, the Qur'an is decisive as to its justice: "And perfected is the word of your Lord in truth and in justice. There is none to change His words. He is the All-Hearing and the All-Seeing" (*al-Anʿām*, 6: 116). We may think of the Qur'an as the spirit of the body of Islam; as the foundations of its building; and as the resource of its constitutional principles, to which all the statutes in Islam are referred, as their parent and safe refuge.

The Prophet's Sunnah is the commentary on this 'constitution', the exposition of it, in the form of both theoretical explanation and practical application: it was his duty to make clear to people what was sent down to them. As the branch does not work against the root, so the explanation does not oppose the explained: the Sunnah turns always within the horizon of the Book, never transgressing it. That is why the *ṣaḥīḥ*, established Sunnah is not found to contradict the injunctions of the Qur'an. If people have supposed such contradiction to exist, then it must be a *sunnah* that is not *ṣaḥīḥ*, or the understanding of which is not *ṣaḥīḥ*, or it may be that the contradiction is not real but merely conjectured.

Understanding the Sunnah in the light of the Qur'an means, to begin with, that hadiths contradicting the Qur'an are rejected. For example:

The hadith about the alleged '*gharānīq*' ('the long-necked ones') is, without a doubt, rebutted because it is contradictory to the Qur'an. One cannot imagine how it could come in the context where the Qur'an is strongly criticizing the false goddesses, where it says: "Have you considered al-Lāt and al-ʿUzzā and Manāt, the third, the other? Are yours the males and His the females? That is indeed an unjust division! They are surely only names that you have named, you and your fathers, for which God did not send any authority. They are not following anything but a whim of the[ir] souls. And assuredly from your Lord the guidance has come" (*al-Najm*, 53: 19–23). How, in the context of this negation of and fleeing from the idols, can one reason that words glorifying them should enter – the alleged words being: "Those *gharānīq* – indeed their intercession is to be hoped for"?![1]

Similarly, the hadith about women – "Consult with them and then oppose them" – is invalid and false in that it contradicts the verse about parents and their arrangements for the nursing of their child: "And if the two of them desire [to engage a wet-nurse] by mutual consent and consulting one another, then it is no sin for either of them" (*al-Baqarah*, 2: 233).

PREFERRING WHAT IS IN THE LIGHT OF THE QUR'AN

Understanding the Sunnah in the light of the Qur'an also means that, if jurists or commentators differ on what they derive from the *sunnah*s, then the best of them and the one to be favored is the one supported by the Qur'an. Consider the verse: "He it is Who produces gardens trellised and untrellised, and the date-palms and crops different in their taste, and the olive and the pomegranate, like them and unlike them. Eat of its fruit when it bears fruit and yield up its due on the day of its harvesting" (*al-Anʿām*, 6: 142).

Now this verse, in what it states in general terms and in what it details, does not omit anything lodged and growing in the earth: for *every* growing thing it indicates a due, and it commands the yielding up of that due. The due as here commanded is *general*: it is what the Qur'an and the Sunnah detailed subsequently, under the categories of zakah (alms-tax).

In spite of this, we see among the jurists those who restrict the liability to zakah on what God has produced out of the earth. They confine it to either (1) four classes only of grains and dates; or (2) to what is used as food in circumstances where one has choice (of what to accept as food), not otherwise; or (3) to produce that can be dried, measured and stored. They remove from liability other fruits and vegetables – plantations of coffee and tea, orchards of apples and mangoes, fields of cotton, sugar-cane, and the like, from all of which wealth flows abundantly for their owners. So far is this so that, when traveling in some Asian lands, I heard that the Communists accuse Islamic fiqh or Islamic Legislation of putting the burden of zakah on small cultivators (probably hired workers on the land, not owners), who grow oats, wheat, barley and cedar, while it exempts from zakah owners of great plantations of coconut, tea, rubber, and the like.

I stand in admiration at the discussion of this issue by Abū Bakr ibn al-ʿArabī, the leading Mālikī of his age. He commented on the verse in his book *Aḥkām al-Qur'ān*, and clarified the doctrines of three jurists – Mālik, Shāfiʿī, and Ibn Ḥanbal – on what, of the plants of the earth, is liable and what is not liable. Among those doctrines is his own, namely the doctrine of Mālik, but (such was his objectivity and depth of knowledge) he pronounced the doctrines of all three schools weak as a whole. Thereafter he said:

> As for Abū Ḥanīfah, he made the verse his looking-glass [i.e. reflected on it intensively] then discerned the truth. He made [zakah] obligatory on the edible [plants], be they nutritious or otherwise. The Prophet explained that in the generality of his saying: "In what the sky waters [i.e. whatever is produced by the action of rain], a tenth (*al-ʿushr*)."

As for the opinion of Aḥmad [ibn Ḥanbal] – that [the liability to zakah] is in what is measured, according to his saying, "There is not [any liability] in what is less than five measures [...]" – it is weak, because that which the outward of the hadith rules upon is the *niṣāb* [minimum value below which wealth is non-liable] in respect of fruit and grain. Then, as for the falling away of the due right from what is other [than fruit or grain], [that] is not within the competency of the statement [it is not covered by the wording in the hadith]. As for the relevance of the nutritional aspect (that is the Shāfiʿī position), then it is [merely] a claim, an idea that does not have a source to which it refers. [The idea is not based on any authority of text or principle.] And ideas, as we have explained in the book on *Qiyās*, are only directed to injunctions according to their sources.

Then how does God, glory be to Him, mention the blessing in the nourishing foods and fruits, and make them liable to the due, all of them, [all] whose condition is classed as the vine and the date-palm, [all] whose kind is classed as cultivated [crops], and [all] to whose nutritional value is adjoined the giving of light, by which the blessing is perfected in the enjoyment of the delight of the eye – [thereby achieving] the fulfillment [above the ground] of the favor in the darkness [under the ground]?

Thereafter Ibn al-ʿArabī said:

Now if it is said: Why was it not conveyed from the Prophet that he took zakah from the vegetables of Madinah and Khaybar? [The people objecting mean: no hadith has reached us, by which the practice of taking zakah on vegetables can be legally established.]

We say [in response]: Just so, that is what our scholars relied on. To be more precise: it [not taking zakah on vegetables] is [based on] an absence of proof, [it is] not [based on] the existence of proof. [The objection is not based on any authority that says *not* to take zakah on vegetables.]

And if it is said: If he took [the zakah], would it not have been conveyed [that he did so]?

We say: What need is there for conveying it [as a practice of the Prophet], when the Qur'an suffices on it?![2]

There is the hadith narrated from the Prophet: "There is no *ṣadaqah* on vegetables". But it is weak in its *isnād*, and one cannot adduce the like of such hadiths in any Legal argument – let alone venturing to specify by them what, in the Qur'an and the well-known hadiths, is general. Al-Tirmidhī narrated the hadith and commented: "The *isnād* of this hadith has no *ṣaḥīḥ*, and in [the hadiths on] this topic not one thing is authenticated as from the Prophet."[3]

The hadith: "The one burying alive and the one buried are [both] in the Fire"

A Muslim must 'refrain from' any hadith that he sees as contradictory to an injunction of the Qur'an, unless he is able to find for that hadith an interpretation easy to accept. So I 'refrained from' the hadith which Abū Dā'ūd and others have narrated: "The one burying alive and the one buried are [both] in the Fire."[4] When I read this hadith I felt dejected at heart. I wondered if the hadith might be weak, for (as the people of this business know) not everything that Abū Dā'ūd has narrated in his *Sunan* is *ṣaḥīḥ*. But I found in a text something in favor of its being *ṣaḥīḥ*. Among those who affirm its being so is Shaykh al-Albānī in *Ṣaḥīḥ al-Jāmiᶜ al-Ṣaghīr* and *Ṣaḥīḥ Abī Dā'ūd*.

An example of the arguments in defence of it: "The one burying alive and the one buried alive are both in the Fire – except if the one burying alive survived until the advent of Islam, then embraced Islam."[5] This means that the one burying alive has some chance of deliverance from the Fire, and the victim, the one buried alive – no chance for her!

Here I raised questions about this – just as the Companions raised questions when they heard from the Prophet: "If two Muslims clash with their swords, then the one who slays and the one slain are [both] in the Fire." They said: "This slayer [we understand the outcome for him], but why the one slain [why should he be in the Fire also?]" He said: "Indeed he [the slain] was coveting the killing of his companion." Thus he explicated for them the aspect of the case justifying the Fire for the one slain – namely, his intention, apparent from him, of killing his companion.

In the same way, I now ask: That the one burying alive should be in the Fire I understand. But why should the one buried alive, the victim, be in the Fire also? Her being consigned to the Fire contradicts the verse: "And when the infant girl buried alive is asked for what sin she was slain" (*al-Takwīr*, 81: 8–9). I have gone back to the commentators to see what they have said on the educational purpose of the hadith, but I have not found anything that gives ease to the mind and heart.

The hadith: "Indeed your father and my father are in the Fire"

Another example is the hadith which Muslim has narrated from Anas: "Indeed your father and my father are in the Fire."[6] The Prophet said this in answering a questioner who asked about his (the questioner's) father: Where is he now (now that he is dead)? I wondered: What sin did ʿAbd Allāh ibn ʿAbd al-Muṭṭalib have that he should be in the Fire, and he was one of the people of the *Fatrah* (the period before the advent of Islam), about whom the *ṣaḥīḥ* reports are that they are saved?

It occurred to me that the words "my father" might be referring to his uncle Abū Ṭālib, who had provided for him, watched over him and cared for him after the death of his grandfather, ʿAbd al-Muṭṭalib. The usage of *ʿamm* (uncle) for *abū* (father) has appeared in the language and in the Qur'an itself: "We worship your God, and the God of your fathers, Ibrāhīm and Ismāʿīl and Isḥāq, and He is One God, and we are *muslim* (wholly submitted to Him)" (*al-Baqarah*, 2: 133). Ismāʿīl was the 'uncle' of Yaʿqūb, but the term in the Qur'an is 'father'. One does not wonder that Abū Ṭālib should be in the Fire, given his refusal, to the last moment of his life, to pronounce the testimony of *tawḥīd.* A group of authenticated traditions inform us that, while under punishment, he would nevertheless be the most easy of the people of the Fire. However, this way of explaining it is most weak in my opinion, because it opposes the immediate aspect of the text. Then, from another aspect: What was the sin of the father of the man who asked the question? The outward sense of what we know of the case is that this man's father died before the advent of Islam. Accordingly, I 'refrain from' this hadith until something appears to me that settles my unease about it.

One of my teachers, Shaykh Muhammad al-Ghazālī, rejected the hadith explicitly, because it controverts what God has said:

> And they are not punished until We have sent a messenger. (*al-Isrā'*, 17: 15)

> And if We had destroyed them with some punishment, they would certainly have said: "Our Lord! If only You had sent us a messenger so that we might have followed Your revelations before we were humiliated and disgraced."(*Ṭāhā*, 20: 134)

> ...lest you should say: "No messenger came to us as a bringer of good news and of warning," a Messenger certainly has come to you as bringer of good news and as a warner. (*al-Mā'idah*, 5: 19)

The Arabs did not have a warner sent to them before Muhammad, as is made explicit in the Book:

> So that you may warn a people whose fathers were not warned so they became heedless. (*Yāsīn*, 36: 6)

> That you may warn a people to whom, before you, no warner came, so it may be they will be[come] guided. *(al-Sajdah*, 32: 3)

> And We did not send to them before you any warner. (*Sabā'*, 34: 44)

However, I prefer, in regard to *ṣaḥīḥ* hadiths, to 'refrain from' them, without rejecting them absolutely, for fear that they have meanings not yet disclosed to me. By great good fortune I went back to what commentators on *Ṣaḥīḥ Muslim* other than al-Nawawī have said. I mean the two most learned scholars, al-Abbī and al-Sanūsī. I found both of them to be 'refraining from' the outward meaning of this hadith. Al-Nawawī commented on the hadith: "He said it in accordance with the goodness of his nature, as a solace for the man, as a sharing in the hardship [of having a father who had not died in the faith]." Then he went on to say: "That one who dies an unbeliever is in the Fire, and the relationship of near relatives does not benefit him." In response to that, al-Abbī said:

> This absolute [statement] needs looking at! Al-Suhaylī has said: "It is not for us to say that, for he has said: 'Do not give hurt to the living on account of the dead.' " And the Exalted has said: "Those who give hurt to God and His Messenger, God has cursed them in this world and the hereafter, and has prepared for them a humiliating punishment" (*al-Aḥzāb*, 33: 57). The Prophet only said it as solace for the man, and it has come that the man had said: "And you, where is your father?", and he said that to him at that time [i.e. in response to the particular form of the question].

Al-Nawawī said: "And in it is [included] that one who died during the *Fatrah*, at which time the Arabs were [immersed] in the worship of idols, is in the Fire, and this is not [an instance] of punishment before preaching, because the call of Abraham, upon him be peace, and other messengers, had reached them."

In response, al-Abbī said:

> Ponder what there is in this statement of contradiction. For those whom the call [to correct worship] reached were surely not of the people of the *Fatrah*. That is known by what is heard [reported from tradition]: for the people of the *Fatrah* are the communities existing between the times of the messengers, those to whom the earlier Messenger was not sent and who did not survive to [the time of] the later [Messenger] – like the Bedouin Arabs to whom Jesus, upon him be peace, was not sent, and they did not survive to the time of the Prophet. The *Fatrah* on this interpretation includes what was between every two messengers.
>
> However, when the jurists use the word *Fatrah* they mean only [the period] which was between Jesus, upon him be peace, and the Prophet. Al-Bukhārī mentioned from Salmān that it was six hundred years.
>
> Since the definitive [proofs] demonstrate there being no punishment until the justification (*ḥujjah*) has been established, we know that they are not [among] the punished.
>
> Then if it is said: [There are] hadiths establishing as correct the punishment of some of the people of the *Fatrah*, like this hadith, the hadith "I saw ᶜAmr ibn Luhayy dragging his entrails (*quṣba-hu*)[7] in the Fire."[8]
>
> I say [in answer]: ᶜAqīl ibn Abī Ṭālib has responded to that with three answers:

First: that they [the hadiths in question] are solitary reports; they cannot go against the definitive [hadiths established from many narrators by many routes].

Second: the punishment is restricted to those [specific individuals mentioned], and God knows the cause [for which they are punished].

Third: the punishment mentioned in these hadiths is restricted to those who changed and altered [the way of life of] the people to some misguidedness[9] that was not forgivable.[10]

CARE IN CLAIMING CONTRADICTION OF THE QUR'AN

It is imperative that we warn here against latitude in claiming contradiction of the Qur'an without well-established foundations for such a claim.

The Muʿtazilis were a group who rode rashly on the vehicle of excess. At times they dared to reject widely known *ṣaḥīḥ* hadiths on the acceptability in the hereafter of the intercession of the Prophet, of his brother prophets, of the angels, and of the righteous ones of the believers. Such intercession is on behalf, among believers in One God, of those who were disobedient. The hadiths tell us that God forgives them by His grace and His mercy, and by the intercession of those who intercede, so that they do not enter the Fire at all, or they enter it and come out of it after a time, and then are proceeded towards the Garden.

This is the munificence of God, Blessed and Exalted is He, to His slaves, which elevates the weight of mercy above the weight of justice. Thus, He has made the recompense of a good deed ten times its like or more, up to seventy times, or He increases it even more. He has made the recompense of an evil deed its like only, or He forgives it. He has appointed for the sins acts of expiation – many of the five prayers, and the Friday prayer, and the fasting in Ramadan, and the vigil therein, and different forms of charitable acts, and the pilgrimage, both hajj and *ʿumrah*, and the recital and remembrance of His Names, and the utterance of the formula of *tawḥīd*, and the magnificat, and the praise of Him, and other kinds of remembrance and supplication. All of these serve to lessen the burden of sin. Moreover, a Muslim does not endure any trouble or hardship, grief or sadness, or offence, so much as the pricking of a thorn – but all of these God offsets against his sins and errors. So also, a part of this munificence of God to His slaves is that He has made the prayer of believers on behalf of one who has died, be they from his family or not, of benefit to the deceased in his grave.

Then, it is not far-fetched that God honors the chosen and elect ones of His slaves, and accepts their intercession for whoever He wills of His creatures from those who died on the word of *tawḥīd*. This is what the hadiths rally around:

> The people come out of the Fire by the intercession of Muhammad, and they enter the Garden, and they will be called the people of hell.[11]

> The people come out of the Fire by the intercession, as if they were *thaʿārir*.[12] (*Al-thaʿārir*: vegetables like asparagus.)

> By the intercession of one man from my Community more [people] will enter the Garden than [the number of people in] the Banū Tamīm.[13]

> The martyr intercedes for seventy of the people of his household.[14]

> The most fortunate of the people by my intercession on the Day of Resurrection is one who says *lā ilāha illa al-Lāhu* (there is no god but God) with sincerity from his heart.[15]

> Every prophet has one supplication [that is accepted by God]. So I intend if God wills that I shall dedicate my supplication to the intercession for my Community on the Day of Resurrection.[16]

> Every prophet has asked a question – or he said: Every prophet has a supplication – he supplicates with it and he is answered. So I have made my supplication the intercession for my Community on the Day of Resurrection.[17]

And in the hadith of Abū Saʿīd, according to the two Shaykhs, al-Bukhārī and Muslim:

> So the prophets and the angels and the believers will have interceded. Then [God] the All-Compelling says: My intercession remains. So He will grasp from the Fire one handful, then let out the people who have been roasted (that is,

> scorched); then by His forgiveness they will be thrown in the river at the mouth of the Garden called the water of life [...].[18]

> Every prophet has one supplication heard and accepted, and every prophet has hastened to submit his supplication. But I have reserved my supplication for intercession for my Community on the Day of Resurrection – then it is accepted – if God wills – for whoever from my Community died not associating anything with God.[19]

But the Muᶜtazilis – because of their giving too much weight to the threat over the promise of God, to His justice over His mercy, and to reason over tradition (rationalism over revelation) – rejected these hadiths, despite the strength and sheer clarity of what establishes them as true. Their doubts, in rejecting those hadiths, were based on the notion that they contradicted the Qur'an which, they claimed, negated intercession. In fact, one who reads the Qur'an does not find in it any negation of intercession except the kind that the Associationists (*mushrikūn*) set their hopes on, and the deviationists from the practitioners of other religions. The Associationists claimed that their gods that they supplicated to, apart from or in spite of God, had the power to intercede for them before God, and hold the punishment back from them. As God has said: "They worship apart from God what neither harms nor benefits them, and they say those are intercessors before God" (*Yūnus*, 10: 18). But the Qur'an pronounces this claimed intercession invalid and false, confirming that their gods do not avail them in anything from God. It says: "Or do they adopt intercessors apart from God. Say: What? Even though they have no power over anything and have no sense or reason? Say: the intercession belongs to God altogether [exclusively]. To Him belongs sovereign power over the heavens and the earth. And then it is to Him you are returning" (*al-Zumar*, 39: 43–44). Also: "And they have adopted gods apart from God so that they may be for them [a source of] might and honor. No indeed! They will reject their worship of them, and they will be adversaries [advocating] against them" (*Maryam*, 19: 81–82).

Without a doubt, the Qur'an negates the notion that the spurious gods have any power of intercession, and that there will be for the Associationists an intercessor who is yielded to: "Warn them of a day …when there will not be for the wrongdoers (*ẓālimīn*) any friend nor any intercessor who is yielded to" (*al-Ghāfir*, 40: 18). The Qur'an frequently uses the term 'wrong' (*ẓulm*) for Associationism and 'wrongdoers' (*ẓālimūn*) for the Associationists, and Associationism is indeed a tremendous wrong. Aside from that, the Qur'an nevertheless establishes the validity of intercession upon certain conditions:

First: That it is only after the permission of God, Exalted is He, to the intercessor that he may intercede. Not one, whosoever he may be, has the power that he can oblige God in any matter. He said in the Verse of the Throne: "Who is he that intercedes before Him except by His leave?" (*al-Baqarah*, 2: 255).

Second: That the intercession is on behalf of 'the people of *tawḥīd*', believers in the Unity of God. As God said about His angels: "And they do not intercede except for him with whom God is well-pleased" (*al-Anbiyā'*, 21: 28).

From the verse about the liars on the Day of Judgment – "Then the intercession of intercessors will not avail them" (*al-Mudaththir*, 74: 48) – one understands that there *are* intercessors, the intercession of other than whom is denied, and they are those who died on the faith.

So the Qur'an did *not* negate intercession absolutely, as those claim who make that claim. Rather, it negated the intercession that the Associationists and deviationists appealed to. It negated that intercession which has been a cause of so much trouble and disorder among the followers of the religions, those who were committing the gravest offences while counting on the expectation that their intercessors and mediators would lift the punishment from them. So also kings and governors commit oppression and injustice in the affairs of this world, expecting to escape the consequences hereafter.

It is regrettable that we find in our time among books associated with Islam those that march side by side with the Muʿtazilis in denying the intercession in the hereafter, and claiming that it is colored by the sort of patronage and intervention on someone's behalf known to people in this world. So they throw to the wall the hadiths that are *ṣaḥīḥ*, explicit and abundant, which are a solace for us, alleging of them that they contradict the Qur'an.[20]

II

GATHERING RELEVANT HADITHS ON A SUBJECT TOGETHER

Also necessary for a correct understanding of the Sunnah is that the *ṣaḥīḥ* hadiths on a single subject be gathered together and juxtaposed – the ambiguous alongside the explicit, the absolute alongside the restricted, the general alongside the particularized. In that way, by interpreting one with the other, we make the meaning intended in them plain and clear. We do not 'strike some of them with others' (i.e. we do not cause some to clash or become confused with others). As it is established and agreed that the Sunnah interprets the Qur'an, and clarifies it – meaning that it details what is general in it, interprets what is obscure in it, particularizes what is universal in it, and restricts what is absolute in it – the maxim 'better followed by better' is most successfully applied within the Sunnah, some elements of it checking other elements of it.

HADITH: WEARING THE *IZĀR* LONG

Take for example the hadiths on wearing the *izār* (the lower garment) long. The threat against doing so is made severe. Many zealous youths rely on that when they rebuke with severity whoever is not wearing his robe above the ankles. They preach on it to the effect of all but making shortening the robe one of the symbols of Islam, or the greatest of duties in it! If they should catch sight of a Muslim scholar or preacher who is not wearing his robe short, how they act! They reproach him among themselves for belittling the religion, and (worse still) they sometimes do so with public proclamation!

If only they had gone back to the whole group of the hadiths related to this issue, and set some of them alongside others, in the light of a comprehensive view of the purposes of Islam for those whom it obligates in their everyday affairs and usages! Had they done so, they would have known the purposes of the hadiths on this point, and they would have lightened their zeal and not ridden rashly on the vehicle of excess. And they would not have made narrow for the people a matter which God had made wide for them.

Consider what Muslim narrated from Abū Dharr, from the Prophet, he said: "[There are] three to whom God will not speak on the Day of Resurrection: the benefactor who does not give anything except as a favor [i.e. he does it for reputation or to bind the recipient]; the quick profiteer[21] whose commodity is [sold] by a lying oath; and the one who wears his *izār* long."[22]

In another narration, also from Abū Dharr: "[There are] three to whom God will not speak on the Day of Resurrection. He will not look at them, and He will not purify them, and theirs will be a painful punishment." He said God's Messenger recited it three times. He (Abū Dharr) said: "They have failed and they have lost! Who are they, O Messenger of God?" He said: "The one who wears his *izār* long; the benefactor; and the quick profiteer who sells his commodity by a lying oath."[23]

What is the intended meaning of 'one who wears his izār long'?

Does it mean anyone who has his *izār* long? Even if, in doing so, he was merely following the conventions of his people, without having in his intention any haughtiness or conceit? Another hadith has perhaps attested to that, one found in the *Ṣaḥīḥ* of al-Bukhārī from Abū Hurayrah: "That which of the *izār* is lower than the ankles, then it is in the Fire."[24] In al-Nasā'ī it has appeared with the wording: "That which of the *izār* is below the ankles, then it is in the Fire."[25] The meaning would appear to be: whatever falls below the ankles of the wearer of the *izār* constitutes 'wearing it long', and it is in the Fire – the outcome for anyone is according to his deed, and here, the robe (used metonymically) alludes to the body and the person it clothes.[26]

However, it becomes clear to one who reads the whole group of hadiths that have come on this that its meaning is as al-Nawawī and Ibn Ḥajar and others judged it on balance to be: namely, the (apparent) absoluteness is to be interpreted by the restriction to 'conceit'. And there is consensus that this 'conceit' is what the threat in the hadith is directed against.[27] So, let us read what has appeared of the *ṣaḥīḥ* from these hadiths.

Al-Bukhārī narrated, under the chapter heading *man jarra izāra-hu min ghayri khuyalā'* (one who has trailed his *izār* without conceit), in a hadith of ʿAbd Allāh ibn ʿUmar from the Prophet, he said: " 'Whoever trails his robe with conceit God will not look at him on the Day of Resurrection.' Abū Bakr said: 'O Messenger of God; one side of my *izār* works loose, unless I am attending to that to [prevent] it.' Then the Prophet said: 'You are not among those who make that [happen] with conceit.' "[28] Also in this chapter is a hadith of Abū Bakrah, who said: "The sun eclipsed, and we were with the Prophet. He stood up, trailing his robe in great haste until he came to the mosque [...]"[29] Then, narrated under the chapter heading *man jarra thawbahu min al-khuyalā'* (one who has trailed his robe with conceit), from Abū Hurayrah that God's Messenger said: "God will not look at one who trails his *izār* with arrogance (*al-baṭar*)."[30] Also from Abū Hurayrah: "He said the Prophet said, (or he said Abū al-Qāsim, said): 'While a man was walking in fine dress, himself admiring himself, his abundant hair well-combed, then God caused the earth to give way to him, so he will be shaking and sinking until the Day of Resurrection.' "[31] And from Ibn ʿUmar – and there is a hadith like it from Abū Hurayrah also – "While a man was trailing his *izār*, then [God] made him sink down, so he will be sinking in the earth to the Day of Resurrection."[32]

Muslim narrated the hadith of Abū Hurayrah, the one last mentioned, and the one before it. Also, he narrated the hadith of Ibn ʿUmar by a number of routes. Among them: "I heard God's Messenger, with these my two ears, saying: 'One who trails his *izār* not meaning by that [anything] but conceit, then indeed God will not look at him on the Day of Resurrection.' "[33] In this narration, the restriction of 'conceit' by way of the clear qualification "not meaning by that [anything] but conceit" has not left any room for interpretation.

Al-Nawawī – and he is not one accused of laxity, rather (as is well known to students), one more inclined to the stricter, more cautious approach – says in commentary on the hadith "One who wears his *izār* long":[34]

> As for his saying, "The one who wears his *izār* long": then its meaning is 'the one who has loosened it for trailing the side of it with conceit'. It has come interpreted in the other hadith "God does not look at the one who trails his robe with conceit", and 'conceit' [means] haughtiness. This limitation to the trailing with conceit particularizes the generality of "one who wears his *izār* long". It is demonstrated that the object of the threat is one who trails it with conceit, for the Prophet, made allowance for Abū Bakr al-Ṣiddīq in that, and said: "You are not among them" when he was trailing it without conceit.

Ibn Ḥajar said in his commentary on the hadiths that al-Bukhārī narrated on the threat against wearing the *izār* long and trailing of the robe:

> In these hadiths: [it is clear] that wearing the *izar* long with conceit is a grave matter. As for wearing long without conceit, then the outward of the hadith forbids it also. However, the inference from the restriction in these hadiths to 'with conceit' is that absoluteness in forcibly preventing the [behavior] mentioned, in rebuking the wearing long, is to be taken alongside the restriction here so that one does not forbid the trailing and wearing long when [this happens in a way that is] safe from conceit.

Ibn ᶜAbd al-Barr said: "The understanding of it is that trailing without conceit will not encounter the threat unless [indeed] the trailing of the shirt and other than that of long garments is [to be censured] in all circumstances."[35]

This confirms that what is aimed at, in the restriction that goes with wearing the *izār* long, and what carries the threat, is the intention of conceit. It confirms also that the threat mentioned in the hadiths is a severe threat, so far so that it has made whoever wears his garment long one of three "to whom God will not speak on the Day of Resurrection. He will not look at them, and He will not purify them, and theirs will be a painful punishment". Indeed, the Prophet repeated that threat three times, which made Abū Dharr so fearful of it that he said: "They have failed and they have lost! Who are they, O Messenger of God?" All of this demonstrates the deeds of those three as being among the gravest of sins, and the gravest of the forbidden things. This is not so except in matters that infringe 'the public good', which the Law came to uphold and to safeguard – in the religion, the soul, the mind, dignity, lineage, and property – the fundamental goals of the Law of Islam.

The bare shortening of the *izār* or robe comes under the heading of the 'refinements' (not essentials), related to good manners and perfections, by which life is graced, tastes elevated, and noble traits of character deepened. As for wearing the garment long or lengthening it when stripped from any evil intention, it belongs in the class of the lesser disapproved acts.

What concerns the religion here, and is deserving of greater attention, is the intentions and sensibility of heart behind the outward behavior. What harms the religion through resistance to it is conceit, pride, haughtiness, self-praise, arrogance, and the like among diseases of the heart and defects of the soul. He does not enter the Garden who has a particle's weight of them in his heart. This supports every confirmation restricting the severe threat mentioned to one who intends conceit in wearing his garment long – as the other hadiths (mentioned above) have demonstrated.

Another meaning, related to what we have said, is this: the command about dress is subject to manners and outward forms familiar to the people and their customs. These vary with variations in heat and cold, wealth and poverty, capacity and incapacity, type of work and standard of living, and other influencing factors. The Law here lightens the restrictions for people, and it does not intervene except in matters related to the fixed bounds, so as to forbid what is visible of waste and extravagance in the outward life, or the intent of arrogance and conceit in the inner life, and the like of that which we have set out in detail elsewhere.[36]

For this reason al-Bukhārī quoted in the beginning of *Kitāb al-Libās* in his *Ṣaḥīḥ*, under the chapter heading *qawl Allāh Taʿāla: Qul: man ḥarrama zīnata al-Lāhi allatī akhraja li-ʿibādihi* (God's saying, Exalted is He: "Say: Who forbids the ornaments of God that He has brought out for His slaves" (*al-Aʿrāf*, 6: 32)). The Prophet said: "Eat and drink and dress, and give in charity, without wastefulness and [with] no conceit."[37] Ibn ʿAbbās said: "Eat what you wish, and wear what you wish, as long as [these] two do not touch you: wastefulness and conceit."[38]

Ibn Ḥajar conveyed from his teacher al-Ḥāfiẓ al-ʿIrāqī that he said, in his commentary on al-Tirmidhī:

> What touches the earth from them (i.e. clothes) is conceit. No doubt as to its being forbidden … And if it is said about the prohibition [that it is] on what exceeds the accustomed [practice], it would not be [going] too far. However, the convention happens to people of lengthening [robes]. Then every class of people begin to notice and know it. The duty in that is [to close] the way to conceit. For no doubt it is forbidden. But [the prohibition] is not on the manner of the custom, and there is no prohibition on it, so long as it does not reach to the forbidden [kind of] trailing of the hem.
>
> Al-Qāḍī ʿIyāḍ conveyed from the scholars: "Aversion is entirely to what is [done] over and above the custom, and beyond the accustomed practice for length and looseness in dress."[39]

So custom has its rule, and convention its influence, just as al-ʿIrāqī said. Departing from custom sometimes makes the doer of it suspected of seeking notoriety, and the robe of notoriety is also reproached in the Law. Then, the good lies in moderation.

Beyond that: one who intends, by the shortening of his robe, following the Sunnah and keeping away from the suspicion of conceit, if he intends abandoning opposition to the scholars, and if he intends his acceptance of the practice as a precaution, then he will be rewarded for that, if God wills. That is on condition also that he does not compel all people to the same, and does not proclaim the rejection of one who, being among those content with the views of the imams and profound commentators that we have cited, has left that practice. The wise maxim is: to every established *mujtahid* his reward, and to every man his intent.

The resort to the outward sense of a single hadith, without looking into the rest of the hadiths and texts relevant to its subject, often causes lapsing into error, and falling far away from the main road of correctness, and from the purposes for which the hadith has come.

THE HADITH IN AL-BUKHĀRĪ ON THE CENSURE OF TILLAGE

Consider the hadith that al-Bukhārī narrated in *Kitāb al Muẓāraʿah* (share-cropping) in his *Ṣaḥīḥ* from Abū Umāmah al-Bāhilī. Abū Umāmah saw an implement of tillage (a plow) and said: "I heard God's Messenger, saying: 'This does not enter the house of a people except that God causes disgrace to enter it [also].' "[40] The outward sense of this hadith does indeed convey the aversion of the Messenger to the plow and tillage, which leads on to censure of workers in it. Orientalists have sought to exploit this hadith to misrepresent the attitude of Islam to agriculture. But is this really the purpose of the outward sense of the hadith, and is Islam really averse to sowing and planting? In point of fact, other clear *ṣaḥīḥ* texts contradict that notion.

The Anṣār (the Muslims native to Madinah) practiced and depended on agriculture and cultivation. But the Prophet did not command them to abandon their agriculture and their cultivation. Rather, the Sunnah clarified, and Islamic jurisprudence detailed, regulations for agriculture and irrigation, and revival of barren lands, and what is related thereto of rights and obligations.

The two Shaykhs (al-Bukhārī and Muslim), as well as others, have narrated from him: "[There is] not one from the Muslims who plants a plant or sows a seed, then a bird eats from it, or a person, or an animal, except that there is from it an act of charity [recorded] for him."[41] Muslim has narrated [it] from Jābir in the words: "[There is] not one of the Muslims who plants a plant except that there is from it an act of charity [recorded] for him. What a beast of prey eats from it, then it is for him an act of charity. What a bird eats from it, then it is for him an act of charity. Not one deprives him (that is, diminishes or takes away from his fruit) except that it is for him an act of charity."[42] Jābir also narrated that the Prophet entered a walled enclosure belonging to Umm Maʿbad, in which there was a date-palm. Then he said: "O Umm Maʿbad. Who planted this date-palm? A Muslim or an unbeliever?" She said: "Indeed, a Muslim." He said: "A Muslim does not plant a plant, then a person eats from it, or an animal or a bird, except that it is for him an act of charity until the Day of Resurrection."[43]

So, for planting, there is recompense and reward with God, just as for an act of charity. The reward is for any fruit taken from what one has planted, even if one did not intend that – for example, what a beast of prey or a bird eats from it, or a thief steals from it, or anyone who diminishes it without taking one's permission to do so. It is an act of charity ongoing, permanent, never cut off, but enduring here while any living creature benefits from the plant or its crop. What virtue is greater than this virtue? What encouragement to agriculture could give greater assurance than this?

An encouragement to planting and sowing even more eloquent and wonderful is what Aḥmad ibn Ḥanbal reported in his *Musnad*, and al-Bukhārī in *al-Adab al-Mufrad* from Anas: "If the Hour approaches and in the hand of any of you there is a seedling, then if he is capable so that it (namely, the Hour) does not come until he plants it, then let him plant it."[44]

In my opinion this is an honoring of the work of building the earth even at the very termination of it. One is urged to plant even with the Hour approaching, even though there is not, after that effort, any profit for the one who plants, or for someone else after him, no expectation that anyone at all will benefit from it! There cannot be a better inducement to planting and producing for as long there is a breath of life to go back and forth. Man has been created to worship God, then to labor and build the earth, and persevere therein, worshipping and laboring until the world at last is in the throes of death. This is the understanding of the Companions and of the Muslims through the centuries. It pushed them to the building of the earth through agriculture and the revival of barren land.

Ibn Jarīr narrated from ʿUmārah ibn Khuzaymah ibn Thābit that he said: "I heard ʿUmar ibn al-Khaṭṭāb saying to my father: 'What prevents you from planting your land?' My father said to him: 'I am an old old man. I may die tomorrow!' Then he, ʿUmar, said to him: 'I stress upon you that you must plant it!' Then I surely saw ʿUmar ibn al-Khaṭṭāb plant it with his hand with my father!"[45] Aḥmad ibn Ḥanbal narrated from Abū al-Dardā' that in Damascus while he was planting a plant a man passed by. This man said to him: "You do this work and you are a Companion of God's Messenger?" Abū al-Dardā' said: "Do not rush at me [do not rush to judgment]. I have heard the Messenger of God say: 'One who plants a plant – no human being nor any creature from the creatures of God eats from it except that it is for him thereby an act of charity.' "[46]

What then should be the interpretation of the hadith of Abū Umāmah which al-Bukhārī narrated? Al-Bukhārī recorded it under the chapter heading *mā yaḥdhuru min ʿawāqib al-ishtighāl bi-ālati al-zarʿi aw mujāwazat al-ḥadd alladhī umira bi-hī* (What warns against the consequences of preoccupation with the implements of tillage, or disregarding the limit commanded for it). Ibn Ḥajar said in *al-Fatḥ*:

> Al-Bukhārī has pointed in the title to reconciling the hadith of Abū Umāmah with the hadith that has come on the virtue of sowing and planting. And that [reconciling] is by one of two ways. Either: that one understands what has appeared of the censure according to the consequence of that [preoccupation with tillage], and the circumstances of it when one is engaged in it – so on account of [preoccupation with tillage] he neglects and fails [in] what he is commanded to keep safe [of other duties] – such as his neglecting and failing the command of obligatory jihad. Or: that one understands [it] according to what he does not neglect and fail in except that he transgresses the limit [prescribed] for it.

> Some commentators have said: This [relates] to one who is near the enemy. For if then he is busy with the plow, he does not busy himself with horsemanship, and the enemy is emboldened against him. And their duty is that they busy themselves with horsemanship, and upon others is [the duty of] helping and supporting them in what they need thereof.[47]

A hadith that throws light on the purpose of the hadith of Abū Umāmah is narrated by Aḥmad ibn Ḥanbal and Abū Dā'ūd from Ibn ʿUmar, from the Prophet: "When you have exchanged by specimen,[48] and taken hold of the tails of cattle, and are pleased with tilling the soil, and you leave the jihad, [then] God gives disgrace mastery over you, and He does not remove [its power over you] until you have returned to the religion."[49] This hadith discloses the reasons for the disgrace that has fallen upon the Community – partly corresponding to its negligence in the commands related to the religion, and its non-observance of those of the commands related to this world whose fulfillment is obligatory.

The exchange 'by specimen' demonstrates that the Community has plunged into what God has forbidden, and forbidden with emphasis, proclaiming on the doer of it war from God and His Messenger – namely, *ribā* (usury), and tricks for the consumption of it by a form of exchange that is, among those who take part in it, outwardly lawful, but within definitely unlawful. Similarly, that 'following the tails of the cattle' and being contented with tilling the soil, demonstrates becoming stuck in agriculture, and particular tasks associated with it, to the point of neglecting other skills, in particular the skills connected to military matters. The abandonment of jihad is the logical consequence of that neglect. For these reasons taken together, disgrace surrounds the Community while it does not return to its religion.

This hadith and those before it make it clear that it is not good for a Muslim to take the Sunnah from a single hadith, without joining to it what else has appeared on the subject in other *ṣaḥīḥ* texts, from what confirms it or contradicts it, or illustrates what is general in it, or particularizes what is universal in it, or restricts what is absolute in it. By this joining of the rest of the *ṣaḥīḥ* hadiths, some of them with others, he enables an integrated and comprehensive view, and he rids his view of partiality and inadequacy. Not doing so lands many who do it in error, even if they did not intend it.

III

RECONCILING DIFFERING HADITHS OR PREFERENCE BETWEEN THEM

The principle for established texts of the Law is that they do not contradict, because the truth cannot contradict the truth. If the existence of a contradiction is supposed, then it is only in the outward of the case, not in actuality or reality. It is incumbent upon us to remove such alleged contradiction. When it is possible, without artifice and arbitrariness, to do that by combining and reconciling the two texts so that one can act according to both together, then it is better than recourse to preference between the two. It is better because preference entails neglecting one of the two texts and giving priority to the other over it.

RECONCILING HAS PRIORITY OVER PREFERENCE

For a good understanding of the Sunnah, it is important to reconcile *ṣaḥīḥ* hadiths that appear contradictory in that, at first glance, their textual meanings are at variance. It is necessary to combine some of them with others, and place each in its correct place, so that they harmonize and do not differ, so that they complement and do not contradict. We say this only about *ṣaḥīḥ* hadiths, because weak and feeble hadiths do not enter into this field. We seek to combine *ṣaḥīḥ* and established texts if they contradict each other. We do not do so for weakly supported texts except as a voluntary service, a supererogatory act – there is no requirement or duty to do that.[50]

For this reason the truth-seeking scholars rebutted the hadith, ("Are you two blind?") found in Abū Dā'ūd and al-Tirmidhī, of

Umm Salmah, which forbids a woman seeing a man even if he is blind. They rebutted it with the hadiths of ʿĀ'ishah and Fāṭimah bint Qays, both of them in the *Ṣaḥīḥ*:

> Umm Salmah said: "I was with the Prophet, and with him too [was] Maymūnah. Then Ibn Umm Maktūm approached, and that was after he had commanded us the *ḥijāb*. Then the Prophet said: 'Cover yourselves from him!' Then we said: 'O Messenger of God, is he not blind? He does not see us or know us.' Then the Prophet said: 'Are the two of you blind? Are you not seeing him?'"

Abū Dā'ūd narrated this hadith, and also al-Tirmidhī who said it was *ṣaḥīḥ* and *ḥasan*.[51] But in its *sanad* – which al-Tirmidhī indeed pronounced *ṣaḥīḥ* – there is Nabhān, the *mawlā* of Umm Salmah, who was not knowledgeable, nor one considered trustworthy except by Ibn Ḥibbān. In *al-Mughnī* al-Dhahabī mentioned him accordingly as among the weak narrators. Also, this hadith is contradicted by what, in the *Ṣaḥīḥ*s of al-Bukhārī and Muslim, demonstrates the permissibility of a woman looking at a stranger. From ʿĀ'ishah, she said: "I saw the Prophet: he screened me with his cloak while I watched the Abyssinians playing in the mosque."[52]

Qāḍī ʿIyāḍ said: "In it there is permission for the looking of women at the action of strangers, because [what is] disliked from [women] is only looking at good looks and taking delight in that." The same idea is expressed in al-Bukhārī's prefatory note on this hadith: "The looking of the woman at the Abyssinians and their like with no suspicion."[53] It confirms what al-Bukhārī has narrated in the hadith of Fāṭimah bint Qays, that the Prophet, said to her, as soon as she was divorced with an irrevocable divorce: "Spend the *ʿiddah* [waiting period before re-marriage is lawful] in the house of Ibn Umm Maktūm, for he is a blind man, you can lay down your cloak, and he will not see you." First he had indicated that she should spend the *ʿiddah* with Umm Sharīk, but then he said: "That woman – my Companions visit her [house]. Spend the *ʿiddah* with Ibn Umm Maktūm […]."

In sum, the hadith of Umm Salmah does not take precedence – because of the weakness in it – over these *ṣaḥīḥ* hadiths. Yet, the effort to reconcile between a weak and a *ṣaḥīḥ* hadith is permitted – by way of voluntary, supererogatory service – even though it is not obligatory. In this regard al-Qurṭubī has said (and others also) on the hadith of Umm Salmah:

> On the assumption of its being *ṣaḥīḥ*: that [which he said] is, from him [and] in view of their elevated status, treating his wives severely, just as he spoke severely to them in the command of the *ḥijāb* – which Abū Dā'ūd and others of the imams have indicated. There remains the meaning of the established and *ṣaḥīḥ* hadith, and it is that the Prophet commanded Fāṭimah bint Qays to take shelter in the house of Umm Sharīk, [but] later he said: "That woman – my Companions visit her [house]. Seek shelter with Ibn Umm Maktūm, for indeed he is blind. You can lay down your cloak and he will not see you."
>
> Some scholars infer from this hadith that a woman is permitted to be seen by a man up to what [one] is permitted to see of a woman, [such] as the head and the earlobe, but as for the *ᶜawrah*, then no.
>
> He only commanded her to remove from the house of Umm Sharīk to the house of Ibn Umm Maktūm because that was better for her than her staying in the house of Umm Sharīk as Umm Sharīk was reported to have many visitors to her [house] so there would be many seeing her. But in the house of Ibn Umm Maktūm no one would see her. So the stopping her being seen by him was more practical and better, so he made it easy for her in that. And God knows better.[54]

HADITHS ON WOMEN VISITING THE GRAVES

Another example of that is the hadith or hadiths which restrain women from visiting graveyards. For example, the hadith of Abū Hurayrah: "God's Messenger condemned women visitors (*zawwārāt*) to the graves". Aḥmad ibn Ḥanbal and Ibn Mājah narrated it, also al-Tirmidhī who called it *ḥasan* and *ṣaḥīḥ*; and Ibn Ḥibbān narrated it in his *Ṣaḥīḥ*.[55] It is narrated also from Ibn ᶜAbbās with the words "women visitors (*zā'irāt*) to the graves", and from Ḥassan ibn Thābit.[56] Supporting that is what has come in other hadiths prohibiting women following funeral processions, from the import of which is derived the prohibition of women visiting the graves.

In opposition to these hadiths, there are others from which one understands the permissibility for women, as for men, of visiting graves. Among them is his saying: "I had forbidden you to visit graves, but [now I say:] visit them."[57] "Visit the graves, for indeed they remind of death."[58] Women are included in the general permission to visit graves, and in the need of everyone to be reminded of death. Also among these hadiths is what Muslim narrated (and al-Nasā'ī and Ibn Ḥanbal) from ʿĀ'ishah. She asked: " 'How shall I address them?' (she meant 'when I visit the graves'). He said: 'Say: Peace be upon the people of the homes of the believers and the Muslims; and God have mercy on the early-comers among us and the late-comers. And indeed we, if God wills, are catching up with you.' "[59] Another example is what the two Shaykhs have narrated from Anas, that "the Prophet passed by a woman weeping at a grave. So he said: 'Fear God and be patient.' Then she said: 'Go away. For indeed you have not suffered the like of my affliction.' And she did not know him [to be the Prophet...]."[60] Now, he forbade her anxiety, but he did not forbid her visiting the grave. Another example is narrated by al-Ḥākim from Fāṭimah, the daughter of God's Messenger, that she used to visit the grave of her uncle, Ḥamzah, every Friday, and she prayed and wept near it.[61]

Moreover, these hadiths demonstrating the permissibility of women visiting graves are more *ṣaḥīḥ* and more common than the hadiths demonstrating the prohibition of it. So combining and reconciling them is possible, in this way: one interprets the 'condemnation' mentioned in the hadith – as al-Qurṭubī said – as referring to over-frequent visiting, which is the connotation of (the intensive form of) *al-zawwārāt*, the expression used in the hadith. He said: "Perhaps the reason for the judgment against it is that she may be neglecting the right of the husband, and the displaying [of herself entailed by frequent visiting], and what intoxicates from the mourning (the wailing), and the like. And it could be said: If all these [matters] are made safe, then there is no impediment to the permission [given] to [women], for the man and the woman [alike] have a need for the reminder of death." And al-Shawkānī commented: "This is an opinion worthy of reliance in reconciling the hadiths contradictory in outward [sense]."[62]

If reconciling two (or more) hadiths contradictory in outward sense is not possible, one resorts to preference between them. This is done according to one of the principles of preference mentioned by the scholars. Al-Suyūṭī, in his book *al-Tadrīb al-Rāwī ʿalā Taqrīb al-Nawāwī*, counted these principles as more than one hundred. This topic – contradiction and preference – is an important one among the sub-disicplines of *uṣūl al-fiqh*, *uṣūl al-ḥadīth*, and the sciences of the Qur'an.

HADITHS ON *AL-ʿAZL (COITUS INTERRUPTUS)*

To illustrate, let us take as an example the hadiths that have come on *ʿal-azl* (*coitus interruptus*) – the withdrawal of the man from his woman during intercourse, whereby he casts the sperm outside the vulva so that she does not conceive by him.

Let us look here at the hadiths which Abū Barakāt ibn Taymiyyah (the grandfather) mentioned in his famous book *al-Muntaqā min al-Akhbār al-Muṣṭafā*, under the heading 'What has come on *al-ʿazl*'.

> From Jābir, he said:
> We used to practice withdrawal with the knowledge of God's Messenger, while the Qur'an was being revealed [i.e. during his lifetime].
> (The hadith is agreed upon.)
>
> A variant, according to Muslim:
> We used to practice withdrawal with the knowledge of God's Messenger. Then that [news of our doing so] reached him but he did not forbid us [from it].
>
> Also from Jābir, that:
> A man came to God's Messenger, and said: "I have a slave girl, she is our servant, and she carries water for us in the date-palms. And I go with her, but I do not want her to conceive."

Then he said: "Practice withdrawal from her if you wish. But indeed there will come to her what is decreed for her."
(Ibn Ḥanbal narrated it, also Muslim and Abū Dā'ūd.)

From Abū Saʿīd, he said:
We went out with God's Messenger, on the expedition to the Banī al-Muṣṭaliq. We took captives from the Arabs, and we desired the women; the abstinence was severe upon us, and we intended to practice *al-ʿazl*, so we asked God's Messenger about that. He said: "[It is] not [incumbent] upon you that you not do [that]. For indeed God, the All-Mighty and Majestic, has already written what He will have created until the Day of Resurrection."
(The hadith is agreed upon.)

From Abū Saʿīd, he said:
The Jews say withdrawal is like burying infants alive. Then the Prophet, said: "The Jews lie. Indeed God, the All-Mighty and Majestic, if He wills to create a thing, no one can rise up to avert it."
(Ibn Ḥanbal narrated it, and Abū Dā'ūd.)

(The variant wording of it):
That a man said: "O Messenger of God, I have a slave girl, and I practice withdrawal from her; I do not want her to conceive, and I want what men want [from women]. And indeed the Jews report that withdrawal is […]."
Ibn al-Qayyim said in *al-Zād*: "Be content with the authenticity of this *isnād*, for all of [its narrators] are *ḥuffāẓ*."

From Usāmah ibn Zayd, that:
A man came to the Prophet, and said: "I practice withdrawal from my woman." God's Messenger, said to him: "Why do you do that?" Then the man said: "I am concerned about her [conceiving] a child, or about her [having] children." Then God's Messenger, said: "If there were harm [in it] it would have harmed the Persians and the Romans [who do that]."
(Ibn Ḥanbal and Muslim narrated it.)

From Judāmah[63] bint Wahb al-Asadiyyah, she said:
I was present with God's Messenger, in [a company of] people, and he was saying: "I had intended that I should forbid intercourse during pregnancy (*ghaylah*). Then I looked to the Romans and the Persians – though they do this it does not hurt their [unborn] children a thing." Then he was asked about

withdrawal, and he, God's Messenger, said: "That is a hidden [form of] burying alive, and she [who is so buried will cry out, as the Qur'an says:] 'When the infant girl buried alive shall ask [for what sin she was slain].' "
(Ibn Ḥanbal and Muslim narrated it.)

From ʿUmar ibn al-Khaṭṭāb, he said:
God's Messenger forbade that one practice withdrawal from a free woman except with her permission.
(Aḥmad narrated it, and Ibn Mājah, but its *isnād* is weak.[64] That is my opinion too – because Ibn Lahīʿah appears in its *isnad*, and there is a well-known discussion about him – but what Ibn ʿAbd al-Barr and Aḥmad ibn Ḥanbal and al-Bayhaqī have reported from Ibn ʿAbbās attests to it: "He forbade withdrawal from a free woman except with her permission" (as cited in *Nayl al-Awṭār*).)

It would appear from the group of hadiths cited that they demonstrate the acceptability of withdrawal. That is the position that the majority of jurists adopt, except that one may not practice withdrawal from a free woman without her permission and consent in view of her right of enjoyment of the act. Nevertheless, there is, in the hadith of Judāmah bint Wahb, the clear statement of its being "a hidden [form of] burying alive". Some among the scholars reconcile this hadith with those before it. So it is interpreted as mildly reprehensible (*ʿalā tanzīh*). That is the approach taken by al-Bayhaqī. Then, there are scholars who pronounce the hadith of Judāmah weak, because of its contradicting what has more routes of transmission. Ibn Ḥajar said: "This rebuts the *ṣaḥīḥ* hadiths by making [them] suspect. But the *ṣaḥīḥ* hadith – there is no doubt in it, and [in any case] reconciling [them] is possible."

Then again, among the scholars are those who have claimed that it is abrogated, but this claim was rejected, following knowledge of the chronology (of the hadiths). Al-Ṭaḥāwī said: "It is possible that the hadith of Judāmah is in agreement with what the command was in the beginning, in line with the People of the Book, in what was not sent down on him. Thereafter, God informed him with the ruling and he called what they had been saying about it false. Ibn Rushd and Ibn al-ʿArabī criticized [that by saying] that the Prophet would not forbid anything following the Jews and then say they were lying about it."

Some among the scholars have preferred the hadith of Judāmah on account of the evidence for its being *ṣaḥīḥ*. They call its opposite weak on account of the variation in its *isnād* and the discrepancy therein. Ibn Ḥajar said: "It is rejected only in that it impairs the [other] hadith, not in that some [part] of it reinforces some [part of the other]. For indeed it is acted upon. And it is the case here. And [in any case] reconciling is possible."

Ibn Ḥazm preferred acting according to the hadith of Judāmah because the hadiths other than hers agreed on the principle of the permissibility of *al-ʿazl*, whereas her hadith demonstrated its being forbidden. He said: "Whoever claims that he permitted [it] after he forbade [it] – it is up to him [to provide] the explanation [for the inconsistency]."

Investigation shows that her hadith is not crystal clear in prohibiting *al-ʿazl*. Also, calling it "a hidden [form of] burying alive" does not necessitate the approach of making the two equal so that *al-ʿazl* should be forbidden in the way that burying alive is. Ibn al-Qayyim reconciled the hadiths and said:

> That in which he said the Jews lied is their allegation that with *al-ʿazl* conception becomes unimaginable altogether. They surely made it of the rank of cutting off the progeny by burying alive, and so he called them liars. He informed [us] that it does not prevent conception if God has willed to create it. If He did not intend its creation it cannot be a burying alive in reality. And [the Prophet] only called it a hidden [form of] burying alive in the hadith of Judāmah because the man withdrew only to avoid conception, and so he brought about his intent [which may well be supposed to be] like what is brought about by burying alive. But the difference between the two is that the actual burying alive is by direct cause of the joining together of the intent and the deed, whereas the withdrawal has to do with intent only. So it is for that [reason] that he described it as being a hidden [form of burying alive]. And this reconciling [of the differing reports] is strong.

Also, the hadith of Judāmah has been pronounced weak. I mean the addition which is there at its end, because Saʿīd ibn

> Abī Ayyūb is alone in narrating from Abū al-Aswad. Mālik narrated it and Yaḥyā ibn Ayyūb from Abū al-Aswad and did not mention [this addition]. [It is considered weak also] on account of its being in contradiction to the group of hadiths under this heading. The people of the four *Sunan* have curtailed [omitted] this addition.[65]

Al-Bayhaqī, in his *Sunan al-Kubrā*, traced and narrated the hadiths and reports judging for the permissibility of *al-ᶜazl*, and they are many. Then he devoted a special chapter to those who dislike *al-ᶜazl*, and who differ in the report from him on it. He did not narrate on its being disliked. But he did cite in that chapter the hadith of Judāmah bint Wahb, which Muslim reported. After that he (al-Bayhaqī) said:

> The opposite has been narrated to us from the Prophet. The narrators of the permissibility [of *al-ᶜazl*] are more common and better at preserving. Those have permitted it whom we have named from the Companions (that is, Saᶜd ibn Abī Waqqās, Zayd ibn Thābit, Jābir ibn ᶜAbd Allāh, Ibn ᶜAbbās, Abū Ayyūb al-Anṣārī, and others). And it [permissibility] is better. And the aversion [to it] is interpreted by those who dislike it as staying aloof [from it] (*tanzīh*) without forbidding [it] (*taḥrīm*). God knows better.[66]

ABROGATION IN THE HADITH

Linked to the topic of contradiction between hadiths is the issue of abrogation, or the abrogating and the abrogated, in hadith. It is an issue common to the sciences of both the Qur'an and hadith. Among Qur'an commentators there are those who exceed the bounds in their claims of abrogation in it – so far so that some of them allege that a single verse, called the 'verse of the sword', abrogates from the Book of God more than a hundred verses, and they make that claim despite not agreeing among even themselves about what the 'verse of the sword' is! In the hadith, some specialists resort to 'abrogation' when reconciling two contradictory hadiths becomes troublesome for them, and when they know which is the later of the two.

In reality the claim of abrogation in the hadith is narrower in scope than the same in the Qur'an. This is so despite the fact that one would expect it to be the other way around, since in principle the Qur'an addresses general and permanent conditions, whereas what the Sunnah deals with includes matters that are partial, circumstantial and temporal, corresponding to the Prophet's leadership of the Community and his consideration for its everyday affairs. Nevertheless, of many of the hadiths of which abrogation is alleged, it becomes evident from precise determination that they are not abrogated.

Among the hadiths there is both what intends stricture, and what intends leniency, and both kinds of injunctions obtain, both together, each in its place. Some hadiths are restricted by a circumstance, and some are otherwise according to another circumstance, but this alteration of the circumstances does not mean abrogation. That has been said, for example, on the prohibition of storing the meats from the Sacrifice after three nights, and its being subsequently permitted. But this is not abrogation, rather the prohibition applies in one circumstance, and the permissibility in another circumstance, as we have clarified elsewhere.

It is worthwhile citing here what al-Bayhaqī has conveyed – in his book *Maʿrifat al-Sunan wa al-Āthār* – with his *sanad* to al-Shāfiʿī, may God have mercy on him. He said:

> Wherever it is feasible of two hadiths that they be acted upon together, let them be acted upon together, and [let] not one of the two be suspended [for] the other. If nothing is feasible of the two hadiths except [their] difference, then the difference in them [can be regarded from] two directions:
>
> One of the two [directions]: that one of the two [hadiths] is abrogating, and the other is abrogated, so one acts according to the abrogating [one], and one leaves the abrogated [one].
>
> And the other [direction]: that the two differ and there is no evidence as to which of the two is abrogating, and which of the two is abrogated. Then we do not go to one of the two and not to the other unless for a cause that demonstrates that the one that we [prefer to] go to is stronger than the one we leave, and that [cause] is that one of the two hadiths is more established [in proof] than the other, so we go to the [one

which is] more established [in proof], or more conformable with the Book of God, the All-Mighty and Majestic, or to the Sunnah of God's Messenger. [We also consider] in what [respects] the hadiths are the same as his Sunnah and [in what respects they] differ from [it], or what is better according to what the people of knowledge know [of the matter], or more correct in [terms of] analogical reasoning, or what the greater number of the Companions of God's Messenger were on.

Al-Bayhaqī reports that al-Shāfiʿī said:

> The summary of this is that one does not accept except a proven hadith, just as one does not accept testimony [in a legal case] except from one whose probity is known. So if the hadith is unknown, or conveyed from those from whom one keeps one's distance, [then] it is as if it had not come, because it is not established.

Al-Bayhaqī said:

> That of which knowledge is obligatory upon one who looks into this book (*Maʿrifat al-Sunan wa al-Āthār*) is that he should know that both Abū ʿAbd Allāh Muhammad ibn Ismāʿīl al-Bukhārī and Abū al-Ḥusayn Muslim ibn al-Ḥajjāj al-Naysābūrī classified and compiled the hadiths, all of them *ṣaḥīḥ*.
>
> The *ṣaḥīḥ* hadiths that remained, they did not trace and report because of their falling, according to both of them, below the rank and quality which they prescribed in their books for authenticity.
>
> Abū Dā'ūd Sulaymān al-Ashʿath al-Sijistānī traced and reported some of them [i.e. of the hadiths not in al-Bukhārī and Muslim]. Abū ʿĪsā Muhammad ibn ʿĪsā al-Tirmidhī [traced and reported] some of them. Abū Bakr Muhammad ibn Isḥāq ibn Khuzaymah [traced and reported] some of them. May God have mercy on them. Each one of them was on [the position] that his ijtihad called him to.
>
> [All] hadiths that are narrated are according to three classes:
>
> Among them: that whose authenticity the people of the knowledge of hadith have agreed upon. So that is [a hadith] that it is not for anyone to find room to differ on – as long as it has not been abrogated.
>
> Among them: that whose weakness they have agreed upon. So that [is a hadith] which it is not for anyone to rely upon.
>
> Among them: that about whose being established they differ on. Then, among [the scholars] there is one who has con-

sidered [a hadith] weak because of a defect that has appeared to him in some of [that hadith's] narrations, [and] that [defect] was hidden from others. Or [one scholar] was not prevented from [knowing] the condition of [a narrator] such that acceptance of his report would be obligatory, [whereas] other [scholars] were prevented from [knowing] it. Or [one scholar saw in] the meaning what he considered a defect [and other scholars] did not see it as a defect. Or [one scholar] 'refrained from' a discrepancy [in the transmission of the hadith], or 'refrained from'] a discrepancy in some of its words, or in some narrations ['refrained from'] the interpolation into the text [proper of the hadith] of the words of the narration, or ['refrained from'] the *isnād* of one hadith entering into [the *isnād* of another] hadith – [all of] that being hidden from other [scholars].

This is what is obligatory upon the people of the knowledge of hadith after [those predecessors in this science]: that they should investigate their differences, and strive for knowledge of the meanings [of the differences] in [view of] acceptance or rejection; then they should choose from their opinions the most correct. And the means to success is from God.[67]

IV

UNDERSTANDING CAUSES, ASSOCIATIONS, AND OBJECTIVES

The best understanding of the Prophet's Sunnah comes by investigation of the particular causes on which hadiths are based, or the specific occasion to which they are attached, specified in the hadith text or discoverable from the hadith, or understood from the actual circumstance to which the hadith is addressed.

A penetrating observer will find that, among the hadith, some are based upon consideration of particular temporal conditions in order to realize a recognized public good, or to ward off a specific harm, or to deal with a difficulty existing at that time. This means that the injunction that the hadith carries appears general and permanent but, on further consideration, is seen to be founded upon a particular reason, and the injunction passes away with the passing away of that reason, just as it stays in force with the continuance of that reason.

This requires profound understanding and subtle perception, as well as comprehensive, integrated study of the texts and mature insight into the goals of the Law and the reality of the religion. It also requires moral courage and inner strength to come out with the truth even if it opposes what the people are used to and what they have inherited. It is not an easy thing. This is the cost exacted from Shaykh al-Islam Ibn Taymiyyah by the enmity of the scholars of his time. They conspired against him until he was put in prison many times, and he died therein, may God be pleased with him.

For an understanding that is sound and subtle, one must know the associated circumstances which the hadith text addresses. This is so because the hadith came to clarify those circumstances and to deal with the conditions thereof. That knowledge helps define the objective of the hadith with accuracy, and does not give scope to meandering speculations, or to unintended running about behind the surface meaning. It is well known that our scholars have stated that part of what is necessary for a good understanding of the Qur'an is knowledge of the occasions of revelation. This is to prevent happening what happened with the extremists among the Khārijis and others, who took the verses that were sent down about the Associationists and applied them to the Muslims. Ibn ʿUmar used to regard them as the worst of creation for that reason – because they distorted the Book of God from what was sent down in it.[68] Now, if the occasions of the revelation of the Qur'an were sought by whoever wished to understand or comment upon it, the occasions of the appearance of the hadith are even more emphatically to be sought. That is because the Qur'an is by its nature general and permanent; there is not in its concern what would allow room for partial matters and details and time-bound considerations – except to take principles and moral lessons from them. The Sunnah on the other hand does often treat of localized difficulties, partial and time-bound matters; and in it there are particulars and details that are not typically found in the Qur'an.

Therefore, it is necessary to distinguish between what is particular and what is general, what is temporal and what is eternal, and what is partial and what is all-comprehensive. Each of these has its appropriate kind and form of injunction. The investigation into the context, and the associated circumstances and occasions, assists in the achievement of a proper, correct understanding, for whomever God enables to achieve that.

HADITH: "YOU KNOW BETTER THE AFFAIRS OF YOUR WORLDLY LIFE"

An example of that is the hadith: "You know better the affairs of your worldly life."[69] It is one on which some people base their evasion of the Legal injunctions in the spheres of economics, civic and political duties, and the like, because these matters – so they claim – are among worldly concerns, and we know them better, and the Messenger, entrusted them to us! But is this really what this noble hadith intends?

By no means. Among the purposes with which God sent His messengers is that they should stipulate for the people the principles of justice, the balanced norms of equity, and the regulations of the rights and duties in their worldly life, so that their standards should not clash, nor their ways differ. As God said: "We surely sent Our messengers with the clear signs, and We sent with them the Book and the Balance so that people may uphold equity" (*al-Ḥadīd*, 57: 25).

So texts of the Book and the Sunnah have come which order and regulate everyday concerns – selling and buying, partnership and mortgaging, leasing and lending, and other matters – to the extent that the longest verse in the Book of God was sent down on the arrangement of a matter that is slight among the worldly matters, namely the writing down of debts. God said: "O believers: when you transact a debt for a settled term, then write it down. And let a scribe write it down between you with justice" (*al-Baqarah*, 2: 282).

The hadith ("You know better your own worldly affairs") is interpreted by the occasion that prompted it, namely the incident of the pollination of date-palms. The Prophet's indication to the people about this was his conjecture, for he was not an agriculturist, he had grown up in a valley not endowed with crops. But the Anṣār supposed his opinion to be by way of a revealed or religious command, and so they abandoned pollination. Its effect was bad for their yield. Then he said: "I was only conjecturing a conjecture, so do not take [from] me [what is] by way of conjecture..." to [where] he said "...You know better your own worldly affairs". And this is the story behind the hadith.[70]

HADITH: "I AM QUIT OF ANY MUSLIM WHO SETTLES [AMONG] THE ASSOCIATIONISTS"

We give as another example, the hadith: "I am quit of any Muslim who settles [among] the Associationists [in such a way that] the fires [of the Muslims and the Associationists] cannot be seen from each other [meaning the two parties are at war]."[71] Some have understood from it the prohibition of settling in a non-Muslim land of any description, despite the multiplication of the needs for that in our time – for education, preaching, work, business, diplomatic missions, flight from oppression, and other reasons – especially as the world is (as one man of letters put it) quickly becoming 'one big village'.

The hadith, as Rashīd Riḍā said, appeared on the obligation of *Hijrah* (emigration) from the land of the Associationists to the Prophet in order to help him. The compilers of the various *Sunan* narrated it. Among them, Abū Dā'ūd narrated it from Jarīr ibn ʿAbd Allāh, noting that the group of narrators did not mention Jarīr, i.e. he narrated it as a *mursal* hadith (one narrated from the Prophet by a Successor, without the Companion narrating to the latter being identified). Al-Nasā'ī mentions only this *mursal* version. Al-Tirmidhī traced and reported it as a *mursal* hadith and pronounced it *ṣaḥīḥ*. He conveyed from al-Bukhārī that he regarded the *mursal* as *ṣaḥīḥ*. However, al-Bukhārī did not report it, as it did not meet his conditions for inclusion in his *Ṣaḥīḥ*. Argumentation from the *mursal* is a famous point of disagreement in the science of the principles of hadith. The text of the hadith:

> God's Messenger sent a detachment to Khathʿam, and [some] people from them took refuge in prostration, but the killing rushed on them [*sc.* they were killed in the rush of battle]. [News of] that reached the Prophet. Then he ordered them [to pay] half the bloodmoney (i.e. bloodwit) and he said: "I am quit of any Muslim who settles [among] the Associationists." They said: "O Messenger of God, why?" He said: "Their fires are not seen by each other." (That is, they are not as neighbors or near kin [who camp close to one another] so that you see the fire of either as the fire of the other. And that implies the distance that is between the two of them.)

He halved the bloodwit for them though they were Muslims, because they had helped against their own and voided the half of their duty[72] by settling among the Associationists at war with God and His Messenger. He was severe about this kind of residence, because it resembled 'sitting out' (i.e. not taking active part in) the call to help God and His Messenger. God says of those who did that: "And those who have believed and do not leave their homes – you have no duty to protect them till they leave their homes. But if they seek help from you in the religion, helping them is your duty, except against a people between whom and yourselves there is a treaty." (*al-Anfāl*, 8: 72)

God repudiated friendship with Muslims who did not emigrate when Emigration was a duty.[73] So the meaning of his saying "I am quit of any Muslim…" is being quit of any liability for that person's life if killed, because he brought that upon himself by settling among those at war with the Islamic state.

The meaning of this is: if the circumstances in which the text was spoken change, then the observed reason behind it is detached from the general good it meant to bring about, or from the harm it meant to avert. So the understanding is that the injunction established by this text before has since been turned away – for the injunction hinges upon its reason being existent and present.

THE WOMAN'S TRAVELING WITH A *MAḤRAM*

An example of that is what has come in the two *Ṣaḥīḥ*s from the hadith of Ibn ʿAbbās and others *marfūʿan*: "A woman may not travel except a *maḥram* is accompanying her."[74]

The reason for the prohibition is fear for the woman traveling alone without husband or *maḥram* at a time when traveling was by camel or mule or donkey, and she was often crossing through desert or barren terrains empty of human settlements or living creatures. Even if, during this kind of journey, the woman did not suffer mischief to herself, she suffered it in her reputation.

But when the conditions change – as in our time – when travel is by airplane or train carrying a hundred or more passengers, then there is not much room to fear for a woman traveling alone. One does not consider this acting in opposition to the hadith. Rather, this position is confirmed by the hadith of ʿAdī ibn Ḥātim *marfūʿan*, according to al-Bukhārī: "[The time] is all but [here when] a woman will leave from Ḥīra heading for the House (i.e. the Kaʿbah), [with] no husband accompanying her."[75] This hadith comes in the context of praising the advent of Islam and the rising of its light, and as a token of its providing safety in the land. It demonstrates the permissibility of a woman traveling alone. Ibn Ḥazm proceeded in accordance with this view.

It is no surprise that we find some of the imams permitting the woman to do hajj without a *maḥram* or husband accompanying her, if she was with trustworthy women, or in trusted company. That is how ʿĀ'ishah did the hajj and *ṭawāf*, as one of the 'mothers of the believers' during the rule of ʿUmar. There was not with them a single *maḥram*; rather, ʿUthmān ibn ʿAffān and ʿAbd al-Raḥmān ibn ʿAwf accompanied them. It is so reported in *Ṣaḥīḥ al-Bukhārī*.

Some people say: A single trustworthy woman is enough as a traveling companion. Others say: She may travel alone if the road is safe. The followers of the Shāfiʿī school have pronounced this view correct for traveling for hajj and *ʿumrah*. Other Shāfiʿīs include any journey in this permission, not just for pilgrimage.[76]

THE LEADERS ARE FROM THE QURAYSH

Another example of that is the hadith "The leaders are from the Quraysh".[77] Ibn Khaldūn commented on it in his *Muqaddimah*. The Prophet saw, in his time, what the Quraysh had of power and group-solidarity, on which, in the view of Ibn Khaldūn, caliphal or monarchical rule is established. He said:

> If it is established that the stipulation of the Qurayshis was only their [capacity for] deterring strife with what they had of group-solidarity and conquering spirit, [then] we know that only that [capacity] is what sufficed [to qualify them for rule]. So we trace it [the stipulation of the Quraysh] to it [possession of group-solidarity]. We move on to the comprehensive reason within the purpose aimed at [in choosing] the Qurayshis [for rule], and it is the existence of group-solidarity. So we stipulate for the person of the commander of the Muslims that he be from the people who have group-solidarity above whoever [else] has it in his time so they can make whoever is like them [in having some group-solidarity] subservient [to them], and the word can come together [i.e. the people can agree] on the best of protection....[78]

THE METHOD OF THE COMPANIONS AND SUCCESSORS IN INVESTIGATING THE REASONS AND CIRCUMSTANCES OF THE TEXTS

This is the method of investigating the surrounding conditions of the hadiths, and of the reasons that constitute their context. The Companions were pioneers in it, and those who followed them in excellence (i.e. the Successors). They abandoned acting on the outward sense of certain hadiths when it was clear to them that these hadiths were attached to the condition fixed in the era of Prophethood, and subsequently that condition had changed.

An example is that the Prophet divided up the lands of Khaybar among the conquerors of it, but ʿUmar did not divide up the fertile land of Iraq (*sawād*). His view was that it should remain in the hands of its owners, and he put the duty of *kharāj* (land tax) on the land, so that it would be a permanent resource for future generations of Muslims.[79] On that, Ibn Qudāmah said: "The dividing up of Khaybar by the Prophet was at the beginning of Islam and [in] the extremity of need, and there was public good in it. The public good in what was after that was in [charitable] public endowment of the land. And it was obligatory."[80]

The attitude of ᶜUthmān to stray camels

An example of that is the Prophet's attitude to stray camels. When he was asked about them, he forbade rounding them up, and said to the questioner: "What is it [to do] with you and with them? You can leave them be. For indeed they have their 'shoes' and their 'waterskins'. They will find water, they will eat [from] the shrubs – until their master finds them."[81]

The matter progressed on this pattern throughout the time of the Prophet. In the time of Abū Bakr al-Ṣiddīq and ᶜUmar ibn al-Khaṭṭāb, the stray camel was left alone in whatever condition it was and, following the command of the Messenger, no one took possession of it – for as long as it was capable of defending itself, and capable of tracking water to drink and to store thereof in its belly what it wished, and it had its 'shoes', i.e. its hoofs, which give it strength in traveling and crossing the desert – until its owner found it.

Then came the time of ᶜUthmān ibn ᶜAffān. Mālik narrates in the *Muwaṭṭā* that he heard Ibn Shihāb al-Zuhrī say: "The stray ones of the camels in the time of ᶜUmar ibn al-Khaṭṭāb were camels giving birth to camels, and no one touched them. Until it was the time of ᶜUthmān ibn ᶜAffān. He ordered the identification of them, then selling [of them]. Then when the owner of them came he was given the price [obtained] for them."[82] After ᶜUthmān, conditions changed a little. ᶜAlī ibn Abī Ṭālib agreed it in permitting the rounding up of the camels and keeping them safe for their owners. However, he took the view that at times there might be some harm in selling them and rendering their price to their owners – because the price did not have the same use for the owners as the camels themselves. Later on he held that rounding up of strays and the expenditure on them should be from the public treasury – until such time as their owner came and they would be given back to him.[83]

In what ʿUthmān and ʿAlī did, there is no opposition to the words of the Prophet. Rather, they looked to his purpose, and to how the character of people had changed – not honoring rights had crept into their ways, and some of them were stretching their hands to the forbidden. The strays from the camels and cattle were left to get lost by themselves, and their being abandoned was a care upon their owners. It is what the Prophet did not intend at all when he forbade rounding them up. Rather, it was to avert this particular harm.

TEXTS BASED ON A USAGE THAT CHANGED LATER

Related to what we have just discussed are issues that come under earlier or later usage. These entail investigation into what some texts are based on in respect of usages ongoing in the age of Prophethood but which, since then, have changed. No harm ensues, in our view, from looking into the objectives of the texts without clinging to their letters. Here is an example:

The opinion of Abū Yūsuf on measuring by volume or weight

Scholars of fiqh know the opinion of Abū Yūsuf on this topic, derived from his discussion of the categories of (what had been) interest-bearing goods. About such goods there has come the well-known *ṣaḥīḥ* hadith of the Prophet: "Wheat for wheat; measure for measure, like for like." That is how it is also for barley, dates and salt. As for gold and silver, he said about them: "Weight for weight."

Abū Yūsuf took the view that that form of expression in what was said, about the categories of goods to be measured by volume or by weight, was based on the usage at the time, and usage had changed. Dates and salt, for example, had come to be sold by weight – as in our age – and action was necessary in accordance with what the new usage had become. So Abū Yūsuf made lawful the selling of, for example, dates and salt, by equal weights, even if they differ in volume.

This is opposed to the position that (his teacher) Abū Ḥanīfah took: namely, that any thing of which God's Messenger stipulated variation in it being forbidden, it was to be measured like for like always – even if people had abandoned measuring it that way. Similarly, anything that he stipulated variation from weighing it as being forbidden, it was to be weighed always – even if the people had abandoned weighing in it. According to this view it is obligatory to go on measuring dates, salt, wheat, barley by volume until the Day of Resurrection. This makes hardship for the people – whereas he ordered that the Law should have no prejudice ensue from it. The correct position is what Abū Yūsuf said, and it is in agreement with the well-being of the people in our time. Indeed all the old volumetric measures for cereals and other produce have come to be replaced by measures by weight.

The existence of two niṣābs for calculating zakah on money

Among the examples that have emerged of a text being based on a usage later altered is the Prophet's decreeing two different *niṣāb*s for calculating zakah on money. One of the two, for silver, he set at 100 dirhams (equivalent to 595 grams), and the second, for gold, he set at 20 *mithqāl*s or dinars (equivalent to 85 grams). For the dinar in that time the exchange rate was equal to ten dirhams.

I have explained in my book *Fiqh al-Zakāh* that the Prophet did not intend to lay down two different *niṣāb*s for zakah. Rather, it is a single *niṣāb*, ownership of which is considered adequate to become liable for zakah on it. He decreed two courses of action following the customary usage of the people during the age of Prophethood. The text came based on that established usage. The *niṣāb* was defined for the two liable kinds of wealth, these two being equivalent always. But conditions have changed in our age – the price of silver has fallen drastically relatively to the fall in the price of gold. It is not permissible for us to set the *niṣāb* for two different kinds of liable wealth that are so extremely different – so that we should say, for example, that the *niṣāb* of money (cash) is what is equivalent to the value of 85 grams of gold, or what is equivalent to 595 grams of silver. At the present time the value of the *niṣāb* for gold is greater than the value of the *niṣāb* for silver by roughly ten times. It does not make sense that we say to a person who has the liable amount fixed in a particular currency: you are considered wealthy if we calculate your *niṣāb* in silver; and we say to another person who possesses many times more: you are counted poor if we calculate your *niṣāb* in gold!

The solution of that is the definition of a single *niṣāb* in our age for money. By it the minimum limit (*niṣāb*) for the wealth liable to zakah under the Law is known.[84] This is the position adopted by the great professor Shaykh Muhammad Abū Zahrah, and his colleagues, Shaykh ʿAbd al-Wahhāb Khallāf and Shaykh ʿAbd al-Raḥmān Ḥasan – God have mercy on them – in their lectures on zakah in Damascus in the year 1952, calculating the *niṣāb* in gold only. This is what I chose and supported with argumentation in my research on zakah.[85]

Again, this is not opposition to the text, as it has been accused of being. Rather, the text is based on a particular custom; with the wearing away of that custom, the injunction relative to that custom has worn away also.

The change in the people liable to pay bloodwit in the time of ʿUmar

Another example of a text based on temporal usage that changed subsequently is the issue of who is liable to pay bloodwit. The Prophet's decision was that the people liable to pay bloodwit for an accidental killing were 'the paternal relatives of the man'. Some jurists took hold of the outward sense of that and made it obligatory that the people liable were always to be the paternal relatives. They did not look to the fact that the Prophet only laid the bloodwit to the charge of the paternal relatives because, in that period, they were the pivot of support and help. Opposing those jurists were others, like the Ḥanafīs. They argued from the action of the caliph ʿUmar, who in his time placed liability on 'the people of the *dīwān* (military register)'. Ibn Taymiyyah discussed the matter in his *Fatāwā*. He said:

> The Prophet judged the bloodwit on the people liable, and they were those who supported the man and helped him. The people liable in his time were [the man's] paternal relatives. Then, in the time of ʿUmar, he [ʿUmar] laid it on the people of the *dīwān*. That is why the jurists have differed on this. The principle of that: are the people liable as defined by the Law or those who supported [the man] and helped him? Those who [held] the first opinion did not act [to shift liability away] from the near relatives because they were the people liable according to the [practice in the Prophet's] time. Those who [held] the second opinion made those liable in any time and place who are [the person's] support at the time. Since, in the time of the Prophet, [those who] supported and helped him were only his near relatives, they were the people liable [to pay bloodwit] – for, in the time of the Prophet, there was no *dīwān*.
>
> When ʿUmar set up the *dīwān* it was known that the [members of the] army of a city supported each other and helped each other, even if they were not near relatives, and so they were the people liable. This is the more correct of the two positions – that [the liability] differs according to the difference in conditions. For otherwise: a man living in the west, and there are there those who support and help him – [but] how can those be liable who are of the east, under another sovereignty, and news of him has been cut off from them?! The inheritance [by contrast] can be preserved for the absent one: for indeed the Prophet judged on the woman who had killed that her bloodwit was due from her paternal relatives, and that her inheritance was for her husband and her sons, so the one who inherits is not of the people liable [to pay the bloodwit].[86]

It is according to this reasoning that I have given a fatwa in our age that the people liable for bloodwit could be assigned from the professional associations: so if a doctor kills by mistake, then his bloodwit is due from the association of doctors, and the engineer's from the association of engineers … and so forth.

About the zakāt al-fiṭr

Among the established sunnahs is that the Messenger used to pay the *zakāt al-fiṭr*, and he ordered its payment after the *fajr* prayer and before the ʿId prayer on the day of the *fiṭr*. That period of time was sufficient for its collection and its distribution to those entitled to it, on account of the society and its members being few in number, and the people in need being well-known, and their places of residence very near, to each other. So there was no difficulty in making the payment in the time he indicated for that.

In the age of the Companions, the society expanded, its members lived further apart, the number of its individuals increased, and new races entered into it. Then the interval between the *fajr* and ʿId prayers was not considered sufficient. The fiqh of the Companions was that they should give *zakāt al-fiṭr* before the ʿId by a day or two days. Then, in the period of the followed imams among the *mujtahid* jurists, the society grew ever more expansive and complicated, so they permitted it to be paid from the middle of Ramadan (as in the Ḥanbalī school), or even from the beginning of Ramadan (as in the Shāfiʿī school).

Moreover, they did not stop at the foodstuffs stipulated in the Sunnah for the payment of *zakāt al-fiṭr*. Rather, they did *qiyās* on those and, by analogy, made it acceptable to give in whatever foodstuffs happened to be prevalent in the area in question. Indeed, some of them broadened the permission to include payment of the cash value (instead of payment in foodstuffs), especially if it was for the greater benefit of the poor. That is the doctrine of Abū Ḥanīfah and his students. Thus the purpose – 'providing for the needy' on this day of generosity, and payment due, in foodstuffs – is rightly served by payment of their cash value. Sometimes the cash value is more perfect in fulfilling the duty of provision than food, and especially in our time. In this, there is preserving of the purpose of the Prophetic text, and applying its spirit, and this is the true fiqh.

The letter of the Sunnah and its spirit, or outward sense and inner objective

For sure, adherence to the letter of the Sunnah amounts on occasion to non-implementation of its spirit and purpose; indeed, it is opposed to it, if adherence is only to the outward form of it. By way of example, consider the strictness of those who totally reject payment of the *zakāt al-fiṭr* in its value in cash – as is permitted according to the doctrine of Abū Ḥanīfah and his students, and the opinion of ᶜUmar ibn ᶜAbd al-ᶜAzīz, and of others among the jurists of the early generations. The argument of those who are strict is that the Prophet made *zakāt al-fiṭr* obligatory on specified categories of foodstuffs – dates, grapes (raisins), wheat and barley. They say it is our duty to stop within the limits that God's Messenger prescribed, and not contradict his *sunnah* with our personal opinion. But if they aspire to obey the command as it should be obeyed, they will find that in reality it is they who are opposing the Prophet by following him only in the outward form of his command. I mean that they are, with due humility, obeying the body of the Sunnah but neglecting its spirit.

The Messenger looked to the circumstances of the situation and the time. So he made the *zakāt al-fiṭr* obligatory on what the people had to hand in foodstuffs. And that was more easy for those giving and more useful for those receiving. Among the Arabs, especially the Bedouins, at that time, ready cash was a rarity while payment in food was easy for them, and the needy were in need of food. In that way the duty of charity was made easy for them. So far is that so that he permitted payment in 'cottage cheese' (it is milk dried with the cream extracted) to whoever had it and it was easy for them, for example among the nomads, for owners of camels, goats and cattle.

Since then, conditions have changed. Money has become abundant, and foodstuffs scarce. Or the poor man has become needy on ᶜId, not of foodstuffs, but of other things for himself or his family. Payment of the value in money is easier for the ones giving and more useful for the ones receiving. And this is acting in accordance with the spirit of the Prophet's teaching and his purpose. In the city of Cairo alone there are more than ten million Muslims. If they were to be charged with the payment of ten million cubic measures of barley or dates or raisins, where would they find them? And what hardship and trouble it would be for them to search for those things in the environs of villages, to track down all or even some of them. But God rejected trouble from His religion, and He intended ease for His slaves, and He did not intend for them hardship. Suppose that they could find those things with ease: then how does the poor man benefit from them, when he has not the means to mill flour, or make dough, or bake, and he can only buy bread ready-made from the baker? Surely, we lay a burden upon him when we give the zakah to him as grain. Then, what follows the giving of grain is selling it (for money to exchange for something else). But then who will buy it, when all the people roundabout are no longer in need of grain?

Nevertheless, it is reported to me that in some lands there are Muslims whose scholars forbid them from payment of the cash value. So what happens is that the one giving the *zakāt al-fiṭr* buys a measure of dates or of cedar, for example, from a merchant for ten riyals, then gives it to the poor man. Then the poor man sells it on the spot to the same merchant for less by one or two riyals than what it was bought for – and sometimes for half the original value, and on occasion the merchant refuses the purchase because of the great quantity of what he already has of it. The measure of foodstuffs continues to be sold and bought in this way, time after time. What happens is that the poor man does not receive food, he receives only money, but with a diminution in the sum he would have received if the zakah-giver had paid the value directly in cash. That is the loss incurred in the difference from the original sum for which the zakah-giver bought from the merchant. Only the sum that the poor man sells it for is his.

Now, did the Law come for the welfare of the poor or for the contrary of that? And is the Law formalistic to this extent? Is the strictness in this really following the Sunnah or opposing the spirit of the Sunnah, whose watchword has always been, 'make it easy, do not make it difficult'?

Further, do not those who disallow payment of the value in *zakāt al-fiṭr*, permit the payment in kind of foodstuffs that the hadith did not stipulate, if such foodstuffs are prevalent in the area in question? That entails a kind of interpretation or analogical reasoning with the text. Their imams have authorized that, and not found any harm in it. It is – in our view – a correct analogy, and an acceptable interpretation. Why then should there be strict rejection of the idea of payment of the value in *zakāt al-fitr*, though its purpose was to make the needy free of the need to run about begging on this day. Perhaps this purpose justifies payment of the value rather more than it justifies payment in the specified foodstuffs. As for the latter, we regard it as obligatory in only one situation, namely the condition of famine, when the people are needy of food much more than of money, when the person has money but cannot find food to buy with it.

V

DISTINGUISHING CHANGEABLE MEANS AND STABLE ENDS

Among the causes of confusion and error in the understanding of the Sunnah is that some people confuse the stable purposes and aims, the realization of which the Sunnah strives for, with the temporal and circumstantial means which sometimes assist the attainment of the sought-for aims. So you see them firmly placing the whole focus on these means, as if they were the purpose itself. By contrast, those who are profound in understanding the Sunnah and its more inward purposes – for them it is clear that the important thing is the aim, which is stable and enduring, whereas the means indeed change with the change in circumstances or epoch or usage or other influencing factors.

Hence you find a common concern among some students of the Sunnah is with the 'medicine of the Prophet'. They focus their energy and concern on the medicines, nutriments, herbs, grains, and other things from what the Prophet described as being medicines in the treatment of some bodily defects or illnesses. They quote well-known hadiths in this regard, for example:

> The best of what you can use as medicine is cupping.[87]
>
> The best of what you can use as medicine is cupping and *qust al-baḥrī* (black cumin).[88]
>
> [It is incumbent] upon you [to treat] with this Indian aloes wood, for there are in it seven healing [properties] …[89]
>
> [It is incumbent] upon you [to treat] with this black seed, for in it there is healing for every ailment except *al-sām*, and that is death.[90]
>
> In the black seed there is healing for every ailment except *al-sām* (i.e. death).[91]
>
> Wear kohl with antimony for it clears the vision and makes the hair grow.[92]

I think these prescriptions and their like are not of the spirit of the Prophetic medicine. Rather, its spirit is preservation of the life and health of the human being, and soundness of the body and its strength, its right to rest when tired, to food when hungry, and to treatment when ill. Its spirit is that the seeking of treatment does not contradict faith in predestination (*al-qadr*), nor reliance upon God. Its spirit is that for every ailment there is a cure, and confirmation of the law of God (*sunnat Allāhi*) in respect of contagion; the legitimization of quarantine for health reasons; the concern for hygiene of the person, the house and the road; and the prohibition of pollution of water and land; the emphasis on prevention above cure; the prohibition of all that (of intoxicants, drugs, noxious aliments or polluting drinks) whose consumption harms the person; the prohibition of any oppression of the body even in the worship of God; the stipulation of relaxation to preserve bodily well-being; and the preservation of the health of the mind alongside bodily health – and other teachings which represent the reality of the Prophetic medicine, in those aspects of it which are true for every time and place.

The means change at times, from age to age, from one situation to another. Indeed it is inevitable that they should change. So, when a hadith stipulates a particular means, that is only to be taken as an explanation of the reality of its time: we are not bound by it, and we are not restricted to it.

Indeed, if a text of the Qur'an itself stipulates a practical measure for a specified time and specified place, then it does not mean that we stop at that measure, and not think of other measures developed since then and elsewhere. Did not the Qur'an say: "Make ready for them all you can of force [of men] and reined horses so that you may thereby dismay the enemy of God and your enemy, and others besides them" (*al-Anfāl*, 8: 60)? Despite this, no one understands that defence against the enemy is not possible except by cavalry, as the Qur'an stipulated in this verse. Rather, everyone who has intelligence and knows the language and the Law understands that 'cavalry' now is tanks and artillery and the like weapons of the age. The texts that have appeared on the virtue of maintaining a cavalry, and the great reward for it – for example, the hadith: "Good is attached to the forehead of the horses until the Day of Resurrection: the reward [hereafter] and the spoils [of war]"[93] – require that one adapt to every means that is invented and has replaced cavalry, or that exceeds it in force of power by many times. An example of such texts is what has come on the virtue of "One who shoots an arrow in the path of God, so he is thus and thus".[94] It applies to any shooting – with an arrow or a shotgun or cannon or missile – to any means thereof that lie hidden in the future.

I hold that the specifying of the *siwāk* for cleaning the teeth is in the same category. For its aim is cleanliness of the mouth so as to please the Lord – as in the hadith: "The *siwāk* is a cleansing of the mouth and a pleasing of the Lord."[95] But is the *siwāk* the purpose itself? Or was it the means suited to and easy for the Arab Peninsula? The Prophet prescribed for the people what was suited to the goal and was not difficult for them. There is no objection that, in different societies where the *siwāk* is not easy, this instrument should change to one (such as the toothbrush) that can be manufactured in mass quantities and that suits many millions of people.

Some jurists have stipulated something like that. In the Ḥanbalī fiqh, the author of *Ḥidāyat al-Raghīb*: said: "The stick is from the [trees or shrubs] *arāk*, *ʿarjūn*, and *zaytūn* (olive), and others. It does not hurt or harm or splinter. To use what hurts or harms or splinters is reproachable (*makrūh*). That which harms: such as the pomegranate (*rumān*) or the *rīḥān* and the tamarisk (*ṭarfā'*) and the like of those ….. He does not rightly observe the sunnah who does his teeth with other than a stick." However, the editor of the book, Shaykh ʿAbd Allāh al-Bassām conveyed from al-Nawawī that he said: "With whatever thing one does the teeth that can remove the change [i.e. restore the teeth to cleanliness], then the cleaning is achieved – even [if the instrument used is] a piece of cloth or a finger…." That opinion is the doctrine of Abū Ḥanīfah, according to the generality of the evidence found in hadiths. We read in *al-Mughnī* "that it observes the *sunnah* to the extent that it achieves some cleaning, and one should not leave the lesser *sunnah* for the sake of the greater". And he mentioned that this opinion is correct.[96] From this we know that toothbrush and toothpaste can take the place of the *arāk* in our age, and especially in the house, and after eating and before sleeping, and in particular as some people do not make proper use of the *siwāk*.

Included in the same category are the hadiths related to table manners, on the virtue of 'licking the bowl', 'licking the fingers', and the like. Al-Nawawī has cited in *Riyāḍ al-Ṣāliḥīn* a good number of these hadiths. One of them is what the two Shaykhs have narrated from Ibn ʿAbbās, who said: "God's Messenger said: 'When one of you eats, let him not wipe his fingers until he has licked them or had them licked.' "[97] Muslim narrated from Kaʿb ibn Mālik, he said: "I saw God's Messenger eating with three fingers, and then he finished off by licking them."[98] He has also narrated from Jābir that God's Messenger commanded licking the fingers and the bowl, and said: "Surely you do not know in which part of your food the blessing is."[99] And from Anas, who said: "When he ate food he licked his three fingers. And he said: 'If a morsel of anyone of you falls, let him pick it up and let him remove from it the harm [i.e. any dirt], and let him eat it and not leave it for Satan.' And he commanded us that we clean out the platter (i.e. that we wipe it out) and he said: 'Surely you do not know in which part of your food the blessing is.' "[100]

One who looks at only the wording of these hadiths will not understand other than that eating with three fingers, and licking them after eating, and licking the bowl or cleaning it out or wiping it, is the *sunnah* of the Prophet. So he may, at times, look with disgust at someone eating with a spoon because, in his opinion, that person is opposing the *sunnah*, behaving as unbelievers do! The reality is that the spirit of the Sunnah that should be taken from these hadiths is his modesty, his acceptance of God's blessing in the food, and the anxious wish that he should not leave from that blessing anything to be wasted without benefit, such as the remnant of food left in the bowl, or the morsel that falls from some people and they are too proud to pick it up, showing themselves as being in affluence and plenty, and distancing themselves from looking like the poor and indigent, who strive for the smallest thing, even if it be a crumb of bread.

The Prophet used the expression that the left-over morsel is left over only for Satan. His *sunnah* in these matters is indeed a moral and economic training at one and the same time. If the Muslims would act upon it, we would not see the waste that is met with every day – rather, at every meal – in every wastebasket and rubbish bin. If the Muslim Community calculated the level of this waste, its economic value every day would amount to millions or tens of millions. Then how much would it be by month or in a whole year? That is the inner spirit behind these hadiths. Many a man who sits on the ground and eats with his fingers, and licks them afterwards, following the words of the Sunnah, is yet far from the character of humility and the character of gratitude, and the character of economy in the use of the blessing of food – which is the desired end behind these manners.

"THE WEIGHT OF MAKKAH" AND "THE MEASURE OF MADINAH"

Another example is the hadith: "The weight is the weight of the people of Makkah, and the [volumetric] measure is the measure of the people of Madinah."[101] In light of the age in which it was said, this contains what some contemporaries would call a 'progressive' teaching. It teaches the unification of the standards of measure or gauge to which the people refer in selling and buying and other transactions. There is reference in that to the smallest unit of the scale that the people knew well.

The people of Makkah were traders, they did their selling and buying in metallic coin, and so depended on the standard weight being well-preserved – the *mithqāl*, *dirham*, *dāniq*, and the like. Accordingly, they gave much attention to the preservation of these weights and their multiples and divisions. Then it is no surprise that their weights were the standards relied upon, the reference against which people resolved any dispute that arose. It is on this basis that the hadith has come with the particular wording: "The weight is the weight of the people of Makkah….." Similarly, the people of Madinah were people of agriculture and tillage, owners of grain and fruit. Their attention was directed to the preservation of volumetric measures – such as the *madd*, the *sa*ᶜ, and others – because of their pressing need of them in the marketing of the produce of their lands, orchards and vineyards. When they sold or bought they made use of these measures and they were more rightfully owners of their regulation. So, no wonder at the wording of the Messenger, that the measure is their measure.

What we mean to establish here is that the meaning of this hadith has to do with the class of practical measures, liable to change with the changing of time and place and circumstance, and it is not a binding command stopped in itself and not permitting any alteration. As for the aim of the hadith – it is, self-evidently, as we have said, the unification of the measures with reference to what man has come to know with greater precision. So the Muslim of today finds no harm in using decimal measures (such as the kilogram and its divisions and multiples), on account of what he distinguishes therein of precision and ease in calculation. Nor does that amount to opposing the hadith in a particular situation. That is why we see it being used by contemporary Muslims in many regions of the world without objection from anyone. The use of metric measures in length is another instance. There can be no objection to it as long as the aim is to arrive at accuracy and unity in the standards. The appropriate maxim to have in mind is: 'Wisdom is the lost property of the believer wherever he finds it, and of all people he has the most right to it.'

SIGHTING THE CRESCENT TO ESTABLISH THE MONTH

It is proper to include in the context of this discussion what has come in the well-known *ṣaḥīḥ* hadith: "Fast upon sighting it (namely, the crescent) and stop fasting upon sighting it. Then if it is hidden from you, estimate (calculate) [the days of the month]." In a variant wording: "Then if it is hidden from you complete thirty days of Shaʿban."

Here the jurist should say: 'Surely this noble hadith points to both an objective, a goal, and to a means.'

Now, as for the objective of the hadith, its explanation is plain to see: that people fast the whole of Ramadan, not missing out a day at the beginning or end of it, or that they fast a day from an adjacent month, namely Shaʿban or Shawwal. That objective is achieved by affirming the start and end of Ramadan by a method practicable and available to the majority of the people, one that does not burden them with hardship or impediment in their fulfillment of the duties of their religion.

Sighting the crescent with the eyes was the easy and available means for the generality of the people in that time. That is why the hadith specifies such sighting. If it had burdened them with another method, such as mathematical calculation – and the Community in that time was ignorant, not versed in writing or calculating – it would have placed a hardship upon them in the matter. And God desires for His community ease and He does not desire for them hardship. And the Prophet said about himself: "Surely God sent me with an easy teaching, and He did not send me with distress."[102]

What then, if another method is found better able to realize the objective of the hadith, and further from erroneous interpretation or conjecture or falsehood in determining the opening of the month? And if this method is no longer difficult to achieve, not beyond the capacity of the Community, given what has come into it of the learning and knowledge of astronomers, geologists and physicists specialized at the global level? And when human knowledge has reached to the extent of man being able to ascend to the moon itself, alight upon its surface, peer about at the fissures of its land, and obtain samples of its rocks and soil? Why then should we adhere to means mentioned in the hadith – and the means is not the intended end itself – and forget the purposes that the hadith aimed at?

The hadith has established the opening of the month by the report of one or two persons proclaiming the sighting of the crescent with the naked eye – where it was the practicable means available to the average member of the Community. Then how can one think of renouncing a means that is closed to error or conjecture or falsehood, a means that attains the rank of certainty and definitiveness? Moreover, it is possible that, by adopting it, the Islamic Community of east and west can come together, and reduce the continual opposition and differences among them in the fasting and breaking fast and the ʿId days.[103] It is something one cannot make sense of or accept, either by logic of knowledge or by logic of the religion, given that, on this matter, it is confirmed beyond dispute that one party must be right and the others wrong.

Acceptance of definitive calculation today surely is the means to establish the months. One must accept it under the heading of 'preferred analogy' in the sense that the Sunnah makes the acceptance of a permissible means lawful for us. Something that entails uncertainty and a need for interpretation – namely, sighting the crescent with the naked eye – cannot cause the rejection of a means higher and more complete, more adequate to the realization of the intended purpose. The more so as this means (definitive calculation) relieves the Community of severe controversy when deciding about the time of its fasting and its Sacrifice, and enables the longed-for unity in its public symbols and rites of worship, stable continuance of what is commanded of the more special affairs of its religion, and what is more relevant for its life and its spiritual being.

The learned and great *muḥaddith*, Aḥmad Muhammad Shākir (may God have mercy on him) reasoned by a different route to the same judgment – that the lunar month should be by astronomical calculation. He based his argument on the fact that the command in respect of sighting the crescent is dependent on the (legal) cause stipulated for it in the Sunnah itself. Now that that cause is no longer found, it is proper that the injunction be negated also, because it is an established and agreed principle that an injunction goes with its cause, existent or non-existent. It is best to cite his text in his own words, because there is strength and clarity in it. He wrote in his essay *Awā'il al-Shuhūr al-ʿArabiyyah*:

> From what there is no doubt [about] is that the Arabs, before Islam and in the early period of Islam, did not know the astronomical sciences, positive scientific knowledge. They were an unlettered Community – they did not write and they did not calculate. One among them who had acquired anything of that knew it only elementarily or the husk of it. He knew it from observation or from following [imitation], or by hearsay and report. [His knowledge] was not based on mathematical roots, nor on definitive proofs deduced from secure axioms. For that [reason] the Messenger of God made the resort for establishing the months in [the people's] rites of worship the definite and witnessed matter that [was] within the capacity of everyone of them, or within the capacity of most of them, and [that] was sighting of the crescent with the naked eye. Then, this was stronger and more regulatory of the times of their [religious] symbols and their rites. It was what joins to itself certainty and firmness from what [was] within their capacity

[to achieve at the time]. And God does not burden a soul except that He gives scope [the capacity to carry that burden].

From what conforms to the commands of the Law there was not [in that time anything to the effect that] one rest the proofs on the devices of calculation and astronomy. They did not know a thing of that in their major cities. Many of them were Bedouin (nomads): the news of the major cities did not reach them, except in occasional intervals of proximity [to the cities], and [that was] infrequently. So if he had made calculation and astronomy [the resort] for them, he would have oppressed them. [For] novelties [as the science of asronomy then was] were not known among them, except by very few, [and that too] from hearsay if it reached them [at all]. It was not known [even] to the people of the major cities except by imitation from some of the people of calculation, and most of them or all of them were from the People of the Book.

Then the Muslims conquered the world, and they took the reins of the sciences. They broadened [their knowledge and competence] in all their arts and crafts. They translated the sciences of predecessors and they distinguished [themselves] therein. They also discovered much from the hidden [hitherto unknown] things and preserved them for those who [were to come] after them. Among those [sciences were] astronomy and astrology and calculation of the stars.

Many of the jurists and hadith scholars did not know astronomy, or they knew [only] some of its rudiments. Some of them, or many of them, were not trusting of one who knew [astronomy], and were not at ease with him. Rather, some of them censured preoccupation with it as deviation and heresy, thinking of it that these sciences led their [practitioners] to claim knowledge of the unseen ('astrology'). Some of them were indeed claiming that, and it brought harm to themselves and to their science. [In fact, some] jurists were excusing [that abuse]. Those who, among the jurists and scholars, knew these sciences, were not capable of defining for them a sound (*ṣaḥīḥ*) position in relation to the religion or to fiqh. Rather, they were indicating them with dread [as something to be feared and avoided].

Their situation was thus – when the cosmological sciences were not as widespread as the religious sciences [were], nor what relates to [those sciences]. Also, according to the scholars, the foundations [of those sciences, in contrast to the religious sciences] were not definitively established.

This spacious and splendid Law will endure through time until God permits the end of the life of this world. It legislates for every community, and for every age. For that [very reason] we see in the texts of the Book and the Sunnah subtle indications to what of the affairs [of humankind that the Law deals with] is renewable. Then, when confirmation of [those affairs] comes, they will be explained and known and understood, even though predecessors had explained them according to [what is] not their reality.

What we are now discussing has been hinted in the authentic Sunnah. So al-Bukhārī has narrated from the hadith of Ibn ʿUmar from the Prophet, that he said: "Indeed we are an unlettered Community. We do not write and we do not calculate. The month [he gestured with his hand] is like this....and like this: that is, at times twenty-nine [days], and at times thirty [days]".[104] Mālik narrated it in *al-Muwaṭṭā'*.[105] Also al-Bukhārī and Muslim and others [narrated it] with the wording: "the month is twenty-nine [days], so do not begin fasting until you see the crescent; and do not stop fasting until you see it. Then if it is obscure for you, then estimate (or calculate) it."

Now our earlier scholars, may God have mercy on them, were right on the explanation of the meaning of the hadith, but they were in error in the interpretation of it. [An example] of their collective opinion on that is the opinion of al-Ḥāfiẓ Ibn Ḥajar:[106] "The intended meaning of the term calculation (*al-ḥisāb*) here is the calculation of the stars and the movement thereof. And [people] were not knowledgeable about that except in a lowly way. So the command to fast and other [commands] are attached to the sighting [of the crescent] so as to lift the burden from them in [respect of] the hardship of knowing the movements [of the stars]. And the command in [respect of] the fasting lasted even though some of them happened to know that [knowledge of the stars' movements]. However, the outward [wording] of the command negates absolutely linking the command [to fast] to calculation [rather than to sighting the moon]. It is clear in his saying in the last-mentioned hadith: 'Then if it is obscure to you, complete the number of thirty'; he did not say 'Then ask the people of calculation'. The wisdom in it is that, when it was obscure, the number [of days to be fasted] is the same for [all] who are under obligation [to fast], so it caused the controversy and dispute to disappear from [among] them. Now in that [matter], one group of people did go to [the position] that resort should be to the people of the movements [of the stars], and they were the Rāfiḍis.[107] Their agreement [with that position] has been conveyed from some of the jurists. [But] al-Bājī said: 'The consensus of the righteous *salaf* is a proof against them.' And Ibn Bazīzah said: 'It is an invalid doctrine. The Law has forbidden delving into the science of the stars because it is surmise and guesswork; there is no definitiveness in it; and conjecture does not outweigh [the definitive, when it comes to making any Legal decision]. Moreover, if the command [of the hadith] is restricted to [astronomers], then it will be narrowed, because [astronomy] is not known except by a few.'

This explanation is correct in that [in the hadith] attention is [indeed directed] to the sighting and not to the calculation. But the interpretation is erroneous [if the claim is] that, even if there happens [to exist] one who knows [calculation], the injunction on fasting remains (i.e. in respect of seeing alone). [It is erroneous] because the command to rely on the seeing alone has come dependent on a Legal cause explicit in the text, and it is the [Community's] being unlettered ('not writing and not counting'). Now, a cause [*ʿillah*, in this case being unlettered] stays within the circle of the effect [*maʿlūl*, in this case being unable to calculate the crescent] being existent and non-existent. [But] then, if the Community has come out of its being unlettered, and become literate and numerate; I mean if there have come into its society [i.e. the collective life of the Community] those who know these sciences; [if] it is possible for the people, the generality of them and the elite of them, to attain to certainty and definitiveness in calculating the beginning of the month; [if] it is possible that they have trust in this calculation [of the same degree as] their trust in sighting, or stronger; when this has become their situation in their collective life and the cause (*ʿillah*) of being illiterate has disappeared [from the society] – [then] it is a duty that they resort to [what yields] established certainty. [It is a duty] also that they adopt in establishing [the month] the instrument of calculation alone, and not resort to sighting, except when knowledge [by calculation] becomes difficult for them – as when people are in the desert or a [remote] village and authentic, reliable reports from the people of calculation do not reach them.

If it is a duty – with the disappearance of the cause [*ʿillah*, which] its being proscribed [was based] on – to resort to calculation alone, then it is also a duty to resort to true calculation according to the instruments [available]. It is [a duty] also to repudiate the possibility of sighting when the possibility of it is non-existent – for the true first of the month is the night on which the crescent disappears from view after the setting of the sun, even if [the event is confirmed by only] a single viewing."[108]

This opinion of mine – that the injunction varies with the variations of the conditions of the people bound by it – is not an innovation among [juristic] opinions Indeed this is [found] commonly in the Law, the people of knowledge know it, and others. Among the examples of that in this question of ours is [the following]: That the hadith "If it is obscure to you, then estimate (or calculate) it" has appeared in other wording. In some of them: "If it is obscure to you, then complete the number of thirty". The scholars explained the summary narration "then estimate (or calculate)" [by joining] to it the detailed narration "then complete the number". However, the great imam of the Shāfiʿīs – indeed he was their leader in his time – and he was Abū al-ʿAbbās Aḥmad ibn Surayj[109] – reconciled the two reports by making them relate to different circumstances. [He argued] that the meaning of his saying "then estimate (or calculate) it" is that [people] should estimate (or calculate) it according to the lunar phase, and that this [command] addresses those whom God has picked out for this science [of astronomy]. And that his saying "then complete the thirty" is an address to the generality [of people who do not know astronomy].[110]

Now my opinion all but sees eye to eye with the opinion of Ibn Surayj except that he has made it particular to when the month is obscured, [for it is in that event only that] he does not accept people doing the sighting. Also he has made the command to adopt calculation [applicable] to the few – in accordance with what was in his time the fewness of the number of those knowledgeable about [astronomy], the non-acceptance of their opinions and calculations, and the slowness of the receipt of reports between one land and another if the month was established in one of them. As for my opinion: it decides generally for the adoption of precise and trustworthy calculation. And the generality of that for the people is [based]

> on what is easy in these days, such as the speed of the receipt of reports and their wide circulation. Reliance on sighting remains for the very few rare [occasions], for those to whom the reports do not come, and they do not find [any means] that establishes [the beginning of the month] from knowledge of the heavens and the descent of the sun and moon.
>
> I see this my opinion as the most just of the opinions, and the nearest of them to a safe understanding, and [nearest] to a correct understanding of the hadiths that have appeared on this topic. [111]

That is what Shaykh Shākir wrote more than half a century ago (Dhu al-Hijjah, 1357 AH, January 1939). Astronomy had not attained at that time what it has since attained by leaps and bounds. It has enbaled people to invade space and ascend to the moon. The science has attained a degree of precision such that, according to one account, the probability of error in calculation by it is as little as one hundred-thousandth of a second!

Shaykh Shākir wrote that, and he was above all things a man of hadith and *āthār*. He lived his life, may God have mercy on him, in the service of the hadith and the Sunnah of the Prophet. He was a pure *salafī*, one who followed, not one who innovated. Yet he did not understand the *salafiyyah* as if it were inflexibly fixed according to what those before us from the *salaf* said. Rather, the true *salafiyyah* is that we take as a method their method, that we imbibe their spirit, that we strive according to our time as they strove according to their time, and that we respond to our reality with our minds, not their minds, without being bound except according to what is definitive in the Law, and the judgments of its texts and its objectives taken as a whole.

This notwithstanding, I read a lengthy article in the month of Ramadan of the year 1409 AH by an esteemed shaykh.[112] In it, he pointed to a *ṣaḥīḥ* Prophetic hadith: "We are an unlettered Community; we do not write, and we do not calculate." He appears to argue that this implies the negation of calculation and lowers the esteem for it among the Community. If this were correct, the hadith would also be an argument for the negation of writing, and the lowering of esteem for that. For the hadith certainly comprises two matters, by which the Community's being unlettered is demonstrated – writing and calculation. No one has said in the past or in the present that, in his view, writing is a matter censured or undesirable for the Community. Rather, writing is a matter sought after; the Qur'an and the Sunnah and the ijma^{c} demonstrate this. The first who took the initiative in spreading writing was the Prophet, as is known from his biography, and his attitude to the prisoners of Badr.

Among the arguments put forward on this subject is that the Messenger did not legislate for us to act on the basis of calculation. He did not command that. He commanded us only in respect of sighting, and adoption of it as the method of establishing the month. In this opinion there is something of error and distortion, in both matters:

First: it does not make sense that the Messenger would command reliance on calculation. In his time, the Community was unlettered, they did not write and they did not calculate. So he legislated for it the means appropriate for it in the time and place, and that is sighting – the practicable method for the majority of the people in his time. However, when a means has been found that is more precise, more secure and further from error and conjecture, then there is nothing in the Sunnah that forbids turning to it.

Second: the Sunnah does point to basing action on calculation in the circumstance of obscurity, when the sky is clouded over. It is what al-Bukhārī has reported in *Kitāb al-Sawm* in *Jāmi^{c} al-Ṣaḥīḥ* by his well-known 'golden chain' of narrators: from Mālik from Nāfi^{c} from Ibn ^{c}Umar from God's Messenger: he mentioned Ramadan, then he said: "Do not fast until you see the crescent; and do not stop fasting until you see it; and if it is obscure to you, then estimate[113] it."

This 'estimating' or 'calculating' is what is commanded. It is possible that reliance on calculation is included in the command for one who would do it well. It joins to the command what settles and contents the soul. It is what has come about, in our age, in the orderly arrangement of the definitive things – as is well-established and well-known to anyone who has the minimum knowledge of the sciences of the age and of what man attains therein, whom his Lord taught what he did not use to know.

I have for years been calling for the adoption of definitive astronomical calculation, at least in the negation, not in the affirmation, of the fact, thereby lessening the big differences happening every year at the beginning of the fasting and at the *ʿĪd al-fiṭr*: at the extreme it leads to three days of difference between some Islamic lands and others. The meaning of adopting calculation 'in the negation of the fact' is that we should continue to establish the crescent by sighting (in conformity with the opinion of most jurists in our age), but if calculation negates the possibility of sighting – if it says it is impossible because the crescent has not been born at all in any place in the Islamic world – it is obligatory not to accept the testimony of eye-witnesses in any way, because the reality (which definitive mathematical science has established) contradicts them. Indeed, in this circumstance, it is not at all required that you give consideration to the testimony of the people, or that the Law courts or a session for fatwas or religious matters be opened to one who wishes to declare a testimony about sighting the crescent.

This is what I was satisfied with and spoke about in many fatwas, in teaching and lectures. Then God willed that I should find it commented on and detailed in the work of one of the great Shāfiʿī jurists, Taqī al-Dīn al-Subkī (d. 756 AH), about whom people said: indeed he reached the rank of ijtihad. He said in his fatwas that, if calculation negates the possibility of sighting with the eyes, the *qāḍī* is obliged to reject the testimony of the witnesses: "Because calculation is definitive, and the testimony and report are conjectural, and the conjectured cannot contradict the definitive, let alone take precedence over it." He stated that it is part of the business of the *qāḍī*, in all cases, to look into the testimony of the witness before him. Then, if he sees that immediate sense-experience or perception contradicts it, he rejects it, and no credit is accorded to it. He said: "The condition of proof is that what is being testified to be possible – perceptible, reasonable and lawful.

Then if the proof of calculation decides definitively on the non-possibility of it, then the impossibility of the opinion becomes the ruling, because of the absurdity of what has been testified to, for the Law does not bring absurdities."[114]

In contrast to mathematical calculation, the testimony of witnesses can be interpreted as suspect, or mistaken, or false. What might al-Subkī have said if he had lived to our time and had seen, of the advance in astronomy (or astrology, as it used to be named), some of what we have pointed to above?

Shaykh Shākir mentioned in his research that the opinion of the great professor, Shaykh Muhammad Muṣṭafa, Shaykh al-Azhar, famous in his time, when he was the head of the Shariʿah High Court, was like the opinion of al-Subkī in rejecting the testimony of witnesses when calculation negates the possibility of sighting. Shaykh Shākir said: "I was, and some of my brothers, among those who opposed the great professor in his opinion. Now I make it clear that he was right. I add [to what he said] the obligatoriness of establishing the crescents by calculation in all circumstances except for one for whom knowledge by it is beyond him."[115]

VI

DISTINGUISHING BETWEEN LITERAL AND FIGURATIVE

Arabic is a language in which the portion of figurative expressions is plentiful. Figurative expression is rhetorically more effective than literal, as is established in the science of rhetoric. The Prophet was most expressive in spoken Arabic, and his sayings most inspired. No wonder then that, in his hadiths, there should be a great number of figurative expressions drawn from their purposes, in most striking form.

'Figurative expression' here means what is included in figurative diction and concepts – metaphor, metonymy, metaphorical simile – all that in a word or sentence departs from the correspondence with the reality they signify. Figurative expression is indicated by markers, in the words themselves or in the context in which the words occur. An example of that is speech or conversation attributed to animals and birds, and inanimate and non-corporeal entities, as in popular sayings like: 'The wood said to the nail: Why are you cleaving into me? It said: Ask the one who is hammering me!' The representation and similitude entailed are not counted as falsehood in a report. Al-Raghīb al-Aṣfahānī said in his valuable book *al-Dharīᶜah ilā makārim al-sharīᶜah* (The means to the most noble of the Law): "Know that speech, when it moves off in the direction of similitude to [convey] a lesson, not a report [i.e. bare information], is not a lie in reality. For this [reason, even] those who are wary do not hold themselves aloof from what is narrated therewith." As an example of that he presented the famous story in which a lion, a jackal and a fox took part in a hunt. They hunted and took an ass, a gazelle, and a hare. The lion said to the jackal: "Divide it out!" The jackal said: "It is divided up like this: the ass is for you; and the gazelle is for me; and the hare is for the fox." The lion pounced on the jackal for saying so and slew him. Then he said to the fox: "Divide it out!" The fox said: "It is divided up like this: the ass is for your breakfast; the gazelle is for your midday meal; and the hare is for your night meal." Then the lion said: "Who taught you this division?" The fox said: "The crimson robe that is on the jackal!"

Al-Raghīb al-Aṣfahānī said: "And [it is] in the light of metaphor [that] one interprets His saying, Exalted is He (*Ṣād*, 38: 23): 'This brother of mine has ninety-nine sheep, while I have one sheep'. Another example of that is what many Qur'an commentators have said about His saying, Exalted is He (*al-Aḥzāb*, 33: 72): 'Surely We offered the trust to the heavens and the earth and the mountains, but they shrank from carrying it and were afraid of it. And man assumed it.' "

Interpreting a saying figuratively is on some occasions precisely appropriate. Otherwise, one stumbles into error. One time, the Messenger said to his womenfolk: "The quickest of you to join me will be the one with the longest hand." ᶜĀ'ishah said: "So they measured, which of them had the longest hand!" Indeed, in some hadiths, it is reported that they took a cane to measure which hand was the longest! But the Messenger had not meant that. He only meant 'long in the hand' in doing good and spending on others in the right way. That is what the event confirmed. For the first of his womenfolk to join him was Zaynab bint Jaḥsh – she was a woman who worked industriously with her hands and she spent in charity.[116]

This kind of error in understanding happens with the Qur'an as it happens with the Sunnah. It happened to ʿAdī ibn Ḥātim who misunderstood this verse on the subject of fasting: "So now have intercourse with them and seek that which God has prescribed for you, and [also] eat and drink until the white thread becomes clear to you from the black thread of dawn. Then hold to the fast until the night" (*al-Baqarah*, 2: 187). Al-Bukhārī narrated from ʿAdī ibn Ḥātim that he said: "When this verse was sent down ('and eat and drink'), I [looked for] two cords, one of them black, the other white. Then I put the two [cords] under my pillow. Then I made [myself] look to the two [cords], and when it was clear to me the white from the black, then I restrained [myself as for fasting]. Then I arose and went in the morning to God's Messenger and informed him of what I did, and he said: 'Then your pillow is indeed spacious! That [verse] is only [pointing to] the day's whiteness [being distinguishable] from the night's blackness.' "[117] (The meaning of "Then your pillow is indeed spacious!" is that it was spacious enough to accommodate the two 'threads', referred to in the verse, the two being the white of the day and the black of the night. So he judged that the pillow was as wide as the east and the west!)

Another example of that is God's saying, in the well-known *ḥadīth qudsī*: "If My slave approaches Me by a hand-span, I approach him by an arm's length; and if he approaches by an arm's length, I approach him by the breadth of a fathom; and if he comes to Me walking, I come to him running."[118] The Muʿtazilis stirred up controversy with *ahl al-ḥadīth* for narrating the like of this text, and accused them of ascribing to God that which is suspected of likening Him to His creation in physical nearness, in walking and running, and this does not befit His Godhood. Ibn Qutaybah rebutted that in his book *Ta'wīl Mukhtalif al-Ḥadīth*:

> This is surely [just] similitude and [figurative] likening. It meant only: whoever comes to Me hastening in obedience, I come to him with reward faster than his coming. Then that has been replaced with 'walking' and 'running'.
>
> An example of that is His saying, Exalted is He: "And those who strive to thwart (*saᶜaw*) Our signs, those are rightful owners of the Fire" (*al-Ḥajj*, 22: 51). The striving to thwart (*saᶜī*) [implies] the speed (or haste) in moving. It does not always mean moving. It only means that they are rushing with their intentions and their actions. And God knows better.[119]

We find some hadiths stirring a kind of ambiguity, specially in the minds of the educated of modern times, when interpreted according to their literal meanings as conveyed in the words in their literal denotations. However, if they are interpreted according to their figurative meaning, the ambiguity is gone, and the face of the intended meaning becomes clear. Let us take as an example of that the hadith of the two Shaykhs from Abū Hurayrah from the Prophet, he said: "The Fire complained to its Lord and said: 'O Lord, one part of me has consumed the other part.' Then He permitted it two breaths – one breath in winter, and one breath in summer. It is the most severe heat that you find, and the most severe cold that you find."[120]

Students in schools in our time study in geography the causes of the variation of the seasons, and the appearance of summer and winter, heat and cold. They are regulated according to the usages of creation, and causes well-known to students. So too, among the well-known witnessed things is that some parts of the terrestrial sphere are in severely cold winter, while others are in severe heat.

Another example is the hadith of Abū Hurayrah in the two *Ṣaḥīḥ*s from the Prophet, he said: "God created the creation, until when He was free from creating it. The womb said; 'Is this the place of refuge with You from the cutting off?' He said: 'Yes. Does it not content you that I will join with one who joins with you, and I will cut off the one who cuts you off.' It said: 'Certainly, O Lord.' He said: 'Then it is for you.' Recite if you wish: 'Would you then, if you were given the command, spread corruption in the land, and sever your ties of kinship?' (*Muḥammad*, 47: 22)."[121]

But is the speaking of the womb (it signifies 'near relations') here literal or figurative? The commentators have disagreed. Qāḍī ʿIyāḍ interpreted the hadith figuratively and said that it is in the class of similitudes. Ibn Abī Jamrah said, in *Sharḥ Mukhtaṣar al-Bukhārī*, in commenting on the meaning of God joining with one who joins his 'near relations': "The being connected with God is a metaphor for a great one of His favors, and He has addressed people [in terms] they understand. And why it is of the greatest [of favors] is that the beloved one is offering, to the one loving him, reunion – and [this] is nearness to him, and providing him with what he desires and helping him to what pleases him. The literal [sense] of that is an absurdity in respect of the due right of God, Exalted is He. [So everyone] knows that that is figurative allusion to a great favor of His to His slave. [...] Similarly, the saying about the cutting off – it is a figurative allusion to being deprived of the favor."

Al-Qurṭubī said:

> It is the same whether we said that the expression referring to the 'womb' is figurative or literal. Or that it is by way of estimation or likening as to what the meaning is. If the 'womb' were something [endowed] with reason and faculty of speech it would say [it] thus. And an example of it: "If We had sent down the Qur'an on the mountain you would see it fearful ..."; and in another [example] "And those are similitudes that we coin for people" (*al-Ḥashr*, 59: 21). Now the purpose of this speaking is to inform [us] of the imperative [nature] of the command [to maintain] the bonds of the 'womb'. And that He, Exalted is He, sent it down [as] a station for one who seeks refuge with Him, then He gives him refuge and enters him into His protection. If it is like that, then the one near to God is not left forsaken. He said: "One who prays the dawn prayer, and he is under the protection of God: if God seeks from him anything from his responsibility [i.e. something he has failed to do], He gets hold of him, then He throws him on

his face in the Fire." Muslim traced the sources of and reported it.

My view is that the kind of interpretation here, taking the hadith as figurative, does not diminish the religion in its power, provided it is accepted without affectation and arbitrariness, and there is a necessity for such interpretation, for departing from the literal to the figurative. Only when the meaning one finds in a text is ruled out by clear reason, or what is right in Law, or certain in knowledge, or certain in reality, does it rule out following the intent of the literal meaning.

Here the controversy arises: in such a case, is it forbidden to take the literal meaning or not? Something that has been regarded as impossible by one man or one group, other scholars may reckon to be possible. It is a matter that demands searching reflection and study. For interpretation (away from the literal sense) without good reason, is not acceptable, interpretation that is arbitrary is not acceptable; on the other hand, to interpret a saying literally when there exists something (in reason or Law or knowledge or reality) forbidding that is also not acceptable.

The rejection of resort to the figurative is here in the category of a trial or test for the intelligent among the people, those whose knowledge of Islam finds no contradiction between the authentically traditional and the clearly rational. Let us read this hadith which the two Shaykhs narrate from Ibn ʿUmar, who said that God's Messenger said: "When the people of the Garden attain to the Garden, and the people of the Fire to the Fire, then death is brought until it settles between the Garden and the Fire, then it is slaughtered, then a caller calls out: 'O people of the Garden: no [more] death. O people of the Fire: no [more] death.' So the people of the Garden increase in the joy of their rejoicing, and the people of the Fire increase in the sadness of their grieving."[122] In the hadith of Abū Saʿīd, according to the two Shaykhs and others, "Death is brought in the form of a handsome ram…"[123]

What does one understand from this hadith? How death is slaughtered, how death dies?

Abū Bakr ibn al-ʿArabī certainly 'refrained from' this hadith. He said:

> This hadith has been regarded as dubious, on account of its being opposed to obvious sense, because death is a quality, and the qualitative is not changed bodily, then how is [death] slaughtered? [...]
>
> One party [altogether] deny the correctness of the hadith and reject it. And its interpretation [according to] one party [is that] they say: "This is by way of simile, and the slaughtering here is not literal."
>
> And a[nother] party say: "Rather, the slaughtering is [to be understood] literally, and the one slaughtered is the one entrusted with [administering] death. And all of [the people] know him, because he is the one charged with the seizure of their spirits."

Ibn Ḥajar said in *al-Fatḥ*: "Some of the later [people] approved this." He conveyed from al-Māzirī his opinion: "In our view death is a quality. According to the Muʿtazilis it lacks meaning. According to both doctrines it is not correct [to say] that [death] could be a ram or [anything] corporeal, and that the intent of this is by way of metaphor and simile." Then he said: "Indeed God created the body [of death], then He slaughtered [the same], then made [it] as an example to [the effect] that death cannot befall the people of the Garden."

Al-Qurṭubī said the like of this in *al-Tadhkirah*. All these explanations are running away from interpreting the saying because of its literal sense being in opposition to simple reason, as Ibn al-ʿArabī said. And that is the beginning of denying the hadith and rejecting it. But it is established by a group of routes that it is *ṣaḥīḥ* from a number of Companions. So its rejection is an act of rashness, and so too is rejection of the possibility of interpreting it.

Ibn Ḥajar also conveyed in *al-Fatḥ* the opinion of a speaker he did not identify, who said: "There is no bar to God bringing qualities into being as substances, appointing for them their particular matter – as is established in *Ṣaḥīḥ Muslim* in a hadith: 'Indeed [the surahs of the Qur'an] *al-Baqarah* and *Āl ʿImrān* will come as if they were like two clouds' and the like of that among the hadiths."[124]

This is the view that Shaykh Aḥmad Muhammad al-Shākir inclined to, in his *Takhrīj* of the *Musnad.* After conveying from *al-Fatḥ* the doubts of Ibn al-ʿArabi about the hadith, and the discussion about its interpretation, he said:

> All this burdens and trespasses upon the Unseen, which God has appropriated exclusively to His knowledge alone. We have no duty other than to have faith in what has appeared as it has appeared, neither denying it nor interpreting it. The hadith is *ṣaḥīḥ*. Its meaning is established also from the hadith of Abū Saʿīd al-Khudrī according to al-Bukhārī, and from the hadith of Abū Hurayrah according to Ibn Mājah and Ibn Ḥibbān. The Knower of the unseen [matter or energy] that is behind substances does not inform about it minds [such as ours] limited by the bodies on earth. Rather, the minds [of human beings] are [already sufficiently] astounded by information about the embodied realities within reach of their capacity for information. So why will they rise to judge what is beyond their [minds'] power and authority? And here we are the first in our age to be informed of the transformation of matter into energy, and we are informed of the transformation of energy into matter, by making and doing – [without clear] knowledge of the reality of the one or the other – and we do not know what will be hereafter, except that human reason is needy and lacking, and [we do not know] what matter is or energy, and quality and substance, except terms of convention approximating the realities [of what they signify]. So the good [thing] for man [to do] is that he have faith and that he act righteously, then leave the Unseen to the Knower of the Unseen – so that he may be saved on the Day of Resurrection. "Say: If the sea became ink for the words of my Lord, the sea would be used up before the words of my Lord were exhausted, even if We brought the like of it to help" (*al-Kahf*, 18: 109).[125]

The Shaykh's discourse, may God have mercy on him, on the reason for refusing interpretation of texts bearing commands on matters unseen is based on strong and convincing logic. However, in this context, exclusion of the hadith text from interpretation is not incontestable. Here, there is no justification for flight from interpretation. For among the perfectly well-known things that reason and tradition agree upon is that death – which separates man from life – is not like a ram or an ox, or any other animal. Rather, it is one of the non-physical realities or, as the earlier scholars put it, 'a quality'. The non-physical does not transform into corporeal or animal form except under the heading of similitude and imaging, which gives (some sort of graspable) form to non-physical and mental realities. This is what is more suited to addressing minds of modern temperament. And God knows better.

THE FIGURATIVE IN HADITHS CONVEYING INJUNCTIONS

Figurative expression occurs in hadiths conveying information and in hadiths conveying injunctions. Being alert to it and alerting others to it is a duty of the people of fiqh. It is for the discharge of duties of this kind that people stipulated conditions for a *mujtahid*: that he should be learned in Arabic, knowledgeable about what is possible to be understood in different arguments or proofs in it, in the way it was understood in the pure Arabic of the time of the Prophet and the Companions. Some knew the language by nature, and some by study, as the Bedouin of old said: "I am no grammarian who has to contort his tongue, rather, I am a natural who pronounces correctly."

Ignoring the distinction between figurative and literal gives rise to many errors – as we clearly see among those who rush to give fatwas in our time, prescribing the forbidden and the obligatory, pronouncing on the heresy or transgression of others, even at times on the unbelief of others, according to texts if they are strong in respect of being correctly established, though not in respect of plainness or clarity of argument.

Take as an example the hadith which some contemporaries adduce for the absolute prohibition against a man shaking hands with a woman. It is what al-Ṭabarānī narrated: "That one of you be pierced with an iron needle is better than that he touch (*yamass*) a woman not lawful to him."[126] Al-Albānī has pronounced the hadith *ḥasan* in his critique of our book *al-Ḥalāl wa al-Ḥarām*, and in his *Ṣaḥīḥ al-Jāmiʿ al-Ṣaghīr*. If – despite the hadith being not well-known in the time of the Companions and their students – we concede its being *ḥasan*, then its wording shows that the hadith does not stipulate the prohibition of shaking hands because, in the language of the Qur'an and Sunnah 'touching' (*al-mass*) does not mean the bare touching of one person touching another. The meaning of *al-mass* here is what the saying of the Qur'an commentator Ibn ʿAbbās demonstrated: that in the Qur'an *al-mass* (touching), *al-lams* (feeling, groping), *al-mulamasah* (contact, sexual intercourse) are ways of naming the act of sexual conjugation. For sure, God in His noble modesty alludes to what He wills by what He wills. This is something that cannot be understood otherwise in the instance of this verse: "O believers: if you marry believing women and divorce them before you have touched them (*tamassū-hunna*), then there is no waiting period for them for you to reckon" (*al-Aḥzāb*, 33: 49).

Now all Qur'an commentators and jurists – until the Ẓāhiris – interpreted 'touching' (*al-mass*) as 'penetration' (*al-dakhūl*), and they linked it to circumstances of strict seclusion because that is the likely situation for it to take place. An example of it is the verse in *Sūrat al-Baqarah* on the divorce that happens before 'touching' (*al-mass*), meaning before consummation (*al-dakhūl*). The saying of the Qur'an on the tongue of Maryam, upon her be peace, confirms this meaning: "How can I have a son when no man has touched me (*yamsas-nī*)?" (*Āl ʿImrān*, 3: 47). Indeed, the proofs for this in the Qur'an and Sunnah are many.

So there is nothing in this hadith that justifies prohibition of a mere shaking hands, in which there is no craving and no fear that, behind it, there lies a cause of disturbance (*fitnah*). This is especially so whenever there is a need for it, such as coming back from a journey, or medical treatment during illness, or escape from persecution, and the like situations which people face. One accepts that when near ones greet one another, when a man needs to shake hands with the wife or daughter of his paternal or maternal uncle, or some other close relative. Especially is this so when she comes to him unexpectedly and extends her hand toward him, and he does not fear in his own heart or in hers any sentiment of lust.

A text that confirms this is narrated by Aḥmad ibn Ḥanbal in his *Musnad* from Anas, he said: "There was 'a slave-woman from among the slave-women' of Madinah and God's Messenger took her by the hand and he did not take his hand from her hand while she went with him wherever she wished [to go]." Al-Bukhārī narrated it with the wording: "There was 'a slave-woman from among the slave-women' in Madinah, and she took the Messenger of God by the hand; then she walked off with him wherever she wished."

The hadith demonstrates the extent of his humility, courtesy and tenderness: though she was a slave-woman she clasped him by the hand and she consulted with him through the city streets of Madinah, so that he decided for her certain needs. He was of extreme modesty and great in character, he did not want to hurt her feelings by withdrawing his hand from her hand. Rather, he shaded her, moving along with her in this situation until she was finished with the judgment of her need. Ibn Ḥajar said in commentary on the hadith of al-Bukhārī:

> The purpose of [this] taking by the hand is the necessary implication of it, and that is [its demonstration of] gentleness and complaisance. Also included are the furthest ranks of humility, because of the mentioning in it of a woman and not a man, of a slave-woman and not a free woman, moreover altogether generalized by the phrase "from among the slave-women", namely that she might be any slave-woman, and by its saying "wherever she wished", meaning any place whatever. The expression "taking by the hand" indicates the extreme of disposition [allowed to the woman], to the extent [that she might have led him anywhere] even if her need were going out of Madinah. The mutual contact with him was her help in that need, so that he helped in that [by not withdrawing his hand while she continued to need to hold it].
>
> And this is proof of the largeness of his humility and his freedom from all the categories of pride.[127]

What Ibn Ḥajar has stated, may God have mercy on him, as a whole is incontestable. However, his diverting the meaning of taking by the hand away from its literal meaning to what it implies only, namely gentleness and complaisance, is not acceptable. This is because the literal and the implied meanings are both intended together. The rule with a saying is that one interprets according to its literal meaning unless one finds some evidence or association that diverts it away from this literal meaning. Here, I do not see what prevents that. Indeed, the narration of Ibn Ḥanbal – "and he did not take his hand from her hand while she went with him wherever she wished [to go]" – clearly demonstrates that the literal meaning is (also) the purpose, and that it is affectation and artifice to depart from it.

THE DANGER OF CLOSING THE DOOR TO THE FIGURATIVE

Closing the door to figurative expression in understanding the hadiths, and stopping at the primary (literal) meaning of the text, blocks many educated contemporaries from understanding the Sunnah, even from understanding Islam, and confronts them with doubts as to its soundness if they take the saying literally. At times they find in the figurative expression what does not please their tastes, and what their education disapproves, and they do not make a way out of this distaste in accordance with the logic of the language and the pillars of the religion.

Similarly, some of the enemies of Islam often exploit some of these primary (literal) meanings to ridicule the Islamic understanding of them, and their (apparent) contradiction of modern science and modern thought. For years one hostile Christian, relying on certain hadiths, has attacked Islamic thinking for its belief in superstitions in the age of science and progress. An example is what al-Bukhārī and others have narrated: "Fever is a heat-haze from hell, so cool it with water."[128] The hostile critic says: Fever is not some heat-haze from hell. Rather it is some heat-haze from the earth. What there is in it is some filth, assisting the generation of germs.

This critic is stupid or pretends to be stupid, is ignorant or pretends to be ignorant of the figurative meaning and purpose of the hadith. Anyone can understand it who enjoys the taste of the Arabic. For example, we say of a day of intense heat – 'this intensity opens from hell' – and speaker and listener alike understand the intended meaning of the expression.

The meaning of "the Black Stone is from the Garden"

One of the ill-intentioned (*maḥsūbīn*) wrote about Islam in ridicule of the hadith "The Black Stone is from the Garden",[129] and the hadith "Pressed dates are from the Garden".[130] This writer ignored the intended meaning of these expressions and similes. The same kind of usage is found in the agreed-upon hadith: "Know that the Garden is under the shade of the sword."[131] No one understands, nor imagines that he understands, that the Garden which God has prepared for the righteous and God-fearing and whose expanse He has made like the expanse of the heavens and the earth, is really under the shade of the sword. One understands only that the jihad in the way of God – and the sword symbolizes it – is the nearest road to Paradise, and especially when God has prescribed being in the Garden as the reward for martyrdom. Another example of that is his saying to one who intended to offer himself in the jihad, and had left his needy mother in someone else's care: "Stick to her: surely the Garden is under her footsteps."[132] Again, anyone who has sense understands that the Garden is not literally by the foot of the mother. He understands only that obedience to the mother and taking care of her are among the widest of the doors that lead to the Gardens of Favor. It is related from one of the righteous that he lagged behind his brothers one day, so they asked him about that. He said: "I have been rubbing my side in a meadow of the Garden; for it has reached us that the Garden is under the footsteps of the mothers!" His brothers did not understand otherwise than that he had been preoccupied in the service of his mother and her care, aspiring thereby to the assurance of God and His Garden.

Hadith: "The Nile and the Euphrates are from the Garden"

Muṣṭafā al-Zarqā' told me that a great professor of modern positive law, among the most learned in Egypt, indeed in the Arab world, said to him one day that he bought the book *Ṣaḥīḥ al-Bukhārī*, then opened it once and his gaze chanced upon a hadith saying "The Nile and the Euphrates are among the rivers of the Garden". As soon as the learned man saw that, contradicting the reality – because the source of these two rivers is well known to every student, and they spring from the earth and not from the Garden – he was opposed to al-Bukhārī's book, the whole of it, and thereafter never thought even to turn its pages. The point of this is the suspicion that settled in his head. For if this man had behaved a little modestly, and referred to one of the commentators on al-Bukhārī, or asked one of the proficient scholars among his contemporaries, the truth would have become as plain to him as daylight to the eyes. But pride and arrogance are among the greatest veils to seeing the reality.

Here I think I should quote the opinion of one of the leaders of Islamic civilization, namely Abū Muhammad ibn Ḥazm, on his understanding of the meaning of the hadith and its explanation. I have chosen Ibn Ḥazm only because he, as is well-known, was a Ẓāhirī jurist. He believed in the letter of the texts and the adoption of their literal (*ẓāhirī*) meanings, without looking to underlying reasons and correlatives in other texts. However, he did believe that in the Arabic language there is both the literal and the figurative. After citing the *ṣaḥīḥ* hadith, "The Sīḥān and the Jīḥān and the Nile and the Euphrates are all among the rivers of the Garden",[133] and the hadith "What is between my house and my pulpit is one of the meadows of the Garden",[134] he said: "These two hadiths are not what the people of ignorance suppose – [namely] that the meadow is cut out from the Garden [literally, as a piece of it], and that the rivers are descended from the Garden. This is invalid and false." Then Ibn Ḥazm explained that the meaning of that space (between the Prophet's house and his pulpit) being a meadow of the Garden is only by way of alluding to the merit of it, to the prayer in it leading to the Garden. Similarly, the rivers, on account of their blessings, are connected to the Garden figuratively. In the same way as one says on good days: 'This is from the days of the

Garden'; and it is said about a flock of sheep: 'These are animals of the Garden'. So too what he said: "Surely the Garden is under the shade of the sword"; another example is the hadith: "The Black Stone is from the Garden". Ibn Ḥazm says of these reports: "The proof is clear from the Qur'an, and from necessity of sense-experience, that they are not [to be understood] on their literal [meaning]."[135]

This was the position of Ibn Ḥazm, well known for his being *ẓāhirī*, and his attachment, to the extreme of strictness, to the literal import of the texts. Yet, despite this, according to him, it was not appropriate that these texts be interpreted by their literal meaning. And – just as he said – only 'the people of ignorance' suppose that they can be so interpreted!

AGAINST LATITUDE IN LEAVING THE LITERAL MEANING

I should warn here that there is a danger in interpretation of hadiths (and the texts generally), and critique of them, at a remove from their literal meanings. From the viewpoint of reason or tradition, it is not commendable for a learned Muslim to enter into it unless the matter necessitates that. Often hadiths are interpreted away from the expressions themselves or their specificities or occasions, only for it to appear to the scrupulous researcher thereafter that it would have been preferable to leave them in their literal meaning.

I cite, by way of example of that, the hadith: "Whoever cuts the lote-tree, God has fixed his head in the Fire."[136] It is often narrated in a different wording. Some commentators explain that the intended referent of the cutting is the sacred lote-tree (*sidr al-ḥaram*), despite the fact that the word here (*sidrah*) is indefinite in the context so that it is general to all lote-trees. However, they find the threat to be so severe that they restricted the reference to the sacred lote-tree.

However, I incline to the view that the hadith informs us of an important matter that people are heedless of, namely the importance of the tree – especially the lote-tree in the land of the Arabs –

because of the usefulness of its shade and its fruit, most particularly in the open desert. So, cutting down this lote-tree – outside of necessity – prevents much good from people collectively, and exposes them to probable harm. Nowadays, this subject comes under what contemporary scholars call 'conservation of plants and the environment'. It is a cause for which societies and political parties have been set up, groups and conferences convened, and institutions and ministries established.

In the *Sunan* of Abū Dā'ūd I found a query by Abū Dā'ūd about this hadith. He said: "This hadith [text] is abridged. That is [in full it is:] one who cuts down a lote-tree in a waterless desert, under which a son of the road [i.e. a traveler] and livestock take shade, [and he cuts it down just] for the sake of it or for wrongdoing without any right [of property over that tree to excuse his cutting it down], God will fix his head in the Fire."

Praise is due to God! This explanation and commentary of Abū Dā'ūd accord with how I had been thinking the hadith should be understood. This hadith and others like it place Islam in the vanguard of the appeal for conservation of the environment and of plants and trees. Let it be entered in the religious temperament of every Muslim who hopes for Paradise and has dread of the Fire.

Rejected interpretations

Among interpretations to be rejected are the vain interpretations for which there is no evidence in the expression used in the text, nor in the context. An example is the opinion of one who said on the hadith, "Take the *saḥūr* [meal before fasting], for there is surely blessing in the *saḥūr*,"[137] that the meaning intended by *saḥūr* was seeking forgiveness! No doubt the seeking of forgiveness in the moments before daybreak is one of the greatest of the actions urged by the Qur'an and Sunnah. However, its being the intended meaning of the hadith here is an aberration on the part of the one who said it, and it is to be rejected. Most particularly so in the light of other hadiths that have come, making clear and certain the intended meaning here. For example, his saying: "How excellent dates are for the *saḥūr*;"[138] and: "the whole of the *saḥūr* is blessing. So do not leave it, even if [it be] that one of you swallows a gulp of water."[139]

Another example is an interpretation of the hadiths that have appeared on the Anti-Christ (*Masīḥ al-Dajjāl*), from the evil of the ordeal of whom we are commanded to seek refuge in God in every prayer. The interpretation is to the effect that the Dajjāl symbolizes the now dominant Western civilization, because it is single-minded (that quality being represented in the Dajjāl's being one-eyed). It looks to life and humanity with just one eye or viewpoint (the material one) and nothing more, so that what goes beyond that, it does not see – so man has no spirit; the creature has no God; and after this life of the world there is no hereafter. This interpretation is opposed to what many hadiths have established – that the Dajjāl is a single individual, who walks here and there, who enters and departs, who summons and seduces and ruins, etc., all that the hadiths have authenticated about the matter. Moreover, these reports are of the rank of *tawātur* (reported by many from many).

Another example of that is the interpretation, by some moderns among the Muslims, of the hadiths that have come on the descent of the Messiah at the end of time. These likewise are hadiths of the rank of *tawātur*, as all the leading hadith experts have explained.[140] The interpretation is that the descent of the Messiah symbolizes an age in which peace and security will predominate, it being widely and popularly supposed that the Messiah is he who will call to peace and tolerance among humankind. This interpretation contradicts completely what the *ṣaḥīḥ* hadiths have demonstrated about the coming of the Messiah: they have described him as the contrary of that: "Ibn Maryam will come down as a just ruler, breaking the crosses, and slaughtering the pigs, and removing the *jizya*",[141] for none will then accept other than Islam. That is but one contradiction of all the contradictions of this interpretation. Even so, it is an interpretation that conforms to the opinions of the ill-meaning and ill-doing missionaries and orientalists, who claim that Islam is a religion of the sword, while Christianity alone is the religion of peace! This, in spite of what the Messiah says in the Gospel (Matthew 10: 34): "Think not that I am come to send peace on earth: I came not to send peace, but a sword." Indeed, some Westerner said that the Messiah did not speak the truth so fully in any of his prophecies as in this one. Perhaps that understanding is why Christendom has been given to so much warring and bloodshed, even within itself – in recent times, the two world wars, whose harvest was scores of millions of human lives.

IBN TAYMIYYAH'S REJECTION OF THE FIGURATIVE

I am aware that Shaykh al-Islam Ibn Taymiyyah rejected the figurative in the Qur'an and the hadith, and in the language, in general terms, and he backed that rejection with diverse arguments and considerations. I know likewise his motives for this opinion. He wanted to bolt the door against those who go to extremes in interpretation of what is connected to the Attributes of God. Ibn Taymiyyah called them '*al-Muʿattilah*'. For them, God's Attributes become all but bare negatives, with no positive in them; so (in effect) they deny, instead of affirming, the Attributes. Ibn Taymiyyah wanted to revive the position that the early generations of the Companions (*salaf*) were on. So he established about God, what He established about Himself in His Book and on the tongue of His Messenger; and he rejected about Him what the Qur'an and the Sunnah rejected about Him. However, in doing that he went to the extreme of rejecting the figurative from the language as a whole.

Now Ibn Taymiyyah is one of the scholars of the Community most dear – perhaps even the very dearest – to my heart. But I approach them with my reason, and I differ from him here, just as he differed from the imams before him. So too he taught us that we should think, and not follow blindly, and that we should follow the proofs and not the individuals, and that we should know the men by the truth, and not the truth by the men. So I love Ibn

Taymiyyah, but I am not a Taymiyyan. Al-Dhahabī said: "Shaykh al-Islam is dear to us; but the truth is dearer to us than he."

Yes: I am with the Shaykh al-Islam in what concerns the attributes of God, what is connected to the world of the Unseen, and the conditions of the hereafter. So it is better that we should not plunge recklessly into imagining referents for Him without proof. It is better not to pretend to knowledge of what we do not know, and to refer it to the Knower of it. We say what those deeply-rooted in knowledge say: "We believe in it; all [of it] is from our Lord" (*Āl ʿImrān*, 3: 7).

This is what I wished to throw some light on in the following section.

VII

DISTINGUISHING THE UNSEEN AND THE VISIBLE

The Sunnah presents subjects related to 'the world of the Unseen', some of them are connected to perspectives other than of this our world – for example, the angels, to the host of whom God has assigned diverse duties: "And none knows the hosts of your Lord except He" (*al-Mudaththir*, 74: 31); or the jinn, inhabitants of the earth, under obligations like us, some of whom see us but we do not see them; and among them the satans, the hosts of Iblīs, who swore before God that he would mislead us and make the false and the evil seem good to us: He said: "By Your power I will certainly mislead everyone of them except those of Your slaves among them of pure heart (*mukhliṣīn*)" (*Ṣād*, 38: 82–83). And among other examples of the same: the Throne, the Chair, the Tablet and the Pen.

Some of these elements of the Unseen are related to the life in the *barzakh*, the interval of life after death and before the resurrection of the Hour – for example, in connection with the interrogation in the grave, and its blessings or its torments. Some of them are related to the life of the hereafter itself – the sending out from the graves, the gathering and the standing, the conditions of the Day of Resurrection, and the supreme intercession, and the Balance and the Reckoning, and the Path, and the ranks of the people therein, and the Fire and the classes of torment therein, touching the senses and the spirit, and the descending degrees of the people therein. All these matters, or most of them, the Qur'an has set out, and the Sunnah has expanded upon and detailed what is summary in the Qur'an.

We are bound to point out that some of the hadiths that have appeared on this do not reach the rank of *ṣaḥīḥ*, which is expected of them, so it is not proper that they be gathered in a discourse on this subject. The discourse should be limited to only the hadiths of the Messenger which are established and authenticated. The duty of the Muslim scholar here is to accept what he has verified as established, according to the principles of the people of knowledge and those of the early generations of the Community who were followed. Rejection of a text is not permitted merely on account of its opposition to what is familiar to us; nor on account of the occurrence of it seeming to us far-fetched in relation to what is familiar to us, so long as it falls within the sphere of the rationally possible. Now there surely is what we customarily consider to be impossible. Yet we also know that even mere human beings have been capable (by virtue of what comes from knowledge) of making things once considered to be in the order of the impossible. Indeed, if such things were reported to predecessors, those who reported them would be represented as madmen. How dare we then measure the power of God, which lacks for nothing in the earth or in the heavens?

For this reason, our scholars affirmed as a principle that the religion brings what reason can marvel at, but it is not possible that it has brought what reason parts from. Accordingly, the authentically conveyed tradition is not contradicted in any circumstance, nor the plainly and clearly reasoned.

One does not suppose any mutual contradiction between the two. It is inevitable that error can indeed have arisen, but only in what has been conveyed but is not authentic, or what has been reasoned but is not plain and clear. I mean matters related to what man considers to be of the religion is not among the truths of the religion, or what he considers to be derived from knowledge or reason is not definitively related to knowledge or reason.

Some schools of thought and Islamic sects surely went to extremes, for example the Muʿtazilis, in rejecting some of the *ṣaḥīḥ* hadiths that seemed far-fetched to their reason. We have seen this in the attitude of some of them to the hadiths that speak of the interrogation by the two angels in the grave, and what ensues of blessing or punishment. Among other examples are: their attitude to the hadith of the Balance[142] and the Path; to the believers' seeing God in the Garden; and to some hadiths that speak about the jinn and their relationship to human beings. Al-Shāṭibī said in his valuable book *al-Iʿtiṣām*:

> It is from the habit-patterns of the people of innovation and deviation that they reject hadiths which entailed non-conformity with their prejudices and doctrines, and made propaganda that [these hadiths] were opposed to what can be reasoned, and [were] without proximity to what [rational] demonstration has necessitated, and so rejection of them was obligatory.
>
> So they are deniers of the punishment of the grave, and the Path and the Balance, and the seeing of God, Mighty and Glorious is He, in the hereafter. In the same way [they deny] the hadith of the fly and its dipping, and that in one of its wings there is harm, and in the other healing, and that it puts in first the one in which there is harm;[143] and the hadith of the one who came complaining about his brother's stomach and the Prophet advised him to drink honey;[144] and what is like that in the *ṣaḥīḥ* hadiths conveyed by people of honorable record.
>
> At times they slandered the narrations from some of the Companions and the Successors – and they are far from deserving that – [whereas] the leading hadith scholars were agreed on their being upright men worthy to be followed. All that they rejected, according to what opposed them in their doctrine. At times they also rejected [the Companions'] fatwas and reviled them in the hearing of the general public so that they frightened the Community away from following the Sunnah and the people of the Sunnah.

They made speaking about the Path or the Balance or the Pool being established and proven a speaking of which one makes no sense! Then indeed one of them asked: "Is unbelief attributed to the one who affirms the [believers'] seeing God in the hereafter?" Then he said: "No. He has not unbelieved insofar as he has said what makes no sense. And one who has said what makes no sense is not an unbeliever."

One faction went to [the position of] negating the reports of the single narrators out of hand, and restricting [what they would accept] according to what pleased their reason in understanding the Qur'an, to the extent that they made wine permissible from His saying, Exalted is He: "There shall be no sin on account of what they consumed upon those who believe and do righteous deeds" (*al-Mā'idah*, 5: 93).

And about those and the like of them God's Messenger said: "Let me not find one of you reclining on his couch: there comes to him one of my commands with what he is commanded [to do] or he is forbidden from [doing], and he says, 'I am not aware [of that]. We did not find our following it [commanded] in the Book of God.'"[145] This is a severe warning, including in it [the warning against] denial [of the Sunnah]. It does not justify the one who perpetrates the crime of rejecting the Sunnah.[146]

Of the same sort as that are the far-fetched calls (from some contemporaries) to reworking of the *ṣaḥīḥ* hadith: "In the Garden there is assuredly a tree in whose shade a rider may travel for a hundred years without crossing through it." The hadith is one agreed upon. The two Shaykhs have narrated it from Sahl ibn Saʿd, and from Abū Saʿīd, and from Abū Hurayrah.[147] Al-Bukhārī has also narrated it from Anas. On this point Ibn Kathīr said in his *tafsīr* of the verse: "And spreading shade" (*al-Wāqiʿah*, 56: 30) – "This hadith from God's Messenger is well-established, indeed definitively *mutawātir* in being *ṣaḥīḥ* according to the leaders of hadith scholarship."

The outward sense is that the hundred years are the years of this world. For this reason, it is said in the narration of Abū Saʿīd: "The rider may travel on a horse specially trained for speed." The outward of this is, again, that it is in this world, but none knows except God the kind of anything between the time of this world and the time of the world that is with God: "And surely one day with your Lord is like a thousand years of what you count" (*al-Ḥajj*, 22: 47). When a hadith has been authenticated there is no scope for us except to say we are content: we believe and we affirm the truth of it, being certain that the particular norms in the hereafter are different from the norms of this world. That is so far so that Ibn ʿAbbās said: "There is nothing from the world in the Garden except the names!"

An example of that is what has come on the punishment of the unbelievers in the Fire: the heaviness of the unbeliever's molar teeth; the distance between his two shoulders; the coarseness of his skin; etc. The acceptance of such hadiths as they are worded is more salutary. As for inquiry into the details thereof – there is no avail in it. The fortunate preacher should not preoccupy the minds of his readers or his audience with this class of hadiths, whose subject-matter gives rise to ambiguities in the contemporary mind, and on knowledge of which neither the practicability of the religion nor contentment in this world are dependent. Only what is appropriate should be mentioned according to the exigency.

Foremost among the things that the Muslim should busy his soul with: to ask of God the Garden, and whatever of speech or act brings him nearer to it, and that by which he may seek refuge from the Fire and from whatever of speech or act brings him nearer to it; and that he behave with the behavior of the people of the Garden, and keep far from his soul the behavior of the dwellers of the Fire. The sound attitude that is incumbent upon him is the logic of faith; and the logic of reason is not incumbent upon him. It is incumbent upon us that we say about all that has been established of the religion in respect of the unseen things: We believe in and we affirm the truth thereof; just as we say about all that has come to us in respect of acts of worship: "We have heard and we obey."

Certainly! We believe in what the text has come to us with, and we do not question about its essence or its modality; nor do we inquire into the details of it. For our intellects are often helpless to comprehend these matters of the Unseen. God, who created man, did not fit him for the like of this perception, because he did not need that for the execution of his duties in the stewardship of the earth (*khilāfah*), and the raising up of its structure, and the worship of God therein.

Now if the school of rational theology, which the Muᶜtazilis exemplify, had been guided to the perception of this truth and the acceptance of it, they would not have needed to reject the *ṣaḥīḥ* hadiths, which establish the believers' seeing of God in the hereafter, and their seeing their Lord as they see the moon on the night of full moon. And the simile is for the seeing distinctly, not for that which is seen, in connection with the outward meaning of the Qur'an, whose interpretation they have caricatured – for example the verse: "That day faces will be radiant, looking toward their Lord" (*al-Qiyāmah*, 75: 22–23).

The fundamental error which has occurred in this is the analogical likening of the Unseen to the visible, of what is to come (hereafter) with what precedes it (in this world). It is a dubious mode of analogy – analogy to the dissimilar – and every mode has its norms and established patterns. For this reason the people of the Sunnah affirm the seeing, together with their consensus that it is not on the pattern of the familiar seeing with the seeing-faculty that is known to us. Rather, it is – as Muhammad ᶜAbduh said – a seeing without modality and without boundaries, and the like of it cannot be except by the seeing-faculty that God will particularly designate for that purpose, for the people of the abode of the hereafter. Or He will make particular alteration in the seeing-faculty so that it then becomes unlike the familiar form known in the life of this world. It is something of which knowledge is not possible for us; nevertheless, we affirm the reality of it when the report of it has been authenticated.[148]

Rashīd Riḍā adhered to the discourse of his teacher (ᶜAbduh) on the means of the seeing in the hereafter. He said:

> The prehension [grasping] of reality belongs to the spirit; and the senses [sight, hearing, etc.] are its instruments. Moreover, it

> is established by the definitive experiments of the scientists of the east and the west in this age that among people there is one who sees and reads while his eyes are blindfolded, in [something] they call reading of concepts; and he sees some things [though] not others in the act of dreaming; and among them [there is another] one who sees a thing despite many veils; and [what is] remote and far away [he sees] like one [directly present and] watching [...]. So then this confirms about the seeing of all people in this world [what is] in opposition to the familiar [modes of seeing]. So does it befit one who has sense that he should be dubious about what, in the Garden, is stranger than [that], and further from the familiar? And [the Garden] is a world of the Unseen, different in its patterns and conventions than the world of the visible. And is the dubiety about and rejection of the seeing [of God in the hereafter] otherwise than on account of an analogy between the world of the Unseen and this world in respect of the seeing and the being seen? It is a vain, false analogy. Its falsehood in respect of the being seen is more evident [than in respect of the seeing].[149]

VIII

ADOPTING THE LEXICAL MEANINGS OF THE WORDS

It is of the utmost importance, for a correct understanding of the Sunnah, to adopt the lexical meanings of the words in which the Sunnah has come. For words surely change in their connotations from one epoch to another, and from one locale to another. This is a matter well known to students of the evolution of languages and vocabularies, and the traces of time and place in that evolution.

CAUTION AGAINST READING CURRENT TERMS INTO OLD TEXTS

People agree by convention on certain words denoting particularized meanings, so there is no dispute among them about terminology. However, the source of anxiety here is the interpretation of what has come in the Sunnah – and another example of that is the

Qur'an – in words belonging to current terminology, and here flaws and errors occur.

Al-Ghazālī informed us about the alteration of terms, in some of the names of the sciences, to meanings removed from what they denoted in the generations of the *salaf*. He cautioned against the danger of this alteration and its misleading those who did not go deeply into the definition of what was being understood. In *al-Iḥyā'*, he addressed a valuable section in his *Kitāb al-ʿIlm* to that. In it he said:

> Know that the source of the confusion of the reproved disciplines in the sciences of the Law is the distortion of the approved names and their alteration. They have been conveyed with ill-intentioned objectives to [introduce] meanings other than what the righteous *salaf* intended. [In] the first century: there were five words – *fiqh* (jurisprudence), *ʿilm* (knowledge, science), *tawḥīd* (God's Oneness), *tadhkīr* (reminding), *ḥikmah* (wisdom) – now these are approved names, by [derivatives from] which are signified office-holders of high dignity in the religion. But nowadays they are conveyed with disapproved meanings. Then the hearts [of people who knew better] shied away from disapproving those who were qualified with their meanings, so that the application of these names to them spread.[150]

Al-Ghazālī elaborated that, may God have mercy on him, in a number of pages. If there were, at that time, these five words, the change in which in the field of science al-Ghazālī took note of, there are now innumerable words in diverse fields that have changed.

Over time this alteration did not fade away. Rather, it widened along with the change in epoch and locale and human development, to the point that there arose a far-reaching gulf between the original Legal connotations of the words, and the connotations known later or used in current idiom. And therein lies the source of unintended error and false understanding, as also of willful deviation and distortion. That is what the brilliant and truth-seeking scholars of the Community cautioned against: namely, reducing the words of the Law to the idioms current with the passing of the ages.

TWO WORDS: *TAṢWĪR* AND *NAḤT*

Whoever does not take due care in this discipline will fall into many errors – as we see in our age. Take for example the word *taṣwīr* (image) which has come in *ṣaḥīḥ* and agreed-upon hadiths. What is the intended meaning of it in the hadiths which threaten those who make images (*muṣawwir*) with the severest torment?

Many of those who preoccupy themselves with hadith and fiqh include under this threat those called *muṣawwir* in our age, a term embracing whoever uses that device called 'the camera', and they put this 'copying a form' (*shakl*) together with what is more properly called an image (*ṣūrah*). But is this naming – calling the operator of the camera a maker of images (*muṣawwir*), and his action image-making (*taṣwīran*) – a linguistically correct naming? No one claims that, when the Arabs coined a usage that occurred to their hearts for this matter, it was not a lexically correct naming. But, at the same time, no one claims that this naming is to do with the Law, because this sort of art or skill was not known in the age of its Legislation. No one imagined that the word *muṣawwir* would apply to the operator of a camera, for the device was then non-existent.

So who then calls him *muṣawwir*, and his action *taṣwīran*? Indeed it is the current usage that does so, it is we Arabs who do so, or we find the ones who demonstrate this art or skill in their time, and we apply to it the name *taṣwīr*, and we mean by it: 'photography'.

It is possible that people call it something else and adopt that as their usage. One such possibility is their naming it *ʿaks* (reflection, reverse, contrast) and call the one who practices it *ʿakkās*, as the people of Qatar and the Gulf do. So if one of them goes to the *muṣawwir* (or *ʿakkās*) and says to him: I want you to 'take a picture of me (*taʿakisu-nī*)'; and the other says to him: 'At what time shall I 'take pictures' (*ʿukūs*) of you? – their conversation is nearer to the reality of the action. For it is not more than a reflection of the form taken by a particular device, just as the form is reflected in the device of a mirror. This is what the learned Shaykh Muḥammad Bakhīt al-Muṭīʿī, the mufti of the lands of Egypt in his time, said in his treatise *al-Jawāb al-Kāfī fī Ibāḥat al-Taṣwīr al-Fūtūghrāfī.*

Just as, in our time, the (photographic) image is called by the term *ʿaks*, an embodied image used to be called *naḥt* (something worked in wood or stone): it is what the scholars of the *salaf* considered as being 'that which has a shadow'. They agreed upon its being forbidden except in the games of children. Now, would calling this (photographic) image *naḥt* take it out of the sphere of what the texts have brought the threat against, in respect of both image and image-makers? The answer is negative emphatically. Because what takes it out of the sphere of that threat is not this name or another, but its nature and function.

In the first place this (photographic) image is that to which the word 'image', in the sense understood in the Law, does not apply in the language or in the Law, because that, to which 'image' in that sense is properly applied, is what resembles and has been made to resemble the creation of God, because the creation of God and its 'image' is an embodied creation, as in the *ṣaḥīḥ ḥadīth qudsī*: "Among the greatest wrongdoers from those who go about is [he who] creates like My creation."

THE OBLIGATION OF PRECAUTION IN COMMENTING ON INDIVIDUAL WORDS OR SENTENCES

One who comments on the eloquent text of a great man of letters or a great poet must study it closely and make fine distinctions in his commentary until he has explained the intended meaning of the text. The research gives expression to the purposes of the author of the text, and it sustains the meaning commensurate with the rhetorical norms of the writer. This is more obligatory and necessary when the text is a religious or sacred one, such as the text of the Qur'an, or a text of the Prophet, which attained the summit of human eloquence, and which turned within the horizon of the Qur'an, clarifying and detailing from the Prophet what was in the Book revealed to him. God gave him weighty sayings (epitomes and maxims), and He taught him the Book and the Wisdom, and He taught him what he did not know, and it was a tremendous favor of God upon him.

It is enough for some words that one refers to the dictionary of the language for their explanation, and the books on the strange materials in the hadith, though with a need for subtlety and refinement in the use of such resources. We find of some words that they shift from the literal to the figurative, from the plainly evident to the secret or hidden. From some words, from the literal ones of the language, the Law is derived, and these were accorded a new meaning not well-known before the appearance of the Law – for example, words related to cleansing of the body (*wuḍu'*, *tayammum*), and to the prayer rite, and the like. Some words are not understood except in the light of their context, and their purposes, and their local and historical situations, as we explained in section IV above.

We have seen how contemporaries, who have intruded what is foreign into the sciences of the Law, play in commentary on the words of the Qur'an and the hadith. It is a matter of regret to all with a kernel of knowledge, and to all with a conscience, for these are commentaries that do not rely upon the logic of religion or of language or of science. They are following only caprice and, as Ibn ʿAbbās puts it, caprice is the worst of what is worshipped on earth: "Have you seen him who makes his caprice his god? God causes him to stray knowingly and seals up his hearing and his heart and makes a covering over his eyes? Then who will guide him after God?" (*al-Jāthiyah*, 45: 23).

Epilogue

In concluding this inquiry we must affirm that the Sunnah of the Prophet is the Muslims' second source of guidance, the reference accompanying the Book of God in the field of Legislation, Legal judgment and fiqh, and in the field of preaching, instruction and education. We must affirm also that the Sunnah is in need of a service befitting its rank and station in Islam, and the standing of the Community at the beginning of the fifteenth century Hijri (the twenty-first of the Christian era). This service must look for its support to the foundations of Islamic knowledge, so that it presents to the world food that is wholesome, fruit that is ripened, and shade that is welcoming in its spaciousness.

The Sunnah is in need of an encyclopedia of the narrators of hadith, including all of them, and all that has been said about them by way of description and characterization, of their trustworthiness or weakness, even of there being among them forgers and frauds. Also needed is an encyclopedia of the texts of the hadiths with their *sanad*s and all their routes, the whole of what has been transmitted as *sunnah* from the person of the Messenger, from every possible source, and covering all manuscript and printed sources to the end of the second third of the fifth century AH.

These two wide domains prepare the way for the third. And this is the manifest aim behind the whole task: the selection, out of the all-inclusive domain, of the domain of the *ṣaḥīḥ* and the *ḥasan*. Such selection must be in agreement with the standards of the precise science, whose foundations the brilliant and critical pioneers of the scholars of the Community laid down. Their effort and achievement is what makes it so important that, first and foremost, those people of the Remembrance, who had a special competence, are read before any contemporary scholars.

Alongside that, it is necessary that this spacious domain of the selected (*ṣaḥīḥ* and *ḥasan*) hadiths is arranged in a new and comprehensive arrangement, indexed with an up-to-date inclusive index. It is necessary too that the thematic arrangement is organized to serve all religious, human and social sciences, and other sciences with which the Sunnah is concerned, and from whose different fields inquirers can benefit. Of particular usefulness in all this – from all that God has taught man in this age and made subservient to him, such as medicines and developed appliances – is the most prominent of those advanced appliances, namely the computer. One Muslim has called it 'the *ḥāfiẓ* of our age'. But it is more than a *ḥāfiẓ*, having more than a capacity for memory. If we excel in benefiting from it, it can enable us to make progress in the service of knowledge, in terms of volume, precision and diversity of the kinds of information we can manage. The pioneers in the service of the Sunnah did not dream of these things, nor did they occur to them. I am hopeful that the Center for Research in the Sunnah and Sīrah in Qatar will make progress, with the help of similar centers and institutes, in its intended role in this field.

Then, the Sunnah is in need of new commentaries, elucidating its truths, making plain the obscurities in it, rectifying the ways of understanding it, and rejecting what is dubious or vain and false. These commentaries should be written in the tongue and idiom of the people in this age, so that we may explain the Sunnah to them effectively.

The Qur'an certainly has won the approbation in our age – and it is its right – of some great scholars. In commentary on it and discovery of its blessings and its jewels, they have addressed, with what has been granted to them of knowledge and culture, the propositions of contemporary reason. This enabled them to put into hearts and minds the most wide-ranging divisions of subject-matter. We have seen that in the Qur'an commentaries of Rashīd Riḍā, Jamāl al-Dīn al-Qāsimī, al-Ṭāhir ibn Āshūr, Abū al-Aʿlā al-

Mawdūdī, Sayyid Quṭb, Muhammad Shaltūt, Muhammad al-Ghazālī, and others.

The books of the Sunnah – and especially the two *Ṣaḥīḥ*s – have not yet been so fortunate in the commentaries of the like of those outstanding people, who reconciled the original and the new in commenting on the Qur'an. Here we must mention the praiseworthy endeavors in commentary on the four books of *Sunan* by colleagues and fellow-Muslims among the scholars of India and Pakistan. But in these commentaries the temperament of copying and imitating predominates, and they do not interact with modern ideas and culture. It may be that God will enable some great preacher to do a commentary on the *Ṣaḥīḥ*s of the two Shaykhs, al-Bukhārī and Muslim, that is at the same time learned and modern. By that Islamic culture would be rendered a conspicuous service.

And, concluding, our prayer:

Praise and thanks belong to God, Lord and Sustainer of all beings.

Notes

NOTES TO CHAPTER ONE

1 [*Ṣalla Allāhu ʿalayhi wa sallam* (the prayer and blessing of God be upon him and peace): a reminder to readers that Muslims say these or similar words after every mention of the Prophet. — Trans.]

2 ['Acceptance' is the literal translation of *taqrīr*. The Prophet was bound, by his duty to give guidance, to express disapproval if he witnessed something wrong. His non-disapproval of something that he witnessed is accordingly understood to mean his acceptance of it. —Trans.]

3 [*Raḍiya Allāhu ʿanha* (may God be pleased with her): a reminder to readers that Muslims say words of this meaning after mention of Companions of the Prophet, and other revered figures. —Trans.]

4 Muslim narrated it in the words "His character was the Qur'an". Also Aḥmad ibn Ḥanbal narrated it, Abū Dā'ūd, and al-Nasā'ī. Cited in Ibn Kathīr's *tafsīr* of *Sūrah Nūn*.

5 As in the verse: "God has certainly shown grace to the believers when He sent among them a Messenger from among themselves who recites to them His signs and purifies them and teaches them the Book and the Wisdom, whereas they were before in manifest error" (3: 164). And addressing the womenfolk of the Prophet: "Keep in mind what is recited in your houses from the Revelation of God and the Wisdom" (33: 34). There is no one with more right to embody the explanation of the Qur'an and the teaching of Islam than the one to whom the Qur'an was revealed and to whom God entrusted the duty of explaining it to the people – and that one was His Messenger.

6 Al-Bukhārī and Muslim narrated it from Anas.

7 Al-Bukhārī narrated it in *Kitāb al-Sawm.*

8 Muslim narrated it from Abū Hurayrah.

9 Muslim and others narrated it.

10 Al-Ḥākim (vol. 2, p. 375) narrated it and authenticated it, and al-Dhahabī confirmed it. Al-Haythamī said in *al-Majmuʿa* (vol. 1, p. 171): "al-Bazzār narrated it and al-Ṭabarānī in *al-Kabīr*; and its *isnād*

(chain of transmitting authorities) is good, and its narrators (*rijāl*) trustworthy."

11 Muslim and Aḥmad ibn Ḥanbal narrated it from Abū Mūsā.

12 Muslim narrated it.

13 See our book *Malāmiḥ al-Mujtamaᶜ al-Muslim* (The characteristics of a Muslim society), ch. *al-Lahw wa al-Funūn* (amusement and arts). See also our treatise *al-Islam wa al-Fann* (Islam and art).

14 Ibn Saᶜd narrated it and al-Ḥakīm al-Tirmidhī as a *mursal* (disconnected) hadith from Abū Ṣāliḥ. Al-Ḥākim narrated it also from him from Abū Hurayrah as a *mawṣūl* (connected) hadith, authenticating it according to the criterion of the two Shaykhs, al-Bukhārī and Muslim, and al-Dhahabī agreed with that. Al-Albānī has authenticated it: see the exposition in our book, *al-Ḥalāl wa al-Ḥarām*, hadith no. 1.

15 Muslim narrated it in *Kitāb al-Talāq*, hadith no. 1478.

16 Agreed upon, from the hadith of Abū Mūsā and Muᶜādh: *al-Lu'lu' wa al-Murjān*, hadith no. 2130.

17 Agreed upon, from the hadith of Anas, *al-Lu'lu' wa al-Murjān*, hadith no. 1131.

18 Al-Bukhāri narrated it, and al-Nasā'ī and al-Tirmidhī, in *Kitāb al-Ṭahārah* from Abū Hurayrah.

19 Al-Ṭabarānī narrated it from Abū Umāmah. In its *sanad* (chain of transmitting authorities) there is a weak narrator, as explained in *Majmaᶜ al-Zawā'id* (vol. 4, p. 302). Al-Khaṭīb and others also narrated it from Jābir by a weak route. In *Fayḍ al-Qadīr* it is said: "But it has three routes so it is not improbable that, because of [that], it will not be deprived of the rank of *ḥasan*." See: *Ghāyat al-Marām* of al-Albānī, hadith no. 8. Ibn Ḥajar cited it in *al-Fatḥ* (vol. 2, p. 444) from al-Sarrāj by way of Abū Zinād from ᶜUrwah from ᶜĀ'ishah in the story of the playing of the Abyssinians in the mosque, and therein: "the Jews should know that in our religion there is space [latitude]. [He said:] 'Indeed I was commissioned with a tolerant true-religion.' What Aḥmad [ibn Ḥanbal] narrated from Ibn ᶜAbbās testifies to [that]: 'It was said to the Messenger of God: "Which of the religions is dearer to God?" He said: "The tolerant true-religion".' Al-Haythamī said: 'Aḥmad [ibn Ḥanbal] narrated it and al-Ṭabarānī in *al-Kabīr* and *al-Awsaṭ*, and al-Bazzār, wherein [it is said]: "Ibn Isḥāq: he [was] a *mudallis* [one who did not name his teacher, claiming instead to narrate directly from his teacher's teacher]"''" (vol. 1, p. 60). Al-Bukhārī made a note of that in his *Ṣaḥīḥ*.

20 Agreed upon, from ʿĀ'ishah: *Ṣaḥīḥ al-Jāmiʿ al-Ṣaghīr*, hadith no. 7887.
21 Muslim narrated it from Ibn Masʿūd.
22 Al-Tirmidhī and al-Ḥākim narrated it from Ibn ʿAmr. Al-Tirmidhī pronounced it *ṣaḥīḥ* in *Ṣaḥīḥ al-Jāmiʿ*.
23 Agreed upon.
24 Muslim narrated it.
25 Aḥmad ibn Ḥanbal and Ibn Ḥibbān narrated it, and al-Bayhaqī in *al-Sunan* from Ibn ʿUmar. Cited in *Ṣaḥīḥ al-Jāmiʿ al-Ṣaghīr*, hadith no. 1775.
26 Aḥmad ibn Ḥanbal and al-Bayhaqī narrated it from Ibn ʿUmar; and al-Ṭabarānī from Ibn ʿAbbās and Ibn Masʿūd. Ibid, hadith no. 1775.
27 Abū Dā'ūd narrated it from Jābir. In it there is also the following: "It was quite enough for him to have done *tayammum*."
28 Ibn al-Qayyim cited the tradition in *Miftaḥ Dār al-Saʿādah* (Beirut: Dār al-Kutub al-ʿIlmiyyah), vol. 1, pp. 163–64, and reckoned it strong by the multiplicity of its routes of transmission. Similarly, Ibn al-Wazīr demonstrated its being *ṣaḥīḥ* or *ḥasan* by the great number of its routes of transmission, alongside what he conveyed of its authentication by Aḥmad ibn Ḥanbal and Ibn ʿAbd al-Barr, and the weight accorded to its *isnād* by al-ʿUqaylī, as well as the breadth of their thorough enquiries and their trustworthiness. All of that demands adherence to it. See: *al-Rawḍ al-Bāsim fī al-Dhabbi ʿan Sunnah Abī al-Qāsim* (Beirut: Dār al-Maʿrifah, vol. 1, pp. 21–23). See also: *al-Rawḍ al-Bāsim* in al-Albānī's *Takhrīj* (commentary on) *Fawā'id Tammām*.
29 Aḥmad ibn Ḥanbal narrated it, also Nasā'ī, Ibn Mājah, al-Ḥākim, Ibn Khuzaymah and Ibn Ḥibbān, from Ibn ʿAbbās. Cited in *Ṣaḥīḥ al-Jāmiʿ al-Ṣaghīr* and its *Supplement*, hadith no. 2680.
30 Muslim narrated it in *Kitāb al-ʿIlm* in his *Ṣaḥīḥ*.
31 See the chapter *Sū' al-Ta'wīl* ('bad interpretation') in our book *al-Murjiʿiyyah al-ʿUlyā fī al-Islām*, pp. 297–330.
32 See ibid, pp. 298–99.
33 [The rationale here is that if a Companion reports on (say) a matter connected with the hereafter, of which he could have no personal knowledge and therefore no personal opinion, then what he reports might be accepted as a report from the Prophet, even if its being from the Prophet is not explicitly stated by that Companion. On the other hand, on matters where the Companion could hold a personal opinion as to what is right or preferable for a believer, then the believers who come after are at liberty to take the report, as they

would the report of any esteemed person, as that individual's personal advice or preference, and act accordingly. — Trans.]

34 See what we have written about the Sunnah in our discourse on 'The principles of fiqh made easy' in our book *Taysīr al-Fiqh li al-Muslim al-Muᶜāṣir* (Making fiqh easy for the contemporary Muslim), part 1 (Cairo: Maktab Wahabah).

35 Shaykh ᶜAbd al-Fattāḥ Abū Ghuddah cited that with censure and disparagement in his commentary on Laknawī's *al-Ajwibah al-Fāḍilah*, (2nd edn., Cairo, 1984) pp. 133–34.

36 Al-Shāṭibī's *al-Iᶜtiṣām* (Safeguarding), vol. 1, pp. 235–37.

37 We count among those scholars the jurist, preacher and *mujāhid*, Shaykh Muṣṭafā al-Sibāᶜī, may God have mercy on him, in his worthy and useful book *al-Sunnah wa Makānātu-hā fī al-Tashrīᶜ al-Islāmī.* May God elevate him in honorable status and rank with Him. Also among them: Muhammad Muṣṭafā al-Aᶜẓamī who rebutted Shacht; Shaykh ᶜAbd al-Raḥmān ibn Yaḥyā al-Muᶜallimī al-Yamānī, author of *al-Anwār al-Kāshifah*; Shaykh Muhammad ᶜAbd al-Razzāq Ḥamzah, author of *Ẓulumāt Abī Rayyah*; Shaykh Muhammad Abū Shahbah, author of *Difāᶜ ᶜan al-Sunnah*; ᶜAjjāj al-Khaṭīb in his *al-Sunnah Qabl al-Tadwīn*, and his book about Abū Hurayrah; and others there is not enough space here to mention.

38 This rebuttal was published in papers and periodicals at the time, and in our book *Fatāwā Muᶜāṣirah* (Contemporary fatwas), part 1.

39 See our fatwas in defence of *Ṣaḥīḥ al-Bukhārī* in ibid.

40 See *Ṣaḥīḥ al-Jāmiᶜ al-Ṣaghīr*, no. 1261. Some scholars have alleged that the hadith is *ḍaᶜīf* (weak). But it is the same by way of ᶜĀ'ishah, and it has not come by only the two routes mentioned.

41 Al-Bukhārī and Muslim narrated it from ᶜĀ'ishah. Ibid, no. 1288.

42 Muslim, al-Tirmidhī and Ibn Mājah narrated it from Ibn Masᶜūd. Ibid, no. 1275.

43 Aḥmad ibn Ḥanbal and Muslim narrated it from Saᶜd ibn Abī Waqqās. Ibid, no. 1882.

44 Aḥmad ibn Ḥanbal and al-Ḥākim narrated it, al-Dhahabī authenticated it and agreed it.

45 Al-Ḥākim and al-Bayhaqī narrated it, in the supplication from Anas. *Ṣaḥīḥ al-Jāmiᶜ al-Ṣaghīr*, no. 1285.

46 Abū Dā'ūd narrated it in *Kitāb al-Malāḥim* (Battles) in his *Sunan*, no. 4270; al-Ḥākim in *al-Mustadrak* (vol. 4, p. 522); al-Bayhaqī in *Maᶜrifat al-Sunan wa al-Āthār*, and others. Al-ᶜIrāqī authenticated it, and al-Suyūṭī cited it in *Fayḍ al-Qadīr*, vol. 2, p. 282.

47 See our study: *Tajdīd al-Dīn fī Ḍaw' al-Sunnah* (2nd edn., Qatar: Markaz Buhūth al-Sunnah wa al-Sīrah), p. 29. Also printed in my book: *Min Ajli Saḥwah Rāshidah* (Beirut: al-Maktab al-Islāmī).

48 Al-Ṭabarānī and al-Ḥākim narrated it from Ibn ᶜAmr. Cited in *Ṣaḥīḥ al-Jāmiᶜ al-Ṣaghīr.*

49 From *Kitāb al-Īmān* in Ibn Taymiyyah's *Majmūᶜ al-Fatāwā*, vol. 7, pp. 314–16.

50 Later printed by Mu'assasat al-Risālah in eight volumes, edited by Shuᶜayb al-Arnā'ūṭ.

51 Al-Haythamī cited it in *Majmaᶜ al-Zawā'id* (vol. 10, p. 190), and said: "Aḥmad [ibn Ḥanbal] narrated it, and its [narrators] are sound men." As for the woman's entering the Fire because of her cruelty to the cat, it is so narrated from Abū Hurayrah by the two Shaykhs and others. See: *Ṣaḥīḥ al-Jāmiᶜ al-Ṣaghīr*, hadith no. 3374.

52 See ibid, the two hadiths, nos. 3995, 3996.

53 Ibid.

NOTES TO CHAPTER TWO

1 Al-Shawkānī *Irshād al-Fuḥūl* (Cairo: Muṣṭafā al-Halabī), p. 33.

2 Ibid. He has attributed it to Yaḥyā ibn Abī Kathīr. Ibn ᶜAbd al-Barr cites it in *Jāmiᶜ Bayan al-ᶜIlm wa Faḍli-hī* (Beirut: al-Muṣawwirah ᶜan al-Munīriyyah), vol. 2, p. 192.

3 Ibid., pp. 191–92.

4 *Irshād al-Fuḥūl*, p. 33.

5 Ibn Khaldūn, *Muqaddimah* (ed. ᶜAlī ᶜAbd al-Wāḥid Wāfī; Beirut: Lajnat al-Bayān al-ᶜArabī, 2nd edn.) vol. 3, pp. 1143–45.

6 That is, that they were not contradicting the *ṣaḥīḥ* and *ṣarīḥ* hadiths with mere opinion, not opposing their own judgments to the revelation of their Lord. Of course, this does not forbid questions seeking explanation and proof. Indeed, how could it be otherwise when the Companions themselves used to ask questions of the Prophet, so that matters were clarified and they were convinced.

7 Al-Suyūṭī, *Miftāḥ al-Jannah*, pp. 49–50.

8 See Ibn Ḥajar, *al-Dirāyah fī al-Hidāyah* (ed. Hāshim al-Yamānī), vol. 2, pp. 205–13.

9 See *Muqqadimah* in *Maᶜrifat al-Sunan wa al-Āthār* in the critical edition of al-Sayyid Aḥmad Saqr (Cairo: al-Majlis al-Aᶜlā li al-Shu'ūn al-Islāmiyyah).

10 See our discourse on this hadith in *al-Ṣaḥwat al-Islāmiyyah bayna al-Ikhtilāf al-Mashrūᶜ wa al-Tafarruq al-Madhmūm* under the heading *'al-ikhtilāf raḥmah'*. The hadith is not established, but its meaning is correct (*ṣaḥīḥ*) if it imports differences in understanding of details, if it does not tend to contention and dissent except in the way that the Companions held differences on such points of fiqh.

11 See the chapter *'Diyat Ahl al-Dhimmah'* in al-Shawkānī, *Nayl al-Awṭār*, vol. 7, pp. 221–24.

12 See the chapter *'Diyat al-Mar'ah'* in ibid., pp. 224–27.

13 He has since finished the work; it has appeared in three volumes.

14 Because it is a narration from ᶜAlī ibn Yazīd al-Albānī. Al-Bukhārī said about him: he is a *munkar* (that is, a weak narrator who brings hadiths that conflict with hadiths from reliable narrators). Al-Nasā'ī said: "He is not trustworthy." Al-Daraquṭnī said: "He is rejected [when he reports] from al-Qāsim Abū ᶜAbd al-Raḥmān." Aḥmad ibn Ḥanbal said about him: "ᶜAlī ibn Yazīd reports from him [al-Qāsim] the most strange [things]!" Ibn Ḥibbāṇ said: "He used to narrate from the Companions *muᶜdillāt* [hadiths with *isnād*s broken in two or more places], and bring from the trustworthy [narrators] *maqlubāt* [hadiths with the *isnād* and the *matn* mixed up]!"

15 Published by the Center for Research in the Sunnah and Sīrah in Qaṭar. It was later printed in Beirut by al-Maktab al-Islāmī, and in Cairo by al-Dār al-Islāmiyyah li-l-Tawzīᶜ, with a supplement of revisions, source-critique, and annotations.

16 *Al-Fatāwā al-Sharᶜiyyah* (Beirut: Dār al-Maᶜrifah), pp. 43–44 (the text cited has been abridged).

17 *Al-Mustadrak*, vol. 1, p. 490.

18 "If we relate from God's Messenger on the lawful and the unlawful, the *sunnah*s and the injunctions, we are strict about the *isnād*s and we criticize [the narrators]. And if we narrate from the Prophet on the virtues of deeds, the reward and punishment [hereafter], the commended [acts] and the supplications, then we relax on the *isnād*s."

19 Al-Khaṭīb, *al-Kifāyah* (al-Madīnah al-Munawwarah: al-Maktab al-ᶜIlm-iyyah), p. 134.

20 Ibn Rajab, *Sharḥ ᶜIlal al-Tirmidhī* (ed. Nūr al-Dīn al-ᶜItr), vol. 1, pp. 72–74.

21 *Tadrīb al-Rāwī ᶜalā Taqrīb al-Nawawī* (ed. ᶜAbd al-Wahhāb ᶜAbd al-Laṭīf; Cairo: Dār al-Ḥadīth), vol. 1, pp. 297, 299.

22 Ibn Rajab, *Sharḥ ᶜIlal al-Tirmidhī*, p. 74.

23 Imam Muslim said in the Preface of his *Ṣaḥīḥ*: "Well then, may God have mercy on you: The proper response to what you requested of discrimination and objective assessment would be easy for us, but for [the following: [1] what we have seen of the evil practice of many of those who give themselves the rank and title of hadith experts – in holding which [title], expelling weak hadiths and rejected nar-rations is incumbent upon them; also, [2] their abandoning the limitation to *ṣaḥīḥ* and famous hadiths from what is conveyed by reliable [narrators] well known for truthfulness and trustworthiness; beyond that, [3] their knowing and their confirming with their tongues that much of the slander against the absent[-minded] ones of the people is detestable; also, [4] the transmission [of reports] from a people not blessed, narration from whom the leading hadith scholars have censured [...] However, on account of what we notified you about – regarding the circulation by the people of rejected reports via weak *isnads* of unknown and weak [narrators], and their bombarding therewith the general public who do not know their defectiveness – it has lightened our heart to answer you what you asked."

24 *Al-Bāʿith al-Ḥathīth: Sharḥ Ikhtiṣār ʿUlūm al-Ḥadīth* (Beirut: Dār al-Kitāb al-ʿIlmiyyah), pp. 91–92. (The text as here quoted has been slightly abridged.)

25 Ibn Ṣalāḥ, *al-Muqaddimah*, and *Maḥāsin al-Iṣtilāḥ* (ed. ʿĀ'ishah ʿAbd al-Raḥmān; al-Hiy'ah al-Miṣriyyah al-ʿĀmmah li-l-Kitāb), p. 217.

26 The hadith is from Ibn Mājah, no. 1388. In its *sanad* there is Abū Bakr ibn ʿAbd Allāh ibn Muhammad ibn Abī Sīrah. Aḥmad ibn Ḥanbal and Ibn Ḥibbān and al-Ḥākim and Ibn ʿAdī have accused him of fabricating the hadith. So too in *Tahdhīb al-Tahdhīb* (there is the same assessment of him).

27 He indicates that, in his view, this hadith is weak despite the number of its routes of transmission. But al-Albānī has pronounced it *ḥasan* in his source-critique of Ibn Taymiyyah's *al-Kalim al-Tayyib.*

28 A part of the hadith – Abū Nuʿaym narrated it in *al-Hilyah* from Ibn ʿUmar. Al-ʿIrāqī pronounced it weak. As cited in *Fayḍ al-Qadīr*, vol. 3, p. 559. Ibn Taymiyyah's discussion of it indicates that he thought it strong.

29 *Majmūʿa Fatāwā Shaykh al-Islām* (Riyadh), vol. 18, pp. 65–67.

30 Ibn Ḥanbal and al-Ḥākim narrated it, and al-Dhahabī authenticated it as *ṣaḥīḥ* and agreed it.

31 See al-Mundhirī, *al-Targhīb* (ed. Muhammad Muḥyī al-Dīn ᶜAbd al-Ḥamīd), hadith no. 4576.

32 In the *Musnad Aḥmad* that Abū Hurayrah said: "I had in my keeping three loads. I distributed two of them." And in *Ṣaḥīḥ al-Bukhārī*, from the hadith of Abū Hurayrah that he said: "From God's Messenger I had two containers. Then as for one of the two, I distributed it. And as for the other, if I had distributed it, this would have cut the windpipes."

33 The ᶜUraniyyūn were a band who approached the Prophet and embraced Islam. They suffered from the climate in Madinah, and he ordered them to come to the camels donated as charity (*ṣadaqah*) and to drink of their milk. They did so and got better. Then they reverted from Islam, killed the camel-herds and drove off their camels. Then he sent people to follow their tracks, and they were brought and punished with a severe and deterrent punishment, until they died. The hadith is in the two *Ṣaḥīḥ*s and other compilations. (Consult *Fatḥ al-Bārī*, vol. 12, p. 98.)

34 The word *abṭala* is used when something comes *bi al-bāṭil*, and *al-baṭalah* stands for witchcraft and the satans. In *Musnad Aḥmad* from the hadith of Abū Umāmah: "Recite *al-Baqarah*. Indeed, taking it is blessing, and leaving it is an affliction, and witchcraft is incapacitated by it [i.e. reciting *al-Baqarah* protects from witchcraft]." And Muslim reported it in *al-Ṣalāh*.

35 So it is in the original. Perhaps it should have read *al-ibāḥiyyah* (meaning 'license'). That was certainly the intent of what was said.

36 The two Shaykhs traced and reported it; also al-Tirmidhī and al-Nasā'ī from the hadith of al-Mughīrah ibn Shuᶜba.

37 *Fatḥ al-Bārī* (Cairo: al-Ḥalabī), vol. 16, p. 227.

38 Ibid.

39 Ibn Mājah narrated it, so also al-Ḥumaydī and al-Ḥākim, from Abū Saᶜīd. Aḥmad ibn Ḥanbal, Ibn Mājah and al-Ṭabarānī, and al-Bayhaqī in *al-Shuᶜab*, narrated it from Abū Umāmah; Ibn Ḥanbal and al-Nasā'ī, and al-Bayhaqī in *al-Shuᶜab*, from Ṭāriq ibn Shihāb. Also al-Ḥākim narrated it from ᶜUmar ibn Qatādah. And others. See *Ṣaḥīḥ al-Jāmiᶜ al-Ṣaghīr* and its *Supplement*, no. 1100.

40 Al-Ḥākim narrated it, and al-Ḍiyā', from Jābir. Al-Albānī pronounced it *ḥasan* in *Ṣaḥīḥ al-Jāmiᶜ al-Ṣaghīr*, no. 3575.

NOTES TO CHAPTER THREE

1 See, on the mythical *gharānīq*, the profound study written up by Muḥammad al-Ṣādiq ʿArjūn, may God have mercy on him, in his book *Muḥammad Rasūl Allāh*, under the heading *'Qiṣṣat al-Gharānīq Ukdhūbah Balhā' Mutazindiqah'*, vol. 2, pp. 30–155.

2 See Ibn al-ʿArabī, *Aḥkām al-Qur'ān* (ʿĪsā al-Ḥalabī), vol. 2, pp. 749–52.

3 See al-Tirmidhī, *Kitāb al-Zakāh, Bāb: 'Mā jā'a fī Zakāt al-Khaḍrāwāt'*; and *Ṣaḥīḥ al-Tirmidhī* with the commentary of Ibn al-ʿArabī, vol. 3, pp. 132–33.

4 Abū Dā'ūd, no. 4717 from Ibn Masʿūd. Ibn Ḥibbān and al-Ṭabarānī have reported the same from al-Hathīm ibn Kalīb. Al-Haythamī said: "Its [narrators] are [narrators] of the *ṣaḥīḥ*" (*al-Fayḍ al-Qadīr*, vol. 6, p. 331).

5 Ibn Ḥanbal and al-Tirmidhī narrated it from Salmah ibn Yazīd al-Juʿfī. Cited in *Ṣaḥīḥ al-Jāmiʿ al-Ṣaghīr.*

6 He narrated it in *Kitāb al-Īmān*, no. 347.

7 *qasba-hu:* that is, his intestines.

8 Agreed upon, from Abū Hurayrah, cited in *al-Lu'lu' wa al-Murjān*, no. 1816. The rest of the hadith is: "Indeed he was the first who sanctified an animal [i.e. made it untouchable] in the name of a god or goddess."

9 For example burying a daughter alive or the like of that act, whose foulness is known to all reasoning beings, and to the followers of all religions.

10 See *Sharḥ* of al-Abbī and al-Sanūsī on *Ṣaḥīḥ Muslim*, vol. 1, pp. 363–73.

11 Ibn Ḥanbal, al-Bukhārī, and Abū Dā'ūd narrated it from ʿImrān ibn Ḥuṣayn. Cited in *Ṣaḥīḥ al-Jāmiʿ al-Ṣaghīr*, no. 8055.

12 Agreed upon, from Jābir. Ibid, no. 7058.

13 Al-Tirmidhī and al-Ḥākim from ʿAbd Allāh ibn Abī al-Jadʿā'. Ibid, no. 8069.

14 Abū Dā'ūd from Abū al-Dardā'. Ibid, no. 8093.

15 Al-Bukhārī from Abū Hurayrah. Ibid, no. 967.

16 Agreed upon, from Abū Hurayrah: *al-Lu'lu' wa al-Murjān*, no. 121.

17 Agreed upon, from Anas. Ibid, no. 122.

18 Agreed upon, from Abū Saʿīd. Ibid, no. 115.

19 Muslim narrated it, and al-Tirmidhī and Ibn Mājah, from Abū Hurayrah: *Ṣaḥīḥ al-Jāmiʿ al-Ṣaghīr*, no. 5176.

20 We have already rebutted this claim in an essay focused on, and reliably established by, the most clear proofs. We called it 'Interces-

sion in the hereafter: between reason and tradition' (Cairo: Dār Nahḍah). We suggested in it that the work of intercession on the Day of Resurrection might be likened to the work of 'committees for extraordinary leniency' in ordinary examinations. Thus, a student may have no just expectation of success if we lay on him measures of strict justice; but if we address him with the logic of leniency, which takes into consideration various extenuating circumstances, and if he can, in light of those, be brought near to the standard of success, he has a right to hope that he will advance from a 'fail' to a 'pass'.

21 *Al-munaffiq* (with doubling of the *fā'* and *kasrah*): *al-murawwij*, namely one who hastens to the quick sale of his commodity and its marketability.

22 Muslim narrated it in *Kitāb al-Īmān* in his *Ṣaḥīḥ*.

23 Ibid.

24 Al-Bukhārī narrated it in *Kitāb al-Libās, Bāb: 'Mā Asfala min al-Kaʿibayn fa-huwa fī al-Nār'*, no. 5787.

25 Al-Nasā'ī narrated in *Kitāb al-Zīnah, Bāb: 'Mā taḥt al-Kaʿibayn min al-Izār'*, vol. 8, p. 207.

26 *Fatḥ al-Bārī* (Dār al-Fikr; a copy of al-Salafiyyah), vol. 10, p. 257.

27 Ibid.

28 Ibid, p. 254, no. 5784.

29 Ibid, no. 5785.

30 Ibid, no. 5788. And *al-baṭar*: self-aggrandizement and arrogance.

31 Ibid, no. 5789. The meaning of "he will be shaking and sinking": he will sink in the earth with a violent buffeting, and he will be falling from one fissure to another.

32 Ibid, no. 5790.

33 *Ṣaḥīḥ Muslim, Bāb: 'Taḥrīm Jarr al-Thawbi Khuyalā'*', with the *Sharḥ* of al-Nawawī (*al-Shuʿab*), vol. 4, p. 790.

34 Ibid, vol. 1, p. 305.

35 *Fatḥ al-Bārī*, vol. 10, p. 263.

36 See our book *al-Ḥalāl wa al-Ḥarām*, the section on clothes and ornaments.

37 Al-Bukhārī mentioned it without *isnād* but in the active voice (implying that he had an *isnād* for it, presented elsewhere). But Ibn Ḥajar stated that there was no *isnād* for it elsewhere. Al-Ṭaylīsī and al-Hārith ibn Abī Usāmah in their *Musnad*s have presented the *isnād* with the hadith of ʿAmr ibn Shuʿayb from his father from his grandfather. In al-Ṭaylīsī's narration the words "without wasteful-

ness, etc." are not found; also lacking in the narration of al-Hārith is the phrase "and give in charity". Ibn Abī al-Dunyā presented the *isnād* with completeness in his book *al-Shukr. Fatḥ al-Bārī*, vol. 10, p. 253.

38 Ibn Ḥajar said: "Ibn Abī Shaybah provided an *isnād* in his *Muṣannaf*." Ibid.

39 Ibid, vol. 10, p. 262.

40 Al-Bukhārī narrated it in *Kitāb al Muzāraᶜah*.

41 Agreed upon, from the hadith of Anas: *al-Lu'lu' wa al-Murjān*, no. 1001.

42 Muslim in *Kitāb al-Musāqāt, Bāb: 'Faḍl al Ziraᶜi wa al-Garsi'*.

43 Ibid.

44 Ibn Ḥanbal narrated it in *Musnad* under 'Anas', vol. 3, pp. 183–84, 191; al-Bukhārī in *al-Adab al-Mufrad*; and al-Albānī (*al-Ṣaḥīḥah*, no. 9) pronounced it *ṣaḥīḥ* by the standard of Muslim (even though it was not included by Muslim in his *Ṣaḥīḥ*). Al-Haythamī presented it abridged in *al-Majmuᶜ*, and said (vol. 4, p. 63): "al-Bazzār narrated and his [narrators] are well-grounded and trustworthy."

45 Al-Suyūṭī, *al-Jāmiᶜ al-Kabīr*. See al-Albānī, *al-Ṣaḥīḥah*, vol. 1, p. 12.

46 Al-Haythamī presented it in *al-Majmaᶜ*, and said (vol. 4, pp. 67–68): "Aḥmad [ibn Ḥanbal] narrated it and al-Ṭabarānī in *al-Kabīr*, and its [narrators] are trustworthy. Among them [there is discussion about the narrators, but] the discussion does not detract [from the worth of the report]."

47 See: *Fatḥ al-Bārī* (al-Ḥalabī), vol. 5: 402.

48 "By specimen": This is a sort of commercial exchange as follows: one sells a thing to another for a deferred price. He surrenders it to the buyer, then buys it back from him, before taking receipt of the price of the first sale, for a price less than that of that first sale, the rate that he pays in cash. In reality it is a sale that was never intended. The purpose was only the cash transfer, and it is a form of trickery about the consumption of *ribā* (usury).

49 Al-Albānī pronounced it *ṣaḥīḥ* and the whole of its authentic routes. See on it the discussion in our book *Bayᶜ al-Murābaḥah li al-Āmir bi al-Shirā'*.

50 As for the hadiths which have no source and no *sanad*, or the fabricated and false hadiths, then preoccupation with them in this field is not worthwhile, except under the heading of exposition of their falsehood and invalidity, and of their opposition to the Book and the

Sunnah, to the decided elements of the creed, and to the purposes of the Law.

51 Abū Dā'ūd, no. 4112, and al-Tirmidhī, no. 1779.

52 The hadith is agreed upon. The two Shaykhs have narrated it, and others with variation in the wording, but the general meaning is one. See *al-Lu'lu' wa al-Murjān*, no. 513, and al-Bukhārī with *al-Fatḥ al-Bārī*, hadith no. 950.

53 *Al-Fatḥ al-Bārī*, vol. 2, p. 445.

54 Al-Qurṭubī, *Tafsīr* (Dār al-Kutub al-Miṣriyyah), vol. 12, p. 228.

55 Al-Tirmidhī in *al-Janā'iz*, no. 1056. And Ibn Mājah, no. 1576, and Aḥmad ibn Ḥanbal, vol. 2, p. 337, and he pointed to it in *Mawārid al-Zam'ān*, 789. Al-Bayhaqī also narrated it in *al-Sunan*, vol. 4, p. 78.

56 See the source-critique of the hadiths nos. 761 and 774 in al-Albānī's *Irwā' al-Ghalīl.*

57 Ibn Ḥanbal and al-Ḥākim narrated it from Anas. Cited in *Ṣaḥīḥ al-Jāmiᶜ al-Ṣaghīr*, no. 4584.

58 Muslim, nos. 976, 977.

59 Muslim narrated it in *al-Janā'iz*, no. 794; and al-Nasā'ī, vol. 4, p. 93; and Ibn Ḥanbal, vol. 6, p. 221.

60 Agreed upon. Cited in *al-Lu'lu' wa al-Murjān*, no. 533.

61 He mentions it in *Nayl al-Awṭār*, vol. 4, p. 166.

62 Ibid.

63 Al-Daraquṭnī (*al-Tahdhīb al-Tahdhīb*, vol. 12, pp. 405–06) said: "[Her name] is [spelled] with a *jīm*, and the *dāl* is undotted. Whoever mentions [her name] with *dhāl* [i.e *dāl* dotted] has misspelled [it]." Al-Ḥāfiẓ Ibn Ḥajar said: "That is how al-ᶜAskarī said [it], and he reported it with *dhāl* (*dāl* dotted) from a group [of narrators]." Al-Ṭabarī said: "Judāmah bint Jandal. The hadith specialists say: 'bint Wahb'. The preferred opinion is that she is the daughter of Jandal al-Asdiyyyah. She embraced Islam early on in Makkah, then she made the Pledge, and she emigrated with her folk to Madinah."

64 *Al-Muntaqā* (Beirut: Dār al-Maᶜrifah), vol. 2, pp. 561–64.

65 *Nayl al-Awṭār* (Dār al-Jīl), vol. 6, p. 346.

66 *Al-Sunan al-Kubrā*, vol. 7, pp. 328–32.

67 Al-Bayhaqī, *Maᶜrifat al-Sunan wa al-Āthār* (ed. al-Sayyid Aḥmad Ṣaqar; Cairo: al-Majlis al-Aᶜlā li-l-Shu'ūn al-Islāmiyyah), vol. 1, pp. 101–03.

68 See what al-Shāṭibī said in *al-Muwāfaqāt.*

69 Muslim narrated it in his *Ṣaḥīḥ, Kitāb al-Manāqib*, no. 2363. From the hadith of ᶜĀ'ishah and Anas.

70 Readers may consult what we wrote concerning this inquiry in the section on 'the Legislative side of the Sunnah' in our book *al-Sunnah Maṣdaran li al-Maʿrifah wa al-Ḥaḍārah* (Cairo: Dār-al-Shurūq).

71 Abū Dā'ūd narrated in *al-Jihād*, no. 1645; al-Tirmidhī in *al-Siyar*, no. 1604.

72 Al-Khaṭṭābī said on the reason for the bloodwit being cut in half: "Because they had taken pains against themselves by settling among the unbelievers, and they were like those who are destroyed by their own crimes, or [the crimes] of others. So the share of their crime cuts from the bloodwit."

73 As the *Hijrah* was obligatory at the beginning of Islam on all who embraced the faith, so that they should be joined to the Prophet and his Companions in Madinah so that he could teach them Islam, and they could strengthen the power of the Islamic society. Then when Makkah was conquered, the need for emigration to Madinah was lifted. God's Messenger said: "No *hijrah* after the Conquest, but the jihad and the intent (*niyyah*) [remain]." Agreed upon.

74 Agreed upon. See *al-Lu'lu' wa al-Murjān*, no. 850, and the three hadiths before it.

75 Al-Bukhārī narrated it in (*Kitāb al-Manāqib*) *Bāb: 'ʿAlāmāt al-Nubuwwah fī al-Islām'*.

76 See *Fatḥ al-Bārī* (Cairo: al-Ḥalabī), vol. 4, p. 447 *et seq*.

77 From the hadith that Ibn Ḥanbal narrated from Anas. Its narrators are trustworthy, as al-Haythamī said in *Majmaʿ al-Zawā'id*, vol. 5, p. 192. Al-Mundhirī said in *al-Targhīb wa al-Tarhīb*: "Its *isnād* is excellent." See our book, *al-Muntaqā*, hadith no. 1299. Ibn Ḥanbal narrated it in another hadith with the wording: "The commanders are from the Quraysh." Al-Haythamī (vol. 5, p. 193) said: "Its narrators are *ṣaḥīḥ* narrators, except for Ibn ʿAbd al-ʿAzīz, and he is trustworthy." Al-Mundhirī said: "The narration of it is reliable." See *al-Muntaqā*, p. 1300.

78 See Ibn Khaldūn, *Muqaddimah* (ed. ʿAbd al-Wāḥid Wāfī; Lajnat al-Bayān al-ʿArabī, 2nd edn.), vol. 2, pp. 695–96.

79 For ʿUmar's stance on the issue of the non-division of the land among its conquerors, see: our book *al-Siyāsah al-Sharīʿyyah: Bayna Nuṣūṣ al-Sharīʿah wa-Maqāṣidi-hā* (Maktab Wahbah), pp. 188–201.

80 Ibn Qudāmah, *al-Mughnī* (Cairo: Maṭbaʿah Nashr al-Thaqāfah al-Islāmiyyah), vol. 2, p. 598.

81 Al-Sharastānī, *Nayl al-Awṭār*, vol. 5, p. 338. It is an agreed upon hadith.

82 *Al-Muwaṭṭā*, vol. 3, p. 129. Camels having camels: i.e. many would be taken into possession.
83 Muhammad Yūsuf Mūsā, *al-Tā'rīkh al-Fiqh al-Islāmī: Fiqh al-Ṣaḥābah wa al-Tābiᶜīn*, pp. 83–85.
84 There is no sense in referring to the same Muslim two different *niṣāb*s of extreme disparity. This is what we have preferred in our discussion of the subject in *Fiqh al-Zakāh*: we hold to the necessity of unifying the *niṣāb* on money. If the *niṣāb* is made one, should it be the *niṣāb* of silver or the *niṣāb* of gold? What I have preferred for the *niṣāb* on money is gold, not silver.
85 See: *Fiqh al-Zakāh*, part 1, pp. 260–61.
86 Ibn Taymiyyah, *Majmuᶜ al-Fatāwā*, vol. 19, pp. 255–56.
87 Ibn Ḥanbal and al-Ṭabarānī narrated it, and al-Ḥākim, who pronounced it *ṣaḥīḥ* from Samurah. Cited in *Ṣaḥīḥ al-Jāmiᶜ al-Ṣaghīr.*
88 Ibn Ḥanbal and al-Nasā'ī narrated it from Anas. Cited in ibid.
89 Al-Bukhārī narrated it from Umm Qays. Cited in ibid.
90 Ibn Mājah narrated it from Ibn ᶜUmar; al-Tirmidhī and Ibn Ḥibbān from Abū Hurayrah; and Ibn Ḥanbal from ᶜĀ'ishah. Cited in ibid.
91 Agreed upon. Cited in *al-Lu'lu' wa al-Murjān*, no. 1430.
92 Al-Tirmidhī narrated it from Ibn ᶜAbbās and said it was *ḥasan gharīb*; no. 1757.
93 Ibn Ḥanbal, the two Shaykhs, al-Tirmidhī, and al-Nasā'ī narrated it from ᶜUrwah al-Bāriqī. Ibn Ḥanbal, Muslim and al-Nasā'ī also narrated it from Jarīr. *Ṣaḥīḥ al-Jāmiᶜ al-Ṣaghīr*, no. 3353.
94 See the hadith that Ibn Ḥanbal, al-Nasā'ī, Ibn Mājah, al-Ṭabarānī and al-Ḥākim narrated from ᶜAmr ibn ᶜAnbasah; and the other hadith that al-Tirmidhī, al-Nasā'ī and al-Ḥakim narrated from Abū Najīḥ. Ibid, nos. 6267, 6268.
95 Ibn Ḥanbal narrated it from Abū Bakr; al-Shāfiᶜī, Ibn Ḥanbal, al-Nasā'ī, al-Dārimī, Ibn Khuzaymah, Ibn Ḥibbān, al-Ḥākim and al-Bayhaqī from ᶜĀ'ishah; Ibn Mājah from Abū Umāmah; and al-Bukhārī in *al-Ta'rīkh* and al-Ṭabarānī in *al-ᶜAwsaṭ* from Ibn ᶜAbbās. Ibid, no. 3695.
96 See Shaykh ᶜAbd Allāh al-Bassām, *Nayl al-Mārib*, vol. 1, p. 40.
97 Agreed upon, as cited in *al-Lu'lu' wa al-Murjān*, hadith no. 1320.
98 Muslim narrated it, no. 2032.
99 Ibid, no. 2033.
100 Ibid, no. 2034.
101 Abū Dā'ūd narrated it in *Kitāb al-Buyūᶜ* (no. 3340), al-Nasā'ī (vol. 7, p. 281), and Ibn Ḥibbān, *al-Mawārid* (no. 1105), al-Ṭaḥāwī in *Mushkil*

al-Āthār (vol. 2, p. 99), and al-Bayhaqī in *al-Sunan* (vol. 6, p. 31), from the hadith of Ibn ʿUmar. Ibn Ḥibbān pronounced it *ṣaḥīḥ*; also al-Dāraquṭnī, al-Nawawī and Abū al-Fatḥ al-Qushayrī. Ibn Ḥajar mentioned it in *al-Talkhīs* (Cairo), vol. 2, p. 175. Al-Albānī mentioned it in his *Ṣaḥīḥ*, vol. 1, hadith no. 165.

102 Muslim narrated it, and others.

103 The difference between one land and another has been as much as three days: in Ramadan of the year 1409 AH, the opening of the month was established as Thursday (6th April 1989) in the Kingdom of Saudi Arabia, Kuwait, Qatar, Bahrayn, Tunisia and other countries – all of them by sighting of the crescent in Saudi Arabia. It was established in Egypt, Jordan, Iraq, Algeria, Morocco and other countries as Friday. As for Pakistan, India, Oman, Iran and other countries, they began fasting on the Saturday!

104 Al-Bukhārī narrated it in *Kitāb al-Sawm.*

105 *Al-Muwaṭṭā'*, vol.1, p. 269.

106 *Fatḥ al-Bārī*, vol. 1, pp. 108–09.

107 "We do not know whom al-Ḥāfiẓ intends by al-Rāfiḍīs [here]. If he meant the Imāmī Shiʿa, we know from their doctrines that, according to them, the adoption of calculation is not permissible. If he meant [some] other people, we do not know who they are."— Shākir.
I think the ones intended are the Ismāʿīlīs, as it has been conveyed that they hold that position. — al-Qaraḍāwī.

108 The opinion on balance is that there remains a period after sunset when the moon's appearance is possible, whereby sighting it with the naked eye also becomes possible, and that is about fifteen to twenty minutes, according to what specialists have said. — al-Qaraḍāwī.

109 "Surayj" with *sīn* carrying a *ḍamma* and *jīm* at the end of it. It is written incorrectly in many printed books "Shurayh" with *shīn* and *hā'*, and it is misspelled. This Abū al-ʿAbbās died in the year 306 AH, and he was a student of Abū Dā'ūd, author of the *Sunan.* Abū Isḥāq al-Shīrāzī said about his person (*Ṭabaqāt al-Fuqahā'*, p. 89): "He was among the greatest of the Shāfiʿīs and of the imams of the Muslims." He was distinguished above all the Shāfiʿīs, including even ʿAlī al-Muzanī; the best biographical notice in al-Khaṭīb's *Tā'rīkh Baghdād* (vol. 4, pp. 278–90) is about him, as also in *Ṭabaqāt al-Shāfiʿiyyah* of Ibn al-Subkī (vol. 2, pp. 67–96). And some have counted him as the *mujaddid* (renewer) of the third century.

110 *Sharḥ* of al-Qāḍī Abū Bakr ibn al-ʿArabī on *al-Tirmidhī* (vol. 3, pp. 207–08); *Ṭarḥ al-Tathrīb*, vol. 4, pp. 111–13; and *Fatḥ al-Bārī*, vol. 4, p. 104.

111 The essay: *al-Awā'il al-Shuhūr al-ʿArabiyyah* (Maktabah Ibn Taymiyyah), pp. 7–17. (I would mention here that among those in modern times who have held this opinion was the great *faqīh*, Muṣṭafā al-Zarqā'. He proposed and supported it in the Academy for Islamic Fiqh but was unable to secure enough backing from other members to achieve the required majority.)

112 He is his eminence Shaykh Ṣāliḥ ibn Muhammad al-Laḥaydān, head of the High Council in the Kingdom of Saudi Arabia. His opinion was printed by the Kingdom in the daily paper in ʿUkāẓ on 21 Ramadan 1409 AH.

113 *Qadara* – with *ḍamma* or *kasrah*, *yaqduru* or *yaqdiru* – with the meaning of *qaddara*. An example of it is the verse: *fa-qadarnā fa-niʿma al-qādirūn* (*al-Mursalāt*, 77: 23)

114 See al-Subkī, *Fatāwā* (Cairo: Maktabat al-Quds), vol. 1, pp. 219–20.

115 The essay, *al-Awā'il al-Shuhūr al-ʿArabiyyah*, p. 15.

116 Muslim narrated the hadith in *Faḍā'il al-Ṣaḥābah*, no. 2453. According to al-Bukhārī there arose a suspicion that the longest in hand of them and the quickest to join him was Sawdah. This is an error found in some narrations which Ibn Jawzī exposed. See al-Dhahabī, *Siyar Aʿlām al-Nubalā'* (Beirut: al-Risālah), vol. 2, p. 213.

117 See: *Tafsīr Ibn Kathīr*, vol. 1, p. 221.

118 Agreed upon. See *al-Lu'lu' wa al-Murjān*, nos. 1746, 1721.

119 *Ta'wīl Mukhtalaf al-Ḥadīth* (Beirut: Dār al-Jīl), p. 224.

120 See *al-Lu'lu' wa al-Murjān*, for what the two Shaykhs are agreed upon, according to Muhammad Fu'ād ʿAbd al-Bāqī, no. 359.

121 Al-Bukhārī narrated it in his *Ṣaḥīḥ*, in *Kitāb al-Adab* and *Kitāb al-Tafsīr*, and Muslim in *al-Birr wa al-Ṣilah*. See: *al-Lu'lu' wa al-Murjān*, no. 1655.

122 Hadith 6548 in *Ṣaḥīḥ al-Bukhārī* with *al-Fatḥ*. It is in *al-Lu'lu' wa al-Murjān*, no. 1812.

123 Ibid, 1811.

124 See on these sayings: *Fatḥ al-Bārī* (Dār al-Fikr), vol. 11, p. 421.

125 See: *al-Musnad* (ed. Shaykh Shākir; Dār al-Maʿarif), vol. 8, pp. 240–41.

126 Al-Haythamī presented it in *al-Majmuʿ* (vol. 4, p. 326) and said: "Al-Ṭabarānī narrated it, and his [narrators] are authentic, from Maʿqil ibn Yasār."

127 *Fatḥ al-Bārī*, vol. 13.

128 Agreed upon, from the hadith of Ibn ᶜUmar, ᶜĀ'ishah, Rāfiᶜ ibn Khadīj, and Asmā' bint Abī Bakr. Al-Bukhārī narrated it also from Ibn ᶜAbbās. See *Ṣaḥīḥ al-Jāmiᶜ al-Ṣaghīr*, no. 3191; and *al-Lu'lu' wa al-Murjān*, nos. 1424, 1426.

129 Ibn Ḥanbal narrated it from Anas, and al-Nasā'ī from Ibn ᶜAbbās. Cited in *Ṣaḥīḥ al-Jāmiᶜ al-Ṣaghīr*, no. 3174.

130 Ibn Ḥanbal, al-Tirmidhī and Ibn Mājah narrated it from Abū Hurayrah; Ibn Ḥanbal, al-Nasā'ī and Ibn Mājah from Abū Saᶜīd and Jābir. Cited in *Ṣaḥīḥ al-Jāmiᶜ al-Ṣaghīr*, no. 4126.

131 Agreed upon, from the hadith of ᶜAbd Allāh ibn Abī al-Awfa. *Al-Lu'lu' wa al-Murjān*, no. 1137.

132 Ibn Ḥanbal narrated it and al-Nasā'ī from Jāhimah. Cited in *Ṣaḥīḥ al-Jāmiᶜ al-Ṣaghīr*, no. 1249.

133 Muslim narrated it from Abū Hurayrah. *Mukhtaṣar Muslim*, 1868.

134 Agreed upon, from ᶜAbd Allāh ibn Zayd al-Māzinī and from Abū Hurayrah. See *Ṣaḥīḥ al-Jāmiᶜ al-Ṣaghīr*, nos. 5586, 5587.

135 Ibn Ḥazm, *al-Maḥallā*, vol. 7, pp. 230–31, *Masā'il* 919.

136 Abū Dā'ūd narrated it in *Kitāb al-Adab* in his *Sunan*, *Bāb: 'Qatᶜ al-Sidr'*, no. 5239. Also al-Bayhaqi narrated it in his *Sunan*, and it is cited in *Ṣaḥīḥ al-Jāmiᶜ al-Ṣaghīr*.

137 Agreed upon, from the hadith of Anas. Cited in *al-Lu'lu' wa al-Murjān*, no. 665.

138 Ibn Ḥibban narrated it, Abū Nuᶜaym in *al-Ḥilyah*, and al-Bayhaqī in *al-Sunan*, from Abū Hurayrah. Cited in *Ṣaḥīḥ al-Jāmiᶜ al-Ṣaghīr*.

139 Ibn Ḥanbal narrated it, and its *isnād* is strong. Cited in al-Mundhirī, *al-Targhīb*.

140 See on that: Anwar al-Kashmīrī's book *al-Taṣrīh bi-mā Tawātur fī Nuzūl al-Masīḥ* (ed. ᶜAbd al-Fattāḥ Abū Guddah). Moreover, he has collected in it forty *ṣaḥīḥ* and *ḥasan* hadiths, not to mention others beyond that.

141 Agreed upon, from the hadith of Abū Hurayrah, with the words approximated. See *Ṣaḥīḥ al-Jāmiᶜ al-Ṣaghīr*, no. 7077, and *al-Lu'lu' wa al-Murjān*, no. 95.

142 Invention in the knowledge of diverse weights and measures in our age makes it possible to measure the heat in the atmosphere or in a person, and to measure things to the very limit of fineness, so far so that certain types of computer can calculate to one part in the million in a second. Then the Balance (that we must face in the hereafter) is not of the sort that has two pans – as the Muᶜtazilis imagined it to be.

143 See our comments on this hadith in our book *Fatāwā Muᶜāṣirah*, vol. 1.

144 What the Messenger commanded is what is advised in present-day medicine: to leave the stomach to empty out what is in it (and thereby relax), and not (as was the practice followed in old times) fight the ailment by putting into it what keeps the stomach taut.

145 Abū Dā'ūd narrated it, no. 4605, and al-Tirmidhī, no. 2665, from the hadith of Ibn Rāfiᶜ. Ibn Ḥanbal narrated it abridged in *al-Musnad*, vol. 6, p. 8.

146 *Al-Iᶜtiṣām* (Sharikat al-Iᶜlānāt al-Sharqiyyah), vol. 1, pp. 231–32.

147 See *al-Lu'lu' wa al-Murjān*, hadith nos. 1799, 1800, 1801.

148 Shaykh Muhammad ᶜAbduh, *Risālat al-Tawḥīd*, pp. 187–88.

149 Ibid.

150 *Iḥyā' ᶜUlūm al-Dīn* (Beirut: Dār al-Maᶜrifah), vol. 1, pp. 31–32.

Index

(Note: in sorting the entries alphabetically, the definite article (prefix al-) and the letter ʿayn (ʿ) are ignored; consonants marked with a dot under are sorted as the same consonant without the dot.)

T